JAMES JOYCE, AUTHORIZED READER

JEAN-MICHEL RABATÉ

JAMES JOYCE,
AUTHORIZED READER

The Johns Hopkins University Press
Baltimore and London

The Johns Hopkins University Press
701 West 40th Street
Baltimore, Maryland 21211
The Johns Hopkins Press Ltd., London

The paper used in this book meets the minimum requirements of
American National Standard for Information Sciences—Permanence
of Paper for Printed Library Materials, ANSI Z39.48-1984.

Library of Congress Cataloging-in-Publication Data

Rabaté, Jean-Michel, 1949–
[James Joyce, portrait de l'auteur en autre lecteur. English]
James Joyce, authorized reader / Jean-Michel Rabaté.
p.   cm.
Translation of: James Joyce, portrait de l'auteur en autre
lecteur.
Includes bibliographical references.
ISBN 0-8018-4140-2
1. Joyce, James, 1882–1941—Critcisim and interpretation.
I. Title.
PR6019.09Z78385   1991
823'.912—dc20   90-49032

For J. D.
for his sixtieth birthday

Contents

Abbreviations and Short Titles

CP   Arthur Power. *Conversations with James Joyce.* London: Millington, 1978.

D   James Joyce. *Dubliners: The Corrected Text.* Edited by Robert Scholes. Frogmore, St. Albans: Panther, 1977.

DD   Stanislaus Joyce. *The Complete Dublin Diary.* Edited by George H. Healey. Ithaca: Cornell University Press, 1971.

FW   James Joyce. *Finnegans Wake.* London: Faber, 1939. Citations are to page and line number and are equivalent in all other editions.

Letters, I   *Letters of James Joyce.* Volume 1. Edited by Stuart Gilbert. London: Faber, 1957.

Letters, 2 and 3	*Letters of James Joyce.* Volumes 2 and 3. Edited by Richard Ellmann. London: Faber, 1966.
P	James Joyce. *A Portrait of the Artist as a Young Man: Text, Criticism, and Notes.* Edited by Chester G. Anderson. Harmondsworth and New York: Viking Critical Library, Penguin, 1977
Selected Letters	*Selected Letters of James Joyce.* Edited by Richard Ellmann. London: Faber, 1975.
SN	Giambatista Vico. *Principi de scienza nuova.* In *Opere.* Edited by F. Nicolini. Minla: Napoli Ricciardi, 1953. Citations are to paragraph number to allow for easy identification in all other editions.
U	James Joyce. *Ulysses.* Edited and revised by Hans Walter Gabler et al. New York: Garland, 1984. Citations are to episode and line number and are equivalent in the new paperback editions by Garland, Random House, Bodley Head, and Penguin.

PREFACE

This book is a self-translation: by which I do not mean only that I myself have translated an essay published in French in 1984 but also that, being simultaneously its author and its translator, I have faced added difficulties and responsibilities. First, I was keenly aware of what could not be translated straightforwardly. Part could be left out without qualms, as ascribed to a dated and awkward tendency in French poststructuralist critical idiom to indulge in systematic punning (an abuse that at the time seemed to have been condoned by Joyce's example). However, the rest of what was lost could always be regained elsewhere. For instance my original title, *Joyce: Portrait de l'auteur en autre lecteur*, suggests that the "author" is an agency that collapses two words, "other" and "reader" (*"aut[re lec]teur"*). The internal rhyme and submerged punning cannot be conveyed in English, but might, if need be, find a slightly distorted equivalent thanks to the near homophony of many words prefixed in "autho-" and "auto-," which would for instance link "authority"

and "autocracy" (defined as "the unlimited authority of an absolute ruler"). Thus, the meaning I wished to convey of a "reader"
who has to "authorize" himself or herself at some point of the
reading could be shifted over to the joint process of writing and
reading in which author(s) and readers share a new and autothelic "auto-rity"—their "aut(h)ority." Needless to say, I have
not systematized these diverging correspondences, nor strained
parallactic linguistic possibilities. They should merely be hinted
at in the course of the essay, permission being given to anglo-
phone readers to try them for themselves.

Being an auto-translator entails resisting another temptation—to rewrite every sentence. This is a temptation I have
resisted whenever the changes derived from a desire to update
the critical issues. I have, for instance, refrained from placing my
argument within the frame of a "genetic" perspective in which
I have since systematically situated myself. This book is more a
theoretical response to Joyce as read in a Lacanian and Derrid-
ian perspective and shows almost no trace of a study of Joyce's
drafts and notebooks, although I had started writing and
researching in that field.[1] I have tried to reassemble several articles dealing with these issues elsewhere.[2] Basically, I do not wish
to deny the "historical" or "contextual" character of what was
originally a doctoral dissertation on Joyce, Pound, and Broch
under the supervision of Hélène Cixous. From this long, unpub-
lished thesis, completed in 1980, I have culled the central parts
of the book, merely adding the first and last chapters (which
have also been published separately in English[3]) to what was
also conceived as an introduction to Joyce.

I have deleted the five pages of the "Synopsis" which gave a
sketch of all the chapters of *Ulysses,* an attempt at stylistic condensation that may have caused more confusion for the uninitiated student of Joyce in view of the complexity of the
argument that followed. Besides, since this book is closer to a
philosophical reading of psychoanalytical issues, it has had a history of its own which could not, for better or for worse, be
silently bypassed. Thus, those who have read *Ulysses Gramophone* will perhaps discover that I am not, after all, a fictional
character invented by Derrida to justify a pun on *oui* and *ouïe,*[4]

even if it is true that I have benefited from real-life chance meetings, numerous encounters and discussions—not all telephonic, absolutely nothing written on postcards—on Joyce and *Finnegans Wake* as early as 1969. This is, however, not (possibly for these same reasons) a "deconstructive" reading of Joyce, but rather a testimony to the fact that "rememembering" an author is both paying homage and undoing (analyzing) at the same time. Undoing myself in a series of "disrememberings" (to quote the Anglo-Irish expression Davin uses in his confession to Stephen Dedalus),[5] I nevertheless decided to delete whatever looked forced, silly, or simplified in the original version and have also modified the introduction and the conclusion.

JAMES JOYCE, AUTHORIZED READER

INTRODUCTION

Perhaps more than any writer of this century, Joyce has forced criticism to acknowledge its theological nature. His ambitions—following Dante's model of a totality of style and belief, channeled through Flaubert and Mallarmé (the two great writers who helped him become aware of the mystical relationship uniting author and language)—have driven his critics to repeat his gesture, to read and write "in memory of him," as Jacques Derrida aptly puts it. Stressing the feelings of resentment and jealousy that are likely to seize any uninitiated reader wading for the first time through *Ulysses* and *Finnegans Wake,* Derrida comments:

> Here the event is of such plot and scope that henceforth you have only one way out: *being in memory of him.* You're not only overcome by him, whether you know it or not, but obliged by him, and constrained to measure yourself against this overcoming. Being *in memory of him*: not necessarily to remember him, no, but to be in his memory, to inhabit his memory, which is henceforth greater than all your finite

memory can, in a single instant or in a single vocable, gather up of cultures, languages, mythologies, religions, philosophies, sciences, history of mind and of literatures.[1]

This implies that no book can now be written on Joyce that would not immediately owe a debt to previous critics, not only because the progress of exegesis is slow, painstaking, and cumulative but also because there is an institution that functions as a necessary passage, a body of books and people who gather regularly to exchange ideas, documents, theories—a collective spirit whose main function is to assuage the feeling of guilt which such a perpetual debt may give rise to in individual scholars.

I do not mean by the preceding remarks that the Joyceans have constituted an unwholesome sect of fanatics, as some might be tempted to hastily conclude. The positive nature of this institutionalized body of texts and critics should, on the contrary, be stressed, and one of its interesting side effects is the current reconsideration of the question of "authority." By *author* we usually mean a name connected with certain books, paintings, scores, works of art, and so on. *Authority* generally implies competence and the right to speak or write in a certain context. However, recent developments of theory have tended to destroy or blur the concepts of author and authority. In 1968, during the heyday of structuralism, Roland Barthes heralded "the death of the author" and indicated the new "birth of the reader" that was to follow. The "text" was invested with all the attributes once conceded to the author, while the reader became the locus of the hermeneutical process.[2] But, as Peggy Kamuf recently showed in a very perceptive discussion of Barthes's "authority," Barthes himself hesitated between a historical analysis (the death of the author being contemporaneous with a refusal of classical realism and psychology) and the timeless essence of all literature: the author has always been displaced by the latent and mobile energies contained by his creations and been reduced to a signature, whose role is both more ominous and less clearly identifiable.[3] And the theological nature of the hermeneutical circle remains unattacked if we merely replace "author" with "reader" as the agency of the (re)constitution of a full meaning, as Barthes seems to imply. The almost religious attitude of a reader who is forced to remain "in memory of Joyce" does not seem to suggest the Nietzschean free play with signifiers which the structuralists saw as a metaphor of political subversion of and as the textual equivalent of continuous revolution. And even if one refuses to move from the "death of the author" to the "birth of the reader," all the theological ambiguities that attached to the ambivalent sentence "God is dead" adhere all the more cunningly to literary hermeneutics.

Joyce, it is true, does not say that the author has died, preoccupied as he is with dead mothers and dying fathers, but states that he has been "refined out of existence": "The personality of the artist, at first a cry or a cadence or a mood and then a fluid and lambent narrative, finally refines itself out of existence, impersonalises itself, so to speak. . . . The artist, like the God of the creation, remains within or behind or beyond or above his handiwork, invisible, refined out of existence, indifferent, paring his fingernails." (*P,* 215) This well-known passage finds its source in Flaubert's letters about the impersonality of the writer. The most obvious source is the letter about the "totally fictitious" nature of *Madame Bovary,* a novel whose truth derives only from its impersonality: "an artist must be in his work like God in creation, invisible and all-powerful; he should be everywhere felt, but nowhere seen."[4] The theory is hardly one entailing a diminished role: the godlike artist disappears tactically; he is not absent but just hidden, and his famous "indifference" is not that of Pascal's *Deus absconditus* but that of a *Deus larvatus,* all the more present because of his invisibility.

While this point has often been made, what has generally been overlooked is that the first stage in Flaubert's theory of invisible omnipotence was not a theory of masks, but rather a theory of an absent object. The godlike author can be invisible because the text, hinged around an idea of style, aims at being itself, as purified of objects as the writer has been refined out of existence. Another letter, which has probably more relevance to Joyce's aesthetics, makes this clear:

What seems beautiful to me, what I should like to write, is a book about nothing, a book dependent on nothing external, which would be held together by the strength of its style, just as the earth, suspended in the void, depends on nothing for its support; a book which would have almost no subject, or at least in which the subject would be almost invisible, if such a thing is possible. . . . it is for this reason that there are no noble subjects or ignoble subjects; from the standpoint of pure Art one might almost establish the axiom that there is no such thing as subject, style in itself being an absolute manner of seeing things.[5]

What is mistakenly credited to Flaubert's "realism" shows here its deep affinity with Mallarmé's dream of a "pure work" or with Blanchot's poetics of "neutrality."[6] Joyce later stated similar beliefs as to the supremacy of style, not cultivated for itself, but seen as the last bolthold of the artist's integrity. The "indifference" of the artist is parallel to the choice of an "indifferent" subject. In French as in English, "subject" alludes here as much to the "object" depicted by language as to the "subjective" attitude of the beholder, in a strategic hesitation which will be constitutive of Joyce's epiphanies.[7]

The common foundation of the new poetics, be they those of Flaubert's, Mallarmé's, or Joyce's, is the autothelic nature of the work's assertion. Its foundation upon the void and upon incertitude replaces the theological model of creation within a more human, but also more unconscious pattern, which uses another metaphor, that of paternity: "Fatherhood, in the sense of conscious begetting, is unknown to man. It is a mystical estate, an apostolic succession, from only begetter to only begotten. On that mystery and not on the madonna which the cunning Italian intellect flung to the mob of Europe the church is founded and founded irremovably because founded, like the world, macro and microcosm, upon the void. Upon incertitude, upon unlikelihood." (U, 9.837–41). These pages will be devoted to an exploration of these "mysteries" and paradoxes. Flaubert's sense of total devotion to his work had an equal only in Joyce's consistency and intransigent attitude. Flaubert may have given Joyce his almost hysterical sense of aesthetic identification (rendered possible precisely by the disappearance of the author as such), which his celebrated "Madame Bovary is myself" sums up so well. In another passage in his letters, he describes how writing is akin to lovemaking, in an embrace that would have him experience both sides of the action: "It is a delicious thing to write, whether well or badly—to be no longer yourself but to move in an entire universe of your own creating. Today, for instance, man and woman, lover and beloved, I rode in a forest on an autumn afternoon under the yellow leaves and I was also the horse, the leaves, the wind, the words my people spoke, even the red sun that made them half-shut their love-drowned eyes."[8] We are indeed not far from Stephen's conception of an androgynous artist-God, "ostler and butcher," "bawd and cuckhold" (U, 9.1050), ultimately based on Shakespeare. And here again, Flaubert can offer a definitive clue, since for him Hamlet is really the modern counterpart of Ulysses: "His [Hamlet's] perpetual state of fluctuation, his constant uncertainty, his irresolution and his inability to solve his problems—these, far from being inconsistent, are what make the play sublime. . . . The truth is that Shakespeare's conception of Hamlet reaches into the remotest corners of the human soul. Ulysses is perhaps the greatest type in all ancient literature, and Hamlet in all modern."[9] Joyce's effort at finding Molly Bloom in himself testifies to a radical feminization of the artist in his wish to vanish and become "impersonal," quite similar to Flaubert's creation of an alter ego with Madame Bovary.

Being "all in all," the artist as God is clearly the supreme "indifference." As Derrida phrases it in his commentary on Husserl's *Origin of Geometry,* "Only infinite being can reduce the difference in presence. In that sense, the name of God, at least as it is pronounced within classical rationalism, is the name of indifference itself."[10] But precisely because the "name of the Artist" is definitively not pronounced by Joyce or Flaubert within the confines of narrow rationalism, God spells out as much difference as indifference for them. What changes the picture completely is that the god-artist first has to embody himself, to suffer the throes of incarnation—or, in other words, to become a "young man"—and furthermore, has to be divided in his being, since he has not only to encompass the two sides of sexuality, masculine and feminine, but also has to invite the "reader" to the same divine production of indifference. The position of divine indifference can thus mobilize the totality of languages and cultures swept away in a multiplication of semantic differences.

Finnegans Wake is, of course, the place of this babelization and multiplication of linguistic atoms, a process that supposes the death of any stable identity. "I swear my gots how that I'm not meself at all" (*FW,* 487.17–18): this could be the battle cry of most characters in this book, if the word *character* had kept any significance. What is more, the generalized assault on characters, identities (to which I shall have to return in more detail), entails a new type of play, in which the reader not only participates in the writing of the book (a feature, after all, common in high modernism) but is there all the time, in dialogue with the writer, who is addressed by the text as if he were a reader: "But how transparingly nontrue, gentlewriter!" (63.9–10); "I can tell you something more than that, dear writer" (476.20–1). The phrases echo Greene's or Fielding's habit of directly addressing an audience, but here the tables have been turned, and the writer is being spoken to from within the text.[11] The "you reder!" (*FW,* 249.13–14) is as much a fictitious audience as a fictitious coauthor, an "anticollaborator" (118.25) working within the "writer complexus" (114.33) as his "shemblable" and "freer" (489.28). The *hypocrite lecteur* of Baudelaire's *Fleurs du Mal* has already been addressed by Eliot in the *Waste Land.* But if Tiresias indeed incorporated both sexes and saw "the substance of the poem," he was not presented as the "incarnation" of the writer-reader complex.[12]

This role is reserved to Stephen Dedalus, Joyce's "altar ego," on the opening page of *A Portrait of the Artist as a Young Man,* as the reader is given a clue of Stephen's budding vocation when Stephen's voice is heard for the first time:

> *O, the wild rose blossoms*
> *On the little green place.*
> He sang that song. That was his song.
> *O, the green wothe botheth.*
> (*P,* 7)

With the distortion of "O the green rose blossoms," baby Stephen conflates the two lines of the song "Lily Dale," thereby positing his first creative gesture, enabling him to really "possess" or own "his" song: he creates a green rose, an ideal rose that bypasses the traditional opposition between a white and a red rose: "White roses and red roses: those were beautiful colours to think of. . . . Lavender and cream and pink roses were beautiful to think of. Perhaps a wild rose might be like those colours and he remembered the song about the wild rose blossoms on the little green place. But you could not have a green rose. But perhaps somewhere in the world you could" (12). The green rose constitutes Stephen's Irish answer to the dilemma set up as a trap by the Jesuits: either York or Lancaster. In so doing, he forges an impossibility, which cannot exist "in the world," but only in language. Such a language is, of course, Anglo-Irish, an Anglo-Irish itself predetermined by another opposition between maroon and velvet. However, Stephen's green rose is not necessarily a proof of his identification with Parnell's green leaf; it is not yet an "ivy leaf." The key to the distortion of the song is the pun: Stephen distorts "blossoms" into "botheth," which should suggest a verbal form based on "both." His refusal to choose between antagonistic colors becomes a verb implying growth and the fusion of the contraries. "Bothing" is a "wild" action, generating a luxuriant and overabundant linguistic procreation, both "in" the world, and more romantically, "anywhere out of the world." A first instance of Stephen's creative mistakes, the "green rose" embodies the linguistic process underlying *Finnegans Wake*.

Thus the process of "forging" cannot be limited to the subjective sphere of the budding artist; on the other hand, Stephen must be made to acknowledge himself as an artist (a little like Proust's narrator at the end of *A la recherche du temps perdu*) so so that the reader can be shown the way towards self-authorization. A similar kind of mistake works emblematically in *Ulysses*, when Stephen meditates on the several pieces of writing he has brought back from his ingloriously short stay in Paris: a few metro tickets some light magazines, and a curiously mangled telegram.

Yes, used to carry punched tickets to prove an alibi if they arrested you for murder somewhere. Justice. On the night of the seventeenth of February 1904 the prisoner was seen by two witnesses. Other fellow did it: other me. Hat, tie, overcoat, nose. *Lui, c'est moi.* You seem to have enjoyed yourself. . . .

. . . Rich booty you brought back; *Le Tutu,* five tattered numbers of *Pantalon Blanc et Culotte Rouge;* a blue French telegram, curiosity to show:

–Nother dying come home father.

The aunt thinks you killed your mother.

(*U*, 3.179–99)

The collation of the two passages, which occur on the same page but are rarely read together, despite their strong thematic ties, would tend to prove that any "text," any piece of paper with printed words or dates on it, constitutes an *alibi*–a proof that otherness is at work in a process that ineluctably entails the murder of some close relative. In this instance, it is the mother who seems to have been dispatched by a blundering Hamlet, but it might have been someone else: the substitution of "Nother" for "Mother," thanks to the felicitous misprint of French telegraphists, suggests the symptomatic resurgence of the "other" in "me" ("other me"). The *Lui, c'est moi* could thus be taken as Joyce's rewriting of Baudelaire's *hypocrite lecteur* already mentioned, if we take it to refer to the reader's progress. In a scene of writing that necessarily repeats some primal fantasy connected with ritual murdering as matricide or parricide, the reader, who involuntarily happens to be taken as an extra witness to the crime, may be thought of as an accomplice.

Or at any rate, this is what Joyce suggests when he makes Stephen remark, "Work in all you know. Make them accomplices" (*U*, 9.158), during a pause in his fictions of Shakespearian paternity, at a point when he compares his speech to the poison which killed the King in *Hamlet*. Once we accept to keep reading, we are forced to become either *lui* or *moi* and are turned into the ideal addressees of a similar telegram sent by our new mystical father, Joyce. In a way, Joyce's alibi (when asked what he had been doing during the War, Joyce proudly answered: "I have written *Ulysses*. And you?") forces us to face the issue of authority as a play with otherness. We cannot deny that we have been changed by our reading of *Ulysses,* that it keeps changing us, that we would not keep reading if we had not been made "other." The famous telegram with a misprint can in its turn be subjected to various misreadings. At first glance, it seems to say, "Another is dying—come back as a father (of your reading)," in the perpetuation of Joyce's central question: How can one become his or her own father?

But a second reading might yield a meaning that would be more consistent with Barthes's argument about the "death of authors," while depriving it of its historical edge. The telegram, still addressed to the reader, would now be "AUTHOR DYING COME BACK OTHER." There must nevertheless always be a place for a gap that cannot be closed by a Homeric *nostos;* the "come back" has desperate overtones, for it is clear that the very structure of the sentence ("X dying come back Y") suggests a return to a different state or level.

The return therefore mimes the Hegelian gesture of final specular reappropriation while shifting its ground, opening the circle of the Spirit as realized in History to the spiral of rereadings. Again, Joyce, as a cunning arranger, takes pains with his allegories. Stephen seems to imply a dialectic of separation and reunification when he says, "When there is a reconciliation, . . there must have been first a sundering" (*U,* 9:334–35). But an excess of meaning is hinted at when we realize that Stephen inadvertently repeats himself, in a strange verbal parapraxis:

—There can be no reconciliation, Stephen said, if there has not been a sundering.
        Said that.

(*U,* 9.398)

The repetition of this truism already points to an excess of pulsional motives, disowns Stephen's tentative theoretical stance, and makes us look for further clues, further proofs of his guilt. And when Stephen leaves Bloom at the end of the book, we realize that the reconciliation has not prevented a final sundering.

In the same way, the Hegelian motive of dialectical reconciliation runs through *Finnegans Wake* but is always found in contexts underlining its inadequacy. Thus, when we find the grandiose marginal annotation in Shaun's hand on the left-hand margin of page 296, "*Zweispaltung as Fundemaintalish of Wiederherstellung*"–which can be glossed as "Division is fundamental to a reunification" and could come straight out of Hegel–we cannot forget that the "reunification" of the warring twins, Shem and Shaun, has left out the bottom of the page, as it were, not deigning to give Issy's feminine voice its due. And she tends to annotate the text in a different key, spelling out difference and above all, hesitation: "Hasitatense?" would be her comment on the same page (*FW,* 296.F4). Shaun's boasts about a totality that would encompass all the members of the family and leave out the original crime or sin are systematically denounced, more often than not by his own slips of the tongue. The "Otherman" is always working against his idealized versions of writing, as in the passage describing the letter he has carried: "I am, thing Sing larynx, letter potent to play the sem backwards like Oscan wild or in shunt Persse transluding from the Otherman or off the Toptic" (419.23–25). He is, of course, trying to answer to the vexed question of authority: who wrote it, who can read its full contents ("read the strangewrote anaglyptics of those shemletters" [419.18–19]) after it has been "Opened by Miss Take" (420.26)? The two joined factors–that the letter is made up of writing and therefore not reducible to the "Larynx," and that the letter cannot be closed and sealed, but has to be "opened" by a feminine agency that shows the "portals of discovery" by using mistakes–work together to prevent any harmonious totalization of meaning.

Just as Bloom and Stephen never merge in the hierarchical relationship of father and son, but part and are superseded by Molly's omnipotent and "indifferent" voice, Shem and Shaun never achieve the "neutrolysis" (612.22) of "unification" and "the spirit of appeasement" (610.23, 27). However, numerous passages tend to promise such a reunification, so that it will be necessary to deal more systematically with this problem. The problem is the function of alterity in the "othering process," which has replaced the issue of authority. In a purely Hegelian scheme, otherness and death are necessary to the system; they are fuel to the dialectical engine. The fact that the great Letter of *Finnegans Wake* never really reaches its (self)destination, since it is and is not identical to the book we are reading, suggests that Joyce's totality is at best "asymptotic," as Derrida has implied:

> The other great paradigm [by comparison with Husserl's phenomenology] would be the Joyce of *Finnegans Wake*. He repeats and mobilizes and babelizes the (asymptotic) totality of the equivocal, he makes this his theme and his operation, he tries to make outcrop with the greatest possible synchrony, at great speed, the greatest power of the meanings buried in each syllabic fragment, subjecting each atom of writing to fission in order to overload the unconscious with the whole memory of man: mythologies, religion, philosophies, sciences, psychoanalysis, literature. This generalized equivocality of writing does not translate one language into another on the basis of common nuclei of meaning.[13]

Such an asymptotic totality would correspond to a broad and vague notion of the "authority" of culture understood in its collective sense as the widest extension of all types of discourses and sciences available to man. But as these discourses are specified by particular idioms, they cannot be subsumed under one single concept. "Authority" cannot help being shifted towards a problematics of alterity and of paternity. Derrida's analysis describes this paradoxical situation quite well:

> *Finnegans Wake* is a little, a little what, a little son, a little grandson of Western culture in its circular, encyclopedic, Ulyssean and more than Ulyssean totality. And then it is, simultaneously, much bigger than even this Odyssey, it comprehends it, and this prevents it, dragging it outside itself in an entirely singular adventure, from closing in on itself and on the event. The future is reserved in it. The "situation" of *Finnegans Wake* is also, because of this, our own situation with respect to this immense text. In this war of languages, everything we can say after it looks in advance like a minute self-commentary with which this work accompanies itself. It

is already comprehended by it. And yet the new marks carry off, enlarge and project elsewhere—one never knows where in advance—a programme which appeared to constrain them. This is our only chance, minuscule and completely open.[14]

We as readers are therefore the grandsons of this grandson, and are required, if we "authorize ourselves" as readers, to become the "fathers" of our reading. This is nevertheless the law of a text that so deftly plays with openness and closure. Just as it would be wrong to take Stephen Dedalus for the author of *Ulysses* and call him "Stephen Joyce," as most commentators seem to imply, it would be historically unsound to deny the coincidence that a real-life Stephen Joyce, the actual grandson of James Joyce, should be mentioned in Derrida's texts, as it were, before he even knew of his existence.[15] The actual presence of a grandson inevitably poses questions of jurisdiction, of legal control over texts, and of the laws of copyright which may set bounds to a given signature. For—this is Derrida's argument— the first instance of an author's authority is to be found in the power of his name, in his signature. Thus, what happens if this signature can be translated?

Joyce, as we know, amused himself with the possible translations of his name. Brody, his publisher and owner of the Rhein Verlag, could explain to him that Jung's strictures on *Ulysses* derived from the fact that his name, translated in German, gave *Freude* ("joy"), hence Freud, but when Joyce came to Paris and decided to be accepted by the French intellectuals, he declared that "the name of Joyce is an old French word, in which one finds the name of M. de Joyeuse."[16] He similarly appreciated the fact that the French pronunciation of his name allowed the "joycity" of his patronymic heritage to resound (his name had become something like *jouasse,* which in French slang means "very happy") and saw a confirmation of this coincidence when the most devoted friend, commentator, and publisher he could find in Paris had a similar name—Jolas.[17] Thus, for Joyce, names can and indeed must be translated: when piling up notes for his *Work in Progress,* he very often used the abbreviation "J.J." as a heading under which he could classify any personal item. But, in typically Flaubertian fashion, if he reserved a siglum for the book itself, described as: □, or the square wheel, the "J.J." category remained private in the notebooks, or else had to be disseminated in the text itself.

In an aside to a jotting in which he decides to let [, or Shem, write the "Preface" to the book, Joyce remarks on his stylistic innovations in *Ulysses:*

[preface
J.J. abolished preface, dedication, notes, letters to press, interviews, chapter titles, capitals, inverted commas[18]

Shem seems to show less daring than his creator, but we know that part of the aim of these stage directions is to multiply the varying and conflicting enunciative strategies contained in the *Wake.*

The endless signifying process of *Finnegans Wake* reinscribes the plurality of translatable signatures set adrift in pure language; they obey the main drift of a language that blurs all clearcut traditional categories of literary genres and linguistic modes. The text thus becomes a "self-signature" in a generalized family in which tensions and rivalries are rife. In a passage reminiscent of the archetypal Cain and Abel story, a Shaunian character says: "Been ike hins kindergardien? I know not, O cashla, I am sure offed habitand this undered heaven, meis enfin, contrasting the first mover, that father I ascend fromming knows, as I think, caused whom I, a self the sign . . . " (483.25–29). (I deliberately cut this long sentence short and leave it unfinished because it is, first of all, impossible to "quote" in the usual sense from *Finnegans Wake,* and then because I only want to exploit a few of its signifiers.) The Cainian denegation alluding to a refusal to repent after the brother's murder generates a series of deliberate paradoxes here: the only surviving son pretends not to know of his brother's fate, whereas in fact he knows; he pretends to revere a father who has begotten him while parading his autonomy; and instead of "descending from" his father, "piously" (*fromm* in German) ascends to the heavens. The purpose of the sentence is to extenuate guilt, and it concludes quite logically on "meas minimas culpads!" (483.35) The "self-reliance" of the sign is parallel to the reliance of the subject: both boast of ill-founded autonomy in an attempt at self-generation. Joyce implies—in a complex Oedipal machinery I shall later explore—that the dream of the Flaubertian artist is now available to each and every "sign," word, letter, phrase, or page in his book. But this dream can only be bought thanks to a murder, a murder that will soon be forgotten when the sun rises and the nightmares of history and sleep are dispelled.

In *Finnegans Wake* this brings about a systematic exploration of human perversities and sins. As most early commentators, from Samuel Beckett to J. S. Atherton, have already pointed out, Joyce's obsession with original sin had slowly become identical with his relentless investment of his signature in language, with his determination to keep writing the Big Book of universal history. The insight, banal as it may sound, may now appear to have been forgotten, since most critics hesitate today to link the religious themes with poststructuralist concerns for a writing that reproduces and perpetuates itself, playing with notions of paternity in order to subvert them. One takes for granted that if one is engaged in "deconstructive" critical strategies, "difference" will be acclaimed as a sort of supreme good and will be endowed with such a potency that it can destroy by itself, as it were, all the values connected with presence and transcendental signifieds. Joyce, like Shaun, would not be so cocksure, and seems to stress subversion, a subversion which in order to remain subversive must at any rate be called a "version," and even perhaps a perversion, of the "truth."

Such a position has been identified with "perversity" by both psychoanalysts and philosophers, or more precisely by two writers whose importance for Joyce remains crucial, even if he probably hardly ever read them: Hegel and Edgar Poe. I shall return to Derrida's idea that Joyce could be called "the most Hegelian of all writers"[19] in my last chapter, and shall only rapidly indicate a first sense in which this can be taken. When Joyce appears to be busy piling "buildung supra buildung" (*FW*, 4.27), recirculating all types of mythologies, folklores, and scientific discourses, he may also be denouncing, as Hegel did in his *Phe-*

nomenology of the Spirit, the reine Bildung ("pure culture") of the Enlightenment. Its particularity is to be circulated among divided subjectivities who use the language of universality only to mask their internal rifts and splits. Their omniscient discourse has already enounced everything and its contrary; the Zerrissenheit of split consciousness sends us back to the perversion (Verkehrung) of empty concepts. "The divided consciousness is the consciousness of perversion, and even of absolute perversion": thus Hegel as he comments upon Diderot's Neveu de Rameau and the "modern" spirit.[20] In such a world, the author and the reader have likewise disappeared, swallowed up by a totalizing discourse that manipulates them. Joyce, if the terms of this analysis can be granted, never falls prey to this seductive position of impersonal mastery, never identifies himself with the word-machine, even if he has to create one.

In Dubliners, the moral and political perversion of Ireland produces a division among the speakers and actors themselves, thereby suggesting the possibility of deducing negatively, a contrario, value judgments which at least expose the roots of symptoms. Ulysses probes in a first moment the paradoxes of paternity, then explodes the limits of psychological positioning in a turn towards encyclopedic knowledge, only to send all plots, stories, and human creations spinning around in a female web of words. Finnegans Wake invests everything in languages, civilizations, and religions but revolves around the limited set of perversions that the familial nexus can map out. These three main steps in the inquiry I wish to lead presuppose a fundamental split within human consciousness, the equivalent of what Hugo von Hofmannsthal calls the Lord Chandos experience, an experience of loss, mutism, and acute schizophrenia that finds its equivalent in Vico's myth of mute though poetic primitive giants.[21] What Joyce suggests is in the line of Hegel's analysis, but without the facility of the final reconciliation provided by a messianic promise of absolute knowledge.

Joyce situates his writing and reading subject in the middle of parody and perversion, in a perversion that adheres to the act of interpretation. As I will try to show with Dubliners, reading is a process in which we make up theories about events and characters, theories which ineluctably repress the parodic division underpinning them. This apparently endless confusion of enunciator and enounced, of quoting subject and quoted texts, determines the essence of writing, and it is a situation very well allegorized by Edgar Poe's tale "The Imp of the Perverse," a brilliant story which can provide a paradigm of literary perverseness. The story begins as a learned and serious disquisition on human faculties, in which one can easily identify a few mischievous digs at Kantian idealism. The considerations we are to read suppose that there exists a primitive impulse that is systematically missed by Reason: "In the pure arrogance of the reason, we have all overlooked it."[22] Moralists, phrenologists, and pure theoreticians have all been unable to acknowledge the fundamental agency of a principle of unreason at work within reason itself: "In theory, no reason can be more unreasonable; but, in fact, there is none so strong" (473). "Theory" should not so much be opposed to "fact" as to "action," or as to the performative gesture accomplished by the cogito of Cartesian metaphysics. The principle of unreason is one that proves itself when we act out our thoughts—for instance, when we try to become certain of our existence: "I am no more certain that I breathe, than that the assurance of the wrong or error of any action is often the one unconquerable *force* which impels us, and alone impels us, to its prosecution" (473). It embodies the parody of the *cogito*, a cogito which, as Lacan reformulated it, can be heard as "I think: 'therefore I am.'" The quotation marks can be deleted, since this thought may be a kind of continuous bass in our sense of identity, but one cannot forget that such a thought is a quotation without paying a high price.

The narrator's idea in "The Imp of the Perverse" is simply that the very act of thinking about transgression generates an irresistible desire to accomplish it; and perversion is defined as either pure *Schadenfreude* (the arbitrary deferral of some task, the withholding of important news) or murderous impulses, whether suicidal (as in the dangerous situation of a man standing at the edge of a precipice who hurls himself into it because he thinks too strongly about his own annihilation) or homicidal (but this is left to the second part of the story). For indeed, while suggesting the material nature of the imp in the very words that call it up ("impulse" and "impel" are repeated several times, along with terms such as "irresistible," "imperceptible," "impossible," "impertinent," and so on), the text produces a conflict within the subject: "We tremble with the violence of the conflict within us, – of the definite within the indefinite – of the substance within the shadow" (475). The "theory" through which reason undoes itself is then very logically set in a more dramatic perspective when we realize that all this discourse is written by a man who sits in a prison, awaiting his execution. He explains that after having perpetrated a perfect murder (he has poisoned the candle of a rich man who was in the habit of reading in bed) he enjoys his riches in peace for some years, until he says to himself one day, "I am safe," and then adds, "if I be not fool enough to make open confession" (478). The very thought that he could betray himself is enough to force him to actually utter the words that send him to the executioner: "Alas! I too well understood that, to *think*, in my situation, was to be lost" (478). With the violence of the return of a terribly repressed sin, the secret is now identical with the "imp," which manifests itself verbally: "The long *imp*risoned secret burst forth from my soul" (478; italics mine).

The theory may have attempted to explain why its author conceived it while he was in prison, or conversely, the story may only serve to exemplify a curious theory. However, the entire situation suggests that the scene of the confession of such a murder emblematically refers to the scene of literature and opposes not a murderer and his victim, but a murderer and his audience as a writer and his readers. As Stanley Cavell aptly puts it, "Both the fiction of the writer's arresting himself and wearing fetters and tenanting the cell of the condemned and the fiction of providing a poisonous wax light for reading are descriptions or fantasies of writing, modeled by the writing before us. There is, or at least we need imagine, no actual imprisoning and no crime but the act of writing itself."[23] What confirms this is the fact that the criminal has found the idea of the candle in French memoirs which provided him with all the necessary "*imp*ertinent details" (477), while he is actually continuing his confession to an audience half-real, half-imaginary. The imp is thus the ghost of the dead man ("And now my own casual self-suggestion, that I might possibly be fool enough to confess the murder of which I had been guilty, confronted me, as if the very ghost of him whom I had murdered—and beckoned me on to death," 478) and the ghost of literature—a vicious circle which leaves us in fetters and offers only the vaguest hope of salvation. "Tomorrow I shall be fetterless!—*but where?*" the criminal asks—a question which might well be that which Stephen Dedalus has to ponder at the end of *Ulysses*, when he wanders out in the dark, free at last but without any fixed abode, a question posed by the cunning "Will" (testament and whim, translated names, and prearranged futurity) which books contain, even when they are not authored by a William Shakespeare:

> Coffined thoughts around me, in mummycases, embalmed in spice of words. Thoth, god of libraries, a birdgod, moonycrowned. And I heard the voice of that Egyptian highpriest. *In painted chambers loaded with tilebooks.*
> They are still. Once quick in the brains of men. Still: but an itch of death is in them, to tell me in my ear a maudlin tale, urge me to wreak their will.

$$(U, 9:352-58)$$

The perversity bequeathed to us by literature is therefore not a negation of otherness—in the sense in which psychoanalytic discourse can define perversity as a kind of "fooling around" with the law or a denial of the others' freedom and autonomy.[24] Perversity simply proves the ineluctable return of the other in the self, an other that cannot be confidently ascribed to an identifiable place (as would be the case with the analysand's transference to the analyst, who then, for him, embodies otherness through silence). For Joyce, however, coming to terms with the peculiar otherness that literature keeps in store meant a uniquely idiosyncrasic combination of "ghost" and "imp" in the act of writing. A letter sent from Rome to his brother Stanislaus reveals this, in a passage in which Joyce seems to lament his sarcastic and negative tone and to deplore his unduly harsh portrayal of Ireland. He acknowledges at the same time that he could not write in a gentler mood: "For were I to rewrite the book as G.R. [Grant Richard] suggests 'in another sense' (where the hell does he get the meaningless phrases he uses) I am sure I should find again what you call the Holy Ghost sitting in the ink-bottle and the perverse devil of my literary conscience sitting on the hump of my pen" (*Letters*, 2:166). Are they fighting, ink versus pen, good angel versus evil genie, holy and perverse spirits playing out again the drama of yes and no, or are they united in a whole-sale denunciation of Dublin? To try to answer this question will be my first step in this reading of Joyce's perverse strategies, a step which will take us to *Dubliners*.

ONE

A PORTRAIT OF THE READER AS A YOUNG DUBLINER

To keep silent, this is what we all strive for when we write.
Maurice Blanchot, L'Ecriture du désastre

Dubliners is a collection of stories haunted by the kind of silence Maurice Blanchot speaks of,[1] a silence against which the chatter of urban gossip reveals its hollowness. Meaning is thus only a limit imposed onto this silence, a border helping to define the diseased mother, the cancerous womb of Dublin. The silence that many commentators—including Ezra Pound and Hermann Broch—have noticed may function like the silence of the analyst or the silence of the priest at confession, since it lets the symptoms speak of themselves. Silence begs the question of textual hermeneutics, for its disturbing effect is the epiphany of meaning.

The question of the silence of interpretation is built within the text, prepared and foreseen in the deceptive game it plays with the reader. This, as I see it, is the primary function of the silences of the text. For there are different kinds of silences: silence can mean the inversion of speech, its mirror, that which structures its resonance, since without silence, speech becomes a mere noise, a meaningless clatter; silence can reveal a gap, a blank space in the text, that can be accounted for in terms of the characters who betray themselves by slips, lapsus, omissions; or in terms of the general economy of the text, silence can be the void element that ensures displacement, hence circulation. Silence can finally appear as the end, the limit, the death of speech, its paralysis. There, silence joins both the mute symptoms (Eveline's aphasia is a good example of this in *Dubliners*) and the work of Thanatos inscribed in the production of writing.

The problematics of silence can offer an approach which would go beyond the facile antagonism between the surface realism of the stories and the suggestions, allusions and quasi-symbolist tactics of inferring by cross-references. The only way to gain a broader perspective is to introduce the silent process of reading into the text. Thus one can keep in mind the insistent ethical function of the stories (Joyce knew he was writing a "chapter of the moral history of my country" [*Letters*, 2:134]) and their political relevance, and see these as confronted with the construction of a real Irish capital through literature ("Is it not possible for a few persons of character and culture to make Dublin a capital such as Christiania has become?" [*Letters*, 2:105]), a construction which opposes any capitalistic exploitation. The mirror held up to the Irish may well be nicely polished; it is not dependent on a theory of pure mimesis or of purely symbolist implications. *Dubliners* is not, on the other hand, a direct consequence of Joyce's current theories of aesthetics, such as Stephen expounds them. It is rather the theory itself, in its wider sense, that is mirrored in the text. There, it is coupled with the utmost degree of precision and particularity in the pragmatics of writing that deconstructs the voices of the characters, narrators, commentators, and paves the way toward the constitution of another rhetoric of silences, the silences of the writing being caught up by the silent reading-writing which transforms a collection of short stories into a text.

My question will then become, In what sense does this book offer a theory of its own interpretation, of its reading, of possible metadiscourses about its textuality? In what way is there the temptation of an identification, with what aspects of the text, and to what effects? If, finally, *Dubliners* rules out any final recourse to a metalanguage, what are the consequences for the ethics and the politics of reading?

I shall start with two theoretical or critical preliminaries. For Broch, who wrote a penetrating review of *Ulysses* in "James Joyce and the Present Time,"[2] Joyce, like Hofmannsthal, reveals through his hatred of clichés the traces of what Broch calls a "Chandos experience," taking this term from Hofmannsthal's fictional letter in which a young and gifted lord tells Bacon that he cannot write any more, nor even speak, after a breakdown of the natural relationship between signifier and signified. Thus, for Hermann Broch, *Dubliners* and *Ulysses* manifest the mutism of a world condemned to silence by the destruction of centered values, in the very hypertrophy of their growth. *Dubliners* marks the reversal from pure individual and sympomatic aphasia to the process of recovering the void; it is to be considered between Lord Chandos's letter (1902) and Wittgenstein's *Tractatus* (begun in 1911). Ezra Pound, too, points out the ethical and political import of *Dubliners*, from a different point of view. He praises the clear, hard prose, which eschews unnecessary detail: "He carefully avoids telling you a lot that you don't want to know."[3] These stories, which are all defined by the special quality of their "vivid waiting" for some impossible escape, render Dublin universal; according to Pound, however, Joyce has not yet surpassed his Flaubertian model of *Trois contes*.

But the reference to Flaubert is decisive, since it enables the critic to stress the ideological relevance of the work. Like Flaubert, who believes that the collapse of France in 1870 might have been avoided if only people had read his books, Joyce also thinks that his "diagnosis" might have been useful to his country in turmoil. In Pound's words, this becomes "if more people had read *The Portrait* and certain stories in Mr. Joyce's *Dubliners* there might have been less recent trouble in Ireland" (*Pound/Joyce*, 90). I shall have to come back to Joyce's use of Flaubert and remark on the limitations of Pound's interpretation; it nevertheless throws a double light on the text of *Dubliners*, which constantly hesitates between the status of a cure, a diagnosis, and that of a symptom, produced by the same causes it attempts to heal. Such an oscillation will become apparent if we try to apply the famous phrase of "silence, exile, and cunning" (*P,* 247) to *Dubliners.*[4]

The theme of exile has been the focus of critical attention, while "silence" seems to have embarrassed everyone. First, the order of the terms in this well-known triad poses a problem; when Stephen decides to be an artist, a "priest of eternal imagination," he selects these three weapons as the only tools he can use against the encroachments of home, fatherland, and church. If the order is chronological, the initial silence defines his refusal to take part in the political and linguistic wrangles of Dublin until he exiles himself and moves to Paris for a start. But then cunning cannot be simply considered as the third step in this movement towards greater intellectual freedom if this freedom is available elsewhere. Could it be that Joyce implies a more logical correspondence between the two triads, silence referring to the family, exile to nationalism, and cunning to the perverse and religious refusal of religion? I shall, in fact, suggest strong affinities between silence and paternity, but as these three "nets" are constantly overlapping, especially in the Dublin of *Dubliners*, it must then be that all three concepts or attitudes work together indissociably and simultaneously. All the dreams of exile to the East in *Dubliners* are part of a ruse that employs silence in different modes of revelation. I shall thus commence by an approach via the silent ruses of interpretation, centered on the notions of perversity, heresy, and orthodoxy, and then move on to an analysis of the exile of "performance" in the enunciative strategies of the text, until finally everything will appear hinged on the silent name of the capitalized Father.

"The Sisters" offers the real starting-point, for it is more than just the first story in the collection; it also provides an elaborate introduction to the discourses of *Dubliners*. What strikes one from the first page is the deliberate suspension of a number of terms: the identity of the dead priest is disclosed through a series of hesitating, unfinished sentences, and even the "now" of the initial paragraph is not related to a precise chronology (it is not directly linked to the supper scene which follows). Several signifiers are given, almost too soon, without explanation (paralysis, simony, gnomon), while the real messenger who brings the news of the priest's decease has already made up his mind as to the signification of the event, but deliberately withholds his own conclusions. "I'll tell you my opinion . . . ," he says, but he never really affords more than hints of a possible perversion. This continuous suspension of meanings introduces a whole series of unfinished sentences, marked by dots; all of Old Cotter's remarks, except for one (*D*, 7-8); the end of the boy's dream (*D*, 12); the aunt's questions (14); and finally the answers given by Eliza ("But still . . .") and her conclusion that "there was something gone wrong with him . ." (16-17).

We must be aware that the child is not a narrator but an interpreter, who also believes that Old Cotter knows more than he does, while constantly suspecting the validity of his information (he has to read the card pinned on the door to be persuaded that the priest is actually dead). The story begins *in medias res*, so that the child may supply the reader with a figure mirroring his own interpretative process. In this process, the child has to come to terms with hints or allusions (Old Cotter *alludes* to the boy as a child, which angers him), from which he attempts to make sense: "I puzzled my head to extract meaning from his unfinished sentences" (9). As he imagines that the face of the dead priest follows him in the dark, it becomes obvious that the symbolic realm of interpretation exhibits gaps which are soon filled by imaginary fantasies. These contaminate the interpretative process with suggestions of sacrilegious communion. Now the roles of the priest and of the old man appear as opposite points of view on the very process of reading.

For, in fact, in the child's view, the meaning only hinted at by Old Cotter through his silences has to be identified with the dream itself. Indeed, the dream supplies meanings which all develop the suspended signifiers of the first paragraph. The face wishes to utter something to the child but fails: "It began to confess to me in a murmuring voice and I wondered why it smiled continually and why the lips were so moist with spittle. But then I remembered that it had died of paralysis and I felt that I too was smiling feebly as if to absolve the simoniac of his sin" (*D*, 9). The absence of "gnomon" will be accounted for later; what matters here is the exchange of sacerdotal functions between the boy and the priest. He confesses the priest, whose voice is heard though not his words, and the perverse enjoyment of the scene in such a "pleasant and vicious region" derives from the inversion of the roles and the transmission of the frozen smile from the priest to the boy. The next time the dream is mentioned, in a flashback, it again is accompanied by speculations about Old Cotter's sentences, and the memories are themselves cut short: "–in Persia, I thought. . . . But I could not remember the end of the dream" (*D*, 12).

The strange complicity between the priest and the child, which is stressed in his recollections of their conversation, enhances two important points: unlike Mr. Cotter, the Reverend Flynn explained to the boy the *meanings* of different ceremonies, of the sacraments and institutions. He also obviously got pleasure from these lessons, and in the parody of the *puer senex* theme, we find the repetition of the uncanny smile that becomes an obscene leer. So, on the one hand, we witness a perverse and seductive exchange of sacraments within an order of faith that appears utterly absurd (until the intricate questions of the catechism are debunked in "Grace"); on the other hand, we find a theory which obstinately refuses to give away its key: "I have my own theory about it, he said. I think it was one of those . . . peculiar cases. . . . But it's hard to say . . ." (8). I would be tempted to read here the disjunction between *orthodoxy*, defined as a theory without a meaning, and *perversity*, as a game of signifiers whose meaning is uncertain.

In order to define this use of the concept of orthodoxy, it might be helpful to consider the very "orthodox" approach to the church by Stephen in a passage of *Ulysses* in which he sees the church triumphing over all heresies: "The proud potent titles clanged over Stephen's memory the triumph of their brazen bells: *et unam sanctam catholicam et apostolicam ecclesiam:* the slow growth and change of rite and dogma like his own rare thoughts, a chemistry of stars. . . . A horde of heresies fleeing with mitres awry . . ." (*U*, 1:650–56).

Orthodoxy in such a picture is not simply the "right opinion"; it is concerned with authority in a special, theological sense, linking it with the idea of tradition, blending the voices of the singers in Stephen's image, and also slowly adding rites and dogmas to the canon. Cardinal Newman is probably the best exponent of such a view of orthodoxy; beside the fact that he is highly praised by Joyce as a prose writer, he gives a very consistent definition of orthodoxy in his writings. For Newman, the particularity of heresy is to appeal to the Scriptures alone and to disdain tradition; in this separation of dogma from living faith, the heresiarchs separate themselves from the body of the true church. It is known that Newman began his theological researches with an examination of the heresy of Arius and founded his main conclusions on this case, which figures in Stephen's list of heresies: "The handful of bishops who supported Arius did not make any appeal to an uninterrupted tradition in their favour. They did but profess to argue from Scripture and from the nature of the case."[5] Orthodoxy is not dependent on revelation alone or on tradition alone; it is the right authority deriving from an exact balance between Scripture and tradition.

It would then remain to prove that the perversion of such an orthodoxy always stems from a reliance on the written word, or a dismissal of oral tradition. The maternal function of heresy is clearer in *Ulysses* than in *Dubliners,* but I must, for the moment, postpone the articulation of the process of writing with the maternal world. In *Dubliners,* nevertheless, the disjunction between orthodoxy and perversity roughly delimits the world of the absent father and that of the mother's smothering attentions. This can be borne out by a comparison with another passage, from "A Painful Case." There is in Mr. Duffy a companion to Mr. Cotter, since he too seems in favor of a separation of the sexes and ages. ("Let a young lad run about and play with young lads of his own age and not be . . . ," says Mr. Cotter [*D,* 8], which appear less drastic than Mr. Duffy's denial of love and friendship, but asserts the same pedagogical repression.) He too has a "theory," while Mrs. Sinico listens to him, probably as amused by the patter of his aphorisms as the reverend was by

the halting answers of the boy: "Sometimes in return for his theories she gave out some fact of her own life. With almost maternal solicitude she urged him to let his nature open to the full;
she became his confessor" (*D*, 123). But when she tries to act out
the implications of what he has left unsaid, as she reads in his
refusal of intimacy a longing for closer contact, he undercuts
such a gross misunderstanding of his own sentences and takes ref-
uge in theoretical equanimity, an enunciated compilation of wisdom without a voice: "He heard the strange impersonal voice
which he recognized as his own, insisting on the soul's incur-
able loneliness" (124). When Mrs. Sinico presses his hand, he
flees, essentially fearing the distortion of an interpretation of his
own voice: "Her interpretation of his words disillusioned him"
(124).

The discrepancy between theory and the interpretation of
symptoms acquires tragic overtones in this story, while in "The
Sisters" it essentially describes the particular infinity of the process. Such an infinity is mentioned by the child when he adds
that he used to enjoy Old Cotter's endless stories before, probably before he had met the priest: the faints and worms can be
adequately replaced by the responses of the mass. But what he
finally hears during his long silence in the last scene after the
visit to the corpse is either the empty gossip of his aunt, or Nannie and Eliza, the ill-fated "Sisters" of destiny, or the silence of
the empty chalice: "She stopped suddenly as if to listen. I too listened; but there was no sound in the house" (*D*, 17). This will be
taken up by the final silence that surrounds Mr. Duffy after
Mrs. Sinico's death ("He could hear nothing: the night was perfectly silent. He listened again: perfectly silent. He felt that he
was alone" [*D*, 131]). The endlessness of the other narratives
relies on such a victorious silence, and this is the real link
between the stories in *Dubliners* and those of *Finnegans Wake*.
When Joyce reordered his notes for the *Work in Progress*, he
mentioned the "story of the invalid pensioner" in a context of
"desperate story-telling": "Arabian nights, serial stories, tales
within tales, to be continued, desperate story-telling, one caps
another to reproduce a rambling mock-heroic tale."[6]

While the masculine theory rests on the gnomic utterance of

clichés which have no proper conclusions and which in their denunciation of bad "effects" are akin to the pompous trivialities of a Polonius, the perversity of the dead symbolic father defines the incompleteness of a gnomon, a significant inadequacy. A gnomon is not only the pointer on a sundial, but more specifically "that part of a parallelogram which remains after a similar parallelogram is taken away from one of its corners," in Euclid. The absent corner hints at the gaping lack revealed not only by the paralysis of the priest, but also by the disjuncture between symptoms and their interpretation. Although the boy is urged by his uncle to "learn to box his corner" (*D*, 8–9)—which also alludes to the confession box in which the priest has been found laughing silently—this foolish assertion of the subject's autonomy and self-reliance is contradicted by the series of dichotomies the child faces. The "lighted *square* of window" (italics mine) has not disclosed such a gnomon yet: it would have taken *two* candles set at the head of the corpse to project a shadow visible from the outside. What the child saw in his fascinated gaze was simply the lack of an expected lack, since death has already begun its "work," but without visible external signs. "We would see a sign . . . " These signs, never ascertainable although working behind the square, are set into motion through the words only.

The words *paralysis, simony,* and *gnomon* become thus inexorably connected through an etymological chain of associations. *Gnomon* implies interpretation and Greek geometry, but is placed curiously beside catechism. Joyce has an illuminating remark in a letter of April 1905: "While I was attending the Greek mass here last Sunday it seemed to me that my story *The Sisters* was rather remarkable. The Greek mass is strange. The altar is not visible but at times the priest opens the gates and shows himself. . . . The Greek priest has been taking a great eyeful out of me: two haruspices" (*Letters*, 2:86–87). The connection Joyce implicitly states is striking, suggesting that the very exposure of a sacrament can become the exposure of the person in what can be termed simony. The series of parallel lines intersecting one another can thus describe the figure of the interlocking signifiers. We know, for instance, that Simon Magus, who was the first to try to buy the power to transmit the Holy Ghost from the Apostles, was also a Samaritan prophet, adored as the first God by the members of his sect. They also coupled him with a goddess named Helena, who was said to have been created by his thought. In his teachings can be found the sources of most subsequent heresies spreading Gnosticism through the early Church. He bears witness to the extent to which the messianic Judeo-Christian heresies had been hellenized. Thus, Persia in the boy's dream also calls up the strong Manichean tendencies of the Simonite heresies, while adding another dimension of exoticism to the composite figure of such a "jew-greek," like Bloom, incestuous and suspected of being homosexual but really in need of a son.

In the same way, *paralysis* eytmologically conveys an idea of dissolution, of an unbinding (*para-lyein*, "to release, to unbind") which is coupled with an anguishing immobility, while *paresis* means "to let fall." The priest's paralysis is both a dropping of some holy vessel (a chalice) in a parapraxis (a slip or lapsus) and the untying of the knots which paradoxically constrict the cramped movements of the protagonists. The fall itself, the *felix culpa* of original sin, links the boy's perverted innocence (it must have been "the boy's fault" in some version of the incident) to the heresy of the condemned priest. In echo to this, Mr. Duffy laments the ruin of their confessional (the meeting place to which Mrs. Sinico came) and fears another "collapse" (*D*, 124) of his feminine confessor—the first collapse he implicitly alludes to being the gesture of Mrs. Sinico when she kissed his hand!

If Mr. Duffy shrinks away, Old Cotter would prefer to cut off, to lop away the gangrened limbs, appearing thus as a real "Old cutter." For the orthodoxy divides in order to anathematize through the particular injunction of lacerated sentences, in a series of performative utterances that stop abruptly before the end. The imitation of Christ is transformed into an apotropaic strategy, such as Stephen practices in the *Portrait* when he tries to become a saint: "His eyes shunned every encounter with the eyes of women. From time to time also he balked them by a sudden effort of the will, as by lifting them suddenly in the middle of an unfinished sentence and closing the book" (*P,* 150). But in *Dubliners,* the maternal tissue of the city, corrupted at its very core by an absent and mute center (indeed, the priest was never heard in the house "you wouldn't hear him in the house any more than now" [*D,* 15]–"now" meaning "now that he is dead"), spreads over, and reforms over the sutured incision, now overgrown with new tissue. This could be why the shop window notice usually reads *"Umbrellas Re-covered"* (*D,* 10). The umbrellas are inscribed both in the series of veils, curtains, and clothes such as the great-coat in which the priest is smothered, priestly vestments which blur the difference, and in the series of parodic phallic substitutes, culminating with O'Madden Burke's gesture as a final law-giver, "poised upon his umbrella" (*D, 168*). In this city of lost property, one cannot recover an absent penis, but the phallus is there as a signifier of the lack to be recovered. The catacombs and the cat-echism organize a space of echoes (*kata-echein*) which allows for the puns on "faints" and "faint," "not long" and "I longed," on the first page of "The Sisters," since the idle play of the signifiers pre-pares for the silent and deadly work of Thanatos in the text.

The recovering of the text by itself when it doubles back in this way describes the necessary process of rereading and mirrors the points where it attaches itself inextricably to ambiguous sig-nifiers, which are floating without mooring. One of these is the term "resignation" used for the priest: "He was quite resigned. . . . He looks quite resigned" (*D,* 14). The signs on his truculent face reveal that this resignation acquires a double edge; the resigned priest has been suspended, so that he is retired and excluded, has resigned his function after his failure to perform his duties. He then assumes the part of the unwilling heretic, perverse precisely because he did not choose to be apart but obeyed the uncon-scious law of the symptom. The word "resigned" yields then another hint, pointing towards "sign." What this double sign (of the cross) leaves open is the symbolic transference of his attri-butes to the boy, whose life, too, is "crossed" by the symptom:

> And then his life was, you might say, crossed.
> –Yes, said my aunt. He was a disappointed man. You could see that.

A silence took possession of the little room, and, under cover of it I approached the table and tasted my sherry.

(16)

The child who has refused the crackers because he would have made too much noise eating them now indulges in this silent communion. Eliza was "disappointed" (13) at his refusal, but this devious acceptance of the wine instead of the Eucharist is another "crossing" of someone's wish. In the first version, the verb used by Joyce to show their first movement when coming into the room was "We crossed ourselves"; the cross was there as a sign, not the sign of the cross, but the crossing of the sign, through the cancellation of a symbol. The silence of confession, from which the priest has been debarred, superimposes the "latticed ear of a priest" (*P*, 221) on that of a boy. The priest was "resigned" because of the crossing between the empty symbol and the transmission of esoteric and perverse powers to someone who is called a "Rosicrucian" (*D*, 9).

The confession is the process of perverse crossing which breeds a rose on a cross in Dublin. This is why Old Cotter vigorously prohibits the boy's confession ("I wouldn't like children of mine . . . to have much to say to a man like that") and utters this unique complete sentence just after he has "spat rudely into the grate" (*D*, 8). The forceful projection of his spittle of course contrasts with the soft oozing of the priest's dribble. The familiar notion of contamination through a poisonous humor can help to explain the curious reversal of the situation of confession. The priest's teaching could have infected the ears of all possible listeners, contaminating by synecdoche the whole of the town. There was a medieval theory of which Joyce was aware which held that heresies could actually poison the atmosphere of a city, as a kind of polluted air (*pestilentia*) penetrating men's viscera.[7] The contagion generated by this infection would surely condemn everyone to excommunication, just as when Henri de Clairvaux found the city of Toulouse so infected with Cathar heresies that no healthy part remained.

The metaphor then develops into that of the cancer, the perverse parasite preying on the whole of the organism, for which the only cure is the amputation of the diseased member. But this cancer is not visible yet, since it still proliferates beneath the skin. The antagonistic forces of division and proliferation can be seen at play in the famous expression used by Saint Paul, who left the formulae that were to be repeated over and over during the later struggles of the church against heresies:

> Study to shew thyself approved unto God, a workman that needeth not to be ashamed, rightly *dividing* the world of truth. But shun profane and vain babblings: for they will increase unto more ungodliness. And their word will eat as doth a *canker*: of whom is Hymenaeus and Philetus [by way of parenthesis, they were followers of Menander, who was very close to Simon Magus in his origin and doctrine]; who concerning the truth have erred, saying that the *resurrection* is past already.
>
> (Timothy 2:15–18; italics mine)

Truth implies a certain concern for division, whereas heresy thrives as perversion on the body of dogma; nowhere is perversion more virulent than in a discourse which attempts to articulate the truth of the subject in his own division, and this is where psychoanalysis and religion exhibit their common logic, a logic Joyce merely displaces—or, rather, warps.

In his reversal of the pattern of confession, Joyce tends to imply that the cancerous contamination of perversion can be effected by the simple, silent act of hearing a confession. The poisoned ear of the murdered king in *Hamlet* becomes the imaginary conch which would magnify parabolically the principle of perversity in the text. To define perversion by simony and simony by perversion points to the idea that the emptying of the symbolic power stems from a negation of the locus of the Other,[8] and thus the difference which constitutes the subject as subject of his desire tends to be displaced, duplicated. The child's wish was utterly dependent on that of the old priest, who had reduced it to a distorted image of his own frustrated desire. Perversion appears then first as a certain confusion on the one hand of duplication, and on the other of division and difference. This entails a derision of the signifiers of the Other's desire. Thus, the pervert erects codes, maxims, laws, so as to dodge past them all the better, and to get around them. Getting around them, he also turns around in them: such is the significance of the meeting with the pervert in "An Encounter." In such a vicious circle, the loss of the object is atoned for by the loss of meaning. But paradoxically, perversion constantly needs the outcrop of sense, its generation as well as the reference to desire and the Law. The law of silence is merely the silence of the Law.

All this does not mean that Joyce is a "pervert" in a trivial sense; rather, he appears as a neurotic who imagines himself to be a pervert in order to assure the continuity of his enjoyment.[9] He was also aware both of his ethical posture and of the perverse nature of his drives in writing. He deplores at one point his failure to express the beauty and glamor of Dublin, for he has started idealizing it by comparison with Rome, and he knows he cannot help distorting the picture: "I am sure I should find again what you call the Holy Ghost sitting in the inkbottle and the perverse devil of my literary conscience sitting on the hump of my pen" (*Letters*, 2:166). But other writers must be judged according to ethical standards: "Maupassant writes very well, of course, but I am afraid that his moral sense is rather obtuse" (*Letters*, 2:99).

Perversion cannot be reduced to parody, and this is how we can, I think, start to distinguish between the strategies of Flaubert (and possibly of Pound) and those of Joyce. Both Flaubert and Joyce have met the problems of censorship, but while *Madame Bovary* and *Ulysses* were attacked on grounds of immorality and obscenity, *Dubliners* was thought litigious, libellous: more perverse than obscene, more subversive than immoral. This can be read in the games the text plays with silence, and it is clear that the first truncated warning given by Old Cotter ("When children see things like that, you know, it has an effect" [*D*, 9]) has been read too literally by the printers. Joyce had been naive enough to reveal the "enormity" of "An Encounter" to his publisher, and the same suspicion crept back in his relationship with Roberts, the second publisher he went to see in Dublin: "Roberts I saw again. He asked me very narrowly was there sodomy also in *The Sisters* and what was "simony" and if the priest was suspended only for the breaking of the chalice. He asked me also was there more in *The Dead* than appeared" (*Letters*, 2:305-6). Everything becomes potentially dangerous, and the fear one is exposed to is paralleled by a desire to name the alleged perversion—a perversion for which, of course, "sodomy" is totally inadequate.

As with Flaubert, a maximum of legibility, of transparence, is coupled with the insinuation of a perversion at work within the signifiers of the text. But Flaubert stops this process before it attacks the structure of the subject. I shall rapidly analyze some parts of "Un Coeur Simple" to substantiate my point, and I shall select three moments which are also three moments of silence. First, a silence spreads over all the objects to stress their weight, their sensual volume, and corresponds to instants of diffuse happiness for a Félicité who is not cut off from the others; she still has to identify with Virginie (The Virgin) and Victor (the defeated heroism and exoticism meeting death). This takes place at Trouville in the summer, when it is too hot to leave the room: "L'éblouissante clarté du dehors plaquait des barres de lumière entre les lames des jalousies. Aucun bruit dans le village. En bas, sur le trottoir, personne. Ce silence épandu augmentait la tranquillité des choses. Au loin, les marteaux des calfats tamponnaient des carènes."[10] After Félicité's complete immersion into the only dominant discourse available, that of religion, her fixation on the parakeet that has been offered to her reveals the limitation of her perception and the dwindling of her circle of reference: "Le petit cercle des ses idées se rétrécit encore, et le carillon des cloches, le mugissement des boeufs, n'existaient plus. Tous les êtres fonctionnaient avec le silence des fantômes. Un seul bruit arrivait maintenant à ses oreilles, la voix du perroquet."[11] The parakeet, Loulou, an obvious parody of the paraclete or Holy Ghost, is there posed as "son and lover," until the last epiphany, which affords the finale of the text, shows her death when she imagines a gigantic parakeet hovering over her head and soaring from the religious procession. This epiphany, like those of *Dubliners*, is a logical denoue-ment, which allows her no other possibility of escape. Slowly crushed in the spiralling metaphor, she has to conclude parodic-ally that the voice of God and the answers she hallucinates are one: "Le Père, pour s'énoncer, n'avait pu choisir une colombe, puisque ces bêtes-là n'ont pas de voix, mais plutôt un des an-cêtres de Loulou."[12] This deduction could have been made by Bourvard and Pécuchet, but here it stresses the sacrilegious inno-cence of her desperation. The effects of perversion in Flaubert's text turn around the problematics of utterance, of enunciation, and in this way Félicité appears as the precursor of Eveline, to whom she may have lent the episode with Victor, when he sails away, like Frank; but these textual effects remain at the level of parody, not because they are limited to an exploration of "style," but because the reader cannot but identify with Félicité's consciousness. The story soars up towards this derisive climax, from which the only fallback to the real happens out-side the text. In *Dubliners*, there is no hysterical identification, but the strategy of silences, not so ordered in their progression, escapes from the brittle dialectics of stylistic parody. Perversity flies from the Pigeon House to the Ballast Office, leaving a deaf Nannie or a mute Eveline in a lurch of the structure—since "c'est le Pigeon" (it is the pigeon or Holy Ghost) of paternity which could alone hold the missing key.[13]

To follow along these lines, *Dubliners* can be divided more simply than Joyce suggests with his four-part pre-Viconian scheme of growth from childhood to adolescence, maturity, and the anarchy of public life. The text falls into two main moments. The first one explores the blind alleys of the possible strategies of interpretation, up to "The Boarding House"; the sec-ond part, starting with "A Little Cloud," hinges on a study of roles and performances, and in fact explores what I would call *enunciation* for short. "Grace," which was meant to be the con-clusion of the book in its first stage, ties all the strands together, as it unites the themes of confession, of interpretation, and of performative utterance. The two significant titles would be "Encounter" for the first part, an encounter with an Other denied and reduced precisely because it denies and reduces the

Other, and "Counterparts" for the second, the system of balances and oppositions encompassing the blocked gestures of the first part and providing them with and endless circulation within the city of paralysis.

Silence means in the first part a teasing seduction to hermeneutics; the moments of interpretation are generally underlined in the text, as in "Araby" ("I could interpret these signs" [D, 34], which foreshadows the final revelation). Lenehan is likewise deliberately ambiguous, since to "save himself" (55) he leaves his expressions open to several interpretations; he also tries to read signs of reassurance in others' gestures or physique. "An Encounter" offers the most blatant clues: the narrator fixes a distant aim, the Pigeon House, and is obviously looking for signs, such as the green eyes which his fantasy lends to Norwegian sailors and which he finds in the pervert's face. He has failed to decipher "the legend" on the boat (23) and remains unclear about his own motivations (". . . for I had some confused notion . . ." [23]). The unfinished sentence is similar to the omission of the end of the first boy's dream.

Every time, the interpretation abolishes itself in a moment of silence, either the missing center of the perverse speech about castigation, this absent secret or mystery never to be disclosed, or the untold action such as the suggested masturbation of the man, which is conveyed by a facile trick of the narration, for the boy has more or less been hypnotized:

> —I say! Look what he's doing!
> As I neither answer nor raised my eyes Mahony exclaimed again:
> —I say. . . . He's a queer old josser!
>
> (26)

The plot contrived to achieve some measure of freedom or escape results in a paltry stratagem, when the boys change their names, and an embarrassed silence. The cunning move is similar to the ruse of Ulysses facing the Cyclops, but here it remains insignificant. In the same way, Corley has been "too hairy" (D, 54) to tell his name to the girl he wants to exploit, and this master trickster exhibits the coin of simony in a silent gesture of mon-stration which gives Lenehan the status of a perverse disciple.

The silence felt in "Araby" ("I recognised a silence like that which pervades a church after a service" [D, 35]) assails the speak-ers as it invades Dublin: Eveline's speechlessness is formulated in "silent fervent prayer," (42), and recognition is lost; she cannot even give a "sign" (43) to Frank. In "The Boarding House" the complicity between the mother and Polly issues in a "persistent silence" (68) which cannot be misunderstood; it is the impetus behind the decisive gesture of the end. Mrs. Mooney's moral cleaver will no doubt cut through the hesitation of Bob Doran as it would do through tender meat. What Polly is waiting for in the end is not told, for she herself has forgotten that she was waiting for something: the castrated body of a man ready to accept all the ties of marriage is a direct anticipation of Tom Kernan's fall and is to be followed by Doran's degradation in *Ulysses*. Both go down the stairs to be met with the loss of some property, be it simply money, freedom and respect, or a corner of the tongue.

Thus, in what I recognize as the second moment, we move towards a definition of failure through the inadequacy of some performance; silence is then constitutive of a discourse, not sim-ply covered or revealed by a discourse. Enunciation refers not simply to direct speech, but assumes the sense of producing meaningful signs in a performance, be it singing or writing. What obviously links the fates of Little Chandler and Farring-ton is their inability to write. In Chandler's case, the main issue is his blindness to the real process of writing: he cannot think of any mediation between an imaginative mood, a certain psy-chological state, and the finished product, the idealized book of poems. He accordingly lives in the world of the clichés of romantic bad taste and finally cannot even read the hortatory consolation afforded by Byron's juvenilia.

Farrington, on the other hand, must find substitutes for what-ever violence he feels threatening to disrupt his servile copying. It is not a mere accident when he repeats the first name in the contract he has to write out. The repetition of "Bernard Ber-nard" (*D*, 100) is structurally similar to the repetition of the same verse sung by old Maria (118). Death drives are branched into repetitive parapraxes, until the pure repetition is identified with the silence of death, as we saw in Mr. Duffy's case. Death is then not a voice repeating itself, but the "laborious drone of the engine reiterating the syllables of her name" (131). The deadly work of the signifiers now seems to undermine the names of the dead, and this appears in "Ivy Day in the Committee Room."

It is in this story that the disjuncture between enunciated and enunciation is brought to the fore in a masterwork of political analysis, and it is emphasized by the intricate punctuation that the text develops through its silences. Pauses and silences mark the appearance and disappearance of the characters ("the room was silent again" seems to be a leitmotiv). For silence maps out the presuppositions of the speakers, their unspoken discourses and their modes of expression expose them much more than their empty speeches. Crofton's arrival releases the longer and most sustained speech by Mr. Henchy, and his silence is twofold: "He was silent for two reasons. The first reason, sufficient in itself, was that he had nothing to say; the second reason was that he considered his companions beneath him" (*D*, 146). The void of the enunciated word is not really sufficient, for we have to understand that what matters most is the *a priori* position of superiority he assigns to himself. Enunciation can reveal this position, without any material being spoken. All the while, this empty enunciated word is the object of the competition between the speakers, who all turn to Crofton and try to gain his mute support. Crofton is addressed twice directly by Henchy but refuses to side with him and does not assent either to O'Connor's pleading asides; only the cork popping out of the bottle can give him the cue. And what he adds to the debate is only the term "gentleman," which will become the object of the derision of "Grace."

In the same way, the adverb "argumentatively" (148), used to qualify the unfinished sentence of Mr. Lyons about the dubious morality of King Edward VII, acquires an ironic significance because the same argument of "let bygones be bygones" buries it in the silence of betrayal and denial. Denial has to be taken in its religious sense here, for it is such a denial that Joyce betrays, slyly putting perversion to work against itself. The final silences which greet the beginning and the end of the bathetic poem on Parnell culminate in the deflation of Mr. Crofton's final reply. The absence of any standard viewpoint from which to judge this poem leaves the reader teased and speechless, with no discourse at his disposal. The "clever" piece by Henchy is suspended in a vacuum of political interpretation, since the name of Parnell has been deprived of all political force and turned into a myth, the myth of the dismembered father devoured and mourned by the parricidal sons. Crofton's silence, resting on the assumption of superiority but unable to voice anything more than the void appears then as the only place the text prepares for the reader—after all, the Conservatives had not "betrayed" Parnell—a place no one can accept.

Names and enunciative strategies are intricately connected in these last stories, but "Counterparts" provides the example that is easiest to analyze. The first thing the reader witnesses is a violent shout—"Farrington!"—which sets the dominant tone of aggression. Being called by his name from the outside, Farrington remains "the man" as a subject of enunciation. But he apparently never utters anything original. We learn that he infuriated Mr. Alleyne by mimicking his Ulster accent, as he will later mimic the flat accent of his terrified son until he finds the felicitous reply which almost escapes his lips. He is then alluded to as the "consignor" (*D*, 102) when he gains his only real victory, derisory as it is: he pawns his watch for six shillings instead of merely five. From then on, he seems to be the subject of his own speech because he appears capable of narrating the incident, repeating it as he amplifies its nature. He stands the drinks as "Farrington," for his utterance has transformed a spontaneous witticism which was almost a slip of the tongue ("could he not keep his tongue in his cheek?" [*D*, 102]) into a decisive retort, now seeming a "smart ... thing" (103). What passes unmentioned, of course, is that his answer was the release of an important rage, the first symptom of which was the paralysis of the hand when he could not write. The circle of his downfall is rounded when, in the last part of the story, he is again called "the man," as he forfeits even his role as a father (109).

But the story "Grace" affords the real conclusion to the problematics of enunciation: from the slip of the cut or hurt tongue to the divine performative utterance of the pope's proclamation of infallibility, the whole gamut of speech acts is depicted, ascending a ladder that goes from infelicities to "happy" results. Even such a minor character as Mr. Fogarty helps to define "grace" in terms of personal appearance and contributes to its connection with utterance: "He bore himself with a certain grace, complimented little children and spoke with a neat enunciation" (*D,* 188), and later: "He enunciated the word and then drank gravely" (190). The text begins to insist on its own metaphoricity, which is brought to the fore twice. The first "metaphor," "we're all going to wash the pot" (184), brings in the theme of confession, while the second, comparing a priest to a "spiritual accountant" (198), introduces simony. Both are linked with enunciation: "He uttered the metaphor with a certain homely energy and, encouraged by his own voice, proceeded" (184). The energy of Martin Cunningham's efforts to lead his friend towards salvation is relayed by the "resonant assurance" of Father Purdon, who asks for permission to use his dominant trope: "If he might use the metaphor . . ." (197). This rhetorical precaution is, of course, superfluous, but it shows that we are invited to difficult readings with possible ruses and tricks, such as the deliberate distortion of the biblical quotation: "It was one of the most difficult texts in all the Scriptures, he said, to interpret properly" (197). In this devious way, Joyce warns us to read the satire along the lines of Dantean exegesis and progression from Hell to Purgatory and Paradise.

This circular structure links the inverted progress towards a parodic Paradiso for the bankrupt petit bourgeoisie of Dublin to the doomed circularity of confession. The forceful tautology of the doctrine of infallibility ("not one of them ever preached *ex cathedra* a word of false doctrine . . . because when the Pope speaks *ex cathedra* . . . he is infallible" [191]) stands out as the keystone of the edifice of empty discourse ("until at last the Pope himself stood up and declared infallibility a dogma of the Church *ex cathedra*" [192]). It is Mrs. Kernan's role to underline the feminine transmission of such a doctrine: on the one hand, she refrains from telling the "gentlemen" that her husband's tongue would not suffer by being shortened (178), while on the other, she feigns "pity" for the priest who would have to listen to their confession (194). The gap in the tongue signifies the first fall, the inscription of the *gnomon* within the apparatus of enunciation. And the fact that their conversation drifts towards the Council of 1870 reveals that it sets up a trap, with which his friends attempt to get at Kernan through his recanted heresy. John MacHale—who, in Mr. Cunningham's narration, suddenly stands up and shouts *"Credo"*—conveys the hysterical contagion of the performative power of authority and orthodoxy: it is the detail "with the voice of a lion" (192) that seems so catching here. The other cardinal (Döllinger, in fact) is disqualified, excommunicated: this is a strategy which pushed Mr. Kernan towards the utterance of such a "Credo." In order to continue speaking with an equivalent authority, he must utter "the word of belief and submission" (192) with the others, but also find his marginal freedom; he then adds another performative verb, fetishistically selecting the most trivial item of pomp: "I bar the candles!" (194). He thus manages to create a similar effect ("conscious of having created an effect on his audience" [194]) which duplicates the unconscious parody of the historical council with its "farcical gravity."

The barred tongue opens to the barring of the phallic substitutes. What remains is only the "retreat business and confession" (194) and their acceptance of a world where business is business. Thus, both the pope and the English king are focal points, helping to expose the undermining of utterance in the void of discourses. The English capital which is demanded by Mr. Henchy and which enables him to condone King Edward's past lapses, and the spiritual accounts which can palliate the most outrageous distortions of the sacred texts and even excuse the aberrations of those "old popes" who are not precisely "up to the knocker" (190), both thrive on the same death and prostitution of values. From this point of view, there remains the possibility of ethical judgements. This will disappear with "The Dead."

"The Dead" is the supplement to the series of stories of *Dubliners* which, added one year after the completion of the rest, not only mirrors the earlier stories, but modifies them retroactively, pushing them into a new mode of writing. Its function is similar to that of the Penelope chapter in *Ulysses*, with the difference that Gretta's secret has been repressed for so long that it cannot really be voiced, so that her voice only resounds muffled through the memories and desires of her husband.

The three aggressions by women, all of whom "discompose" Gabriel (*D*, 230), bring about a new askesis, which puts off the work of perversion, because the subject enjoys his own dissolution. This can be examined through a study of the uses of silence as a musical pause in the narration. There are different moments of silence, which enhance the progressive undoing of the subject. First, a silence greets Lily's bitter retort (203), a silence which is then mirrored negatively in the silence by which the three young ladies snub Mr. Browne (209). Gabriel is silent when he fails to answer Miss Ivors (214) after which he concentrates on the preparation for his speech: "He . . . took no part in the conversation with which the table covered Lily's removal of the plates" (226). Even this conversation, lively as it appears, reveals its weak points and allows for the lurking menace of death to hush the gossips, as when someone mentions the monks who sleep in their coffins: "As the subject had grown lugubrious, it was buried in a silence of the table" (230). The uneasy silence of this parodic last supper is transformed into the general silence marking the signal for Gabriel's speech. His empty rhetoric soars on the background of a willingness to forget the silence of vanished ghosts.

When Gretta, entranced, listens to the song Bartell d'Arcy finally sings, Gabriel tries to arrest her movement in a permanent vision which is blind to the musical qualities of the scene, precisely because he asks the wrong question of the symbolical meaning of such a picture: he wonders "what is a woman standing on the stairs in the shadow, listening to distant music, a symbol of" (240). The sense he is groping for is of course the deferred meaning he has promised to tell Gretta, this hidden truth which allows him to cope with the task of sewing clichés together to entertain his aunts. This truth can in fact never be uttered, for in the destruction of the symbol, it is exposed as a sham.

Like Tom Kernan, Gabriel refuses the candle offered by the porter, preferring the complicity of shadows to "that handsome article" (247); he prepares a little scenario of seduction, in which he would be the master of the revels, ready to "overmaster" (248) his wife when she seems aloof. It is not simply that he cannot hold a candle to the secret and past love between Michael Furey and Gretta, but rather that he fears that the simple light of a candle could pale the fire he feels in his blood. It might also be that he unconsciously fears that their tête-à-tête would look like a mortuary vigil, a wake, watched from the outside by some unknown and wistful youth.

For the music of desire is also one of hackneyed phrases quoted from old letters; the silence of his lust is curiously linked with the ineffability of her name: *"Why is it that words like these seem to me so dull and cold? Is it because there is no word tender enough to be your name?* Like distant music these words that he had written years before were borne towards him from the past" (244). It is well known that Joyce quotes from one of his letters to Nora, but it must be stressed that the context of this model is one of dejection and also of an utter failure to speak; Joyce wrote in September 1904:

> The energy which is required for carrying on conversations seems to have left me lately and I find myself constantly slipping into silence. . . . I know that when I meet you next our lips will become mute. . . . And yet why should I be ashamed of words? . . . What is it that prevents me unless it be that no word is tender enough to be your name?
>
> (*Letters*, 2:56)

Gretta's bare and artless enunciation of a fact that pierced her yields the symbolic otherness for which Gabriel was vainly looking in his own past.

Thus, silence assumes a double function in "The Dead," and it is, for instance, such a silence that explains Gabriel's misunderstanding of Gretta's mood. The same expression as in "The Sisters" is used: "Under cover of her silence" (*D,* 246) he indulges in his erotic fantasies, while such a silence is echoed twice in the following paragraph. The mounting tension toward physical desire is contrasted sharply with the desexualized truth of Gretta's past love, an infinite love because it has been unbounded by the death of Michael; and the climax of their misunderstanding comes when she tells him, "You are a very generous person" (249) as he entangles himself in sordid details. When she breaks down, he approaches her and passes a mirror: "He caught sight of himself in full length . . . the face whose expression always puzzled him when he saw it in a mirror and his glimmering gilt-rimmed eye-glasses" (249). The mention of the mirror is strategic here; first, it duplicates itself, towards the imaginary fascination for the image of the self, captured in the smaller mirrors of his spectacles, which screen him from the real as visual goloshes. This glance is still caught in the generality of the series of glances which *always* startle Gabriel, and appears as an indulgence. When the couple he visualises comes to the fore, the mirror is shattered: "While he had been full of memories of their secret life together, full of tenderness and joy and desire, she had been comparing him in her mind with another. A shameful consciousness of his own person assailed him." He can now reinterpret the "pitiable fatuous fellow he had caught a glimpse of in the mirror" (251), a mirror in which Gretta had looked rapidly at herself only to go beyond it.

But then the duplication gives way to division, to splitting, to the fading of the subject. An evanescent Gabriel becomes the frozen stone guest who comes in symptoms to disturb the banquet of his desires, to paraphrase Lacan. He understands that he has to play the role of the Other in relation to his wife, an Other absolutely cut off from any hearing; the generous ear he lends to his wife brings no real atonement. His tears of remorse, similar to those of little Chandler, betray only his self-indulgence: "Generous tears filled Gabriel's eyes" (255). The generosity of impossible love brings no analytic position: he only listens to the fall of snow—that is, of a natural descent—without a subject. The generous is then swallowed up by the general

("Snow was general all over Ireland"), a general of death whose last charge rounds off everything. Gabriel is poised between the pleasure of his own disappearance ("His own identity was fading out into a grey impalpable world: the solid world itself which these dead had one time reared and lived in was dissolving and dwindling"), and the anguish of such a "bitter ending"; a delicate balance is established between the reversed signifiers of "swoon" and "snow" in their slow downfall (255–56): potentiality dissolves into entropy.

The last oceanic silence which concludes "The Dead" cannot be reduced by interpretation; in its rhythmic beauty, it calls up an ecstasy such as *The Portrait* describes with "the soft peace of silent spaces of fading tenuous sky above the waters, of oceanic silence" (*P*, 225–26) before the conclusion of *Finnegans Wake*. The dissolution of the subject implies an infinite interpretation, not reducible to the antagonisms between East and West. The critical controversy around the value of "westward" (*D*, 255) seems a little idle; what Joyce simply suggests is that a cycle has been completed, since perversion has exhausted its own possibilities. The pure annihilation of differences proposes to the subject the empty place of the other and silent listener, "playing possum," as Earwicker will have to do to save himself in the *Wake*. The symbolic structure has been so violently fractured for Gabriel that we are left gazing at the empty mirror of the sky, in much the same way as we stand as readers metamorphosed into a horned and paralytic Shakespeare at the end of the "Circe" episode in *Ulysses*.

Silence is not a mere symptom, then; it defines the vanishing point of all assertion, exhibits the empty space which the writing of the text constantly re-covers and recovers, in its multiplication. The "few light taps upon the pane" made by the snow are echoed in *Finnegans Wake* by the taps of the branches on the shutters expressed by the recurrent "Zinzin" motif.

   —Now we're gettin it. Tune in and pick up the forain counties! Hello!
   —Zinzin.
   —Hello! Tittit! Tell your title?

> −Abride!
> −Hellohello! Ballymacarett! Am I thru' Iss? Miss? True?
> −Tit! what is the ti . . ?
>   SILENCE.
>
>   (*FW,* 500.35–501.5)

In the *Wake*, the recurrent "Silence" incorporates the same symptom into a historical movement; it marks the *tabula rasa* of the
last stage of a Viconian ricorso: "And all's set for restart after the
silence" (*FW,* 382.14). This dialectical silence breaks with the silences of *Dubliners*; the metaphor of confession which was
applied to "Grace" (with the "washing of the pot") does not
apply to "The Dead." Gretta feels no regret, no contrition, she
never "confessess" to Gabriel; hence the impression of strange-
ness of her diction. Moreover, she may not have told everything, as Gabriel suddenly realizes. As with Anna Livia, washing
not the pots and kettles of supper but the dirty linen of the capital, the only silence that produces the space of otherness necessary to the weaving of the serial stories will be that of an almost
inaudible murmur, the deep flow of the river of time.

The first fourteen stories try to set up the possibility of an
ethical discourse criticizing the paralysis of Dublin; this is
finally left outside the scope of the subject's discourse in "The
Dead," as in *Finnegans Wake*. Like Wittgenstein, Joyce tends to
affirm the salvation of ethics through silence, since with the loss
of any metalanguage, one can only show, not enunciate, the possibility of direct action or of mythical contemplation. This is
why there is a real break and a real loss in the last silence in
Anna's final monologue, and not a mere expectancy of the
restart for a new beginning. There a certain "tacebimus" can provide a foundation for the ethics of critical reading. Maurice Blanchot remarks in his introduction to *Lautréamont and Sade* that
Heidegger has compared the poems of Hölderlin to a bell held
up in a still air, which a soft snow, falling on it, could make
vibrate; likewise, the commentary should not be more than a little snow, sounding or ringing this ancient bell.

Finally, the text approaches the region where a supreme
silence reigns, returning to the original condition from which it

emerges. The space of our reading is suspended between these two blanks, which are necessary to understand our position as subjects of a desire to read, a desire which can be that of losing oneself in the difference of the written signs. This process, indefinitely postponing the absolute loss of the self, manifests itself in fiction as an equivalent of the work of mourning, especially when the text is absorbed by its reenacting the killing and burial of the dead father, like *Finnegans Wake*. At this point reader and author lose their identities to fuse with the general system of the textual unconscious, a concept which is necessary to facilitate a reading of the *Wake* such as I shall endeavor to develop in the next chapters.

The constant rereading of Joyce's works by his later texts yields some clues to the symbolic strategies he employs, and such is the case with the parody of all the titles of the stories in *Finnegans Wake*. This comes after the description of the way Shem writes over his own body with his excrements, thereby displaying universal history in this "dividual chaos" (*FW*, 186.4–5). All the stories are then quoted, and their grouping is interesting, since it does not follow the order of the book. The first to be mentioned is "Ivy Day . . ." ("circling the square, for the deathfête of Saint Ignaceous Poisonivy, of the Fickle Crowd" [*FW*, 186.12–13]), and it is the only title to be so developed as to seem to refer to the *Wake* itself. Saint Ignatius has replaced Parnell, but their wake is held by the same fickle crowd of politicians.

Then twelve stories are jammed together in one paragraph and play the role of the twelve jurymen, here answering the call of "constable Sistersen" (alluding of course to the Sisters). The police inquest into this "painful sake" does not forget the "fun the concerned outgift of the dead med dirt" (*FW*, 187.10) and seems to have spotted a case of murder, a murder which is then distorted at the beginning of the following paragraph in "What mother?" (187.15). The two stories "Ivy Day" and "A Mother" have thus been carefully isolated; the first seems to define the general structure of the quadrature of the circle, the last the problematics of the murdering mother. The shaunish figure of Justius, who appears to defend the rights of the father's law, addresses the shemish heresiarch directly but also speaks to "himother," to himself made other through the mother's alterity. It is very fitting that he too refuses a "confession" and advises his brother to "conceal himself" (188.2): "You will need all the elements in the river to clean you over it all and a fortifine popespriestpower bull of attender to booth" (188.5–7).

I have already commented on enunciation in "Ivy Day" but have not yet touched on "A Mother." This is one of the key stories in that it shows a mother who is ready to jeopardize or even destroy her daughter's musical career because of her obstinacy in enforcing the law of a contract she has drawn herself. She has married Mr. Kearney out of spite and to silence the slander of her friends, but she soon capitalizes on his name: she seizes the opportunity to introduce her daughter into nationalist circles to promote her piano-playing. In this story we find the unique example of a father who is depicted as a "model": "For his part he was a model father" (*D,* 154). We soon realize that this comes from the perspective of Mrs. Kearney, who really acts in his place but still needs the moral caution of an abstract paternal function: "She respected her husband in the same way as she respected the General Post Office, as something large, secure and fixed; and though she knew the small number of his talents she appreciated his abstract value as a male" (159). He is conspicuously silent during the whole scene of crisis and seems capable only of getting a cab, after his wife has shouted at him to do so. Perhaps he is also capable of an epiphany, like the clock of the Ballast Office in Dublin! But undoubtedly his role prepares for the figure of the gigantic Finn, buried in the landscape of Phoenix Park. His name and his real absence are indispensable for the mother to become "A" Mother, another symptom of paralysis; and the echoes of Lot's wife turned into an "angry stone image" (168) add a mythological layer to the signification of her frozen gestures.

Mrs. Kearney insists on the literal respect of an abstract law, taking no account of the other codes, of economic, political, cultural, human concerns. She manifests the drive to a reduction of character to type, and *Finnegans Wake* will develop itself in the proliferation of such stereotypes. To stress the link between *Dubliners* and *Finnegans Wake,* a link attested by the notebooks,

I would be tempted to say that the father hesitates between the paralysis of heresy and sexual sin—this would be best figured out by the GPI, or syphilitic "general paralysis of the insane"[14] affecting Father Flynn, and the paralysis of mute orthodoxy, the GPO, or General Post Office, the pure ballast of an empty symbolic structure, defining the void center of the capital "to the wustworts of a Finntown's generous poet's office" (*FW,* 265.27–28). The shift from *i* to *o* could describe the range of the IOUs the fathers bequeath to their sisters and sons alike. This could also explain why Father Flynn had told the boy that the works of the fathers were as bulky as the Post Office Directory, and why Gabriel proudly announces his arrival to his aunts with these words: "Here I am as right as the mail" (*D,* 201). Shaun the Post and Shem the Penman are there implicitly portrayed in the gnomon of the father, squaring the circle of a city with a corner less or too much.

For the gnomon itself will have to be identified as the name of the father, a name ruling the silences, exiles and ruses of Noman, Outis, or Ulysses: "First you were Nomad, next you were Namar, now you're Numah and it's soon you'll be Nomon" (*FW,* 374.22–23). This name is both ineffable, like the tetragrammaton, and endlessly translatable. It must be kept silent, in a silence that cannot be "kept," as Maurice Blanchot again suggests: "Keep silent. Silence cannot be kept, it has no truck with works which would keep it—it is the demand of a waiting without any object, of a language which, supposing itself to be a totality of discourse, would spend itself all at once, would undo itself and fragment itself endlessly."[15]

TWO

THY NAME IS JOY

Paternity, thy name is joy
When the wise sire knows which is which.
James Joyce, *"Epilogue to Ibsen's* Ghosts*"*

By an ironic twist of fate, now that we have stopped believing
that any text can be reduced to its original meaning by questions such as, Who speaks to whom? Who's who? and Which is
which? (probably because we are now aware that a great part of
the authority these questions take for granted in the ascertain-
ing of precise identities has been shifted over to the reader), even
if we can see in *Ulysses* the paradigm for a modernity defined by
a new conception of textuality, there is nevertheless no denying
that the novel keeps returning to a central issue of paternity: the
question of the origins and the endless aporias of artistic self-
begetting.

Paternity in fiction may be treated either as a function or as
a locus, a thematic and rhetorical topos. Even if we all readily
agree that paternity constitutes one of the major themes of
Ulysses, no critical agreement seems to be at hand concerning
the narrative functions of the theme. Is it a part of the central
"plot," if any? Is it rather a decoy? Has it to be treated as a first

stage in the development of the writing process, along the lines followed by Michael Groden concerning the genesis of the book?[1] Does paternity retain a primary meaning, a meaning which may imply that we have to deprive the theme of the more psychological overtones it possesses? If paternity is merely a metaphor for artistic creation, are we so sure that we understand what a metaphor is, how it works, without having recourse to some sort of theory of paternity or, of course, of maternity?

In order to avoid the circularity of a round of questions all begging further questions, I would like to suggest that Joyce's main thesis about fathers is that paternity implies, or more directly proves, the existence of the Unconscious—as Stephen explains about Shakespeare: "Fatherhood, in the sense of conscious begetting, is unknown to man. It is a mystical estate, an apostolic succession, from only begetter to only begotten" (*U,* 9.837–39). What the language of the church describes well enough for Joyce can be apprehended only through the language of psychoanalysis, and particularly through Lacan's version of the Unconscious structured as a language. For Lacan, the paternal function is the key to the metaphors which underpin our Unconscious, and it is divided into three levels or modes:

1. the real father, or actual genitor, who is the historical father inside or outside the family, always inadequate to his role or to expectations;
2. the symbolic father, who is reduced to the pure agency of the Father's Name through which the Law and castration come into play;
3. the imaginary father (or the invented substitute father whom children may evolve in infantile dreams, fantasies, or wish-fulfilments), who occupies the space of the paternal "fantasms" between the symbolic structure and the real lack or absence.

Ulysses clearly exploits the distance between Simon Dedalus, the real father—present in fact among the Dublin drunkards and cronies, but absent from his home and role—and Bloom, who can be Stephen's "symbolic father" only for the hurried reader or for the "interpreter" deceived by metaphysical fictions, since Stephen is obviously looking for a substitute mother much more than for another father, at the psychological level of the fiction at least. All of this raises the problem of "atonement," an atonement that is savagely demolished in "Ithaca": at best, it boils down to the "nocturnal perambulation to and from the cabman's shelter, Butt Bridge (atonement)" (*U,* 17.2057–58); at worst, it is exposed as a theological fallacy. It is not enough to state that there is no atonement for purely negative reasons, Stephen's failure to coincide with the ideal pattern of the son's return to the father: the entire conception of paternity as founded upon the void and incertitude rules out any such reunion and stresses differences. Thus the difference between the symbolic and the imaginary fathers shows, first, that a gap remains for the son's imaginings of what it means to be a father, and, second, that if the son may have to redeem the failed father, it is not by any appeal to a symbolic father, whoever he might be, but by becoming himself a kind of symbolic father: that is, by a deeper comprehension of the process of naming.

Atonement should not be confused with redemption or forgiving, as the poem "Ecce puer" shows, when the union or even fusion of mystical persons is achieved only by an evocation of no fewer than four generations:

A child is sleeping:
An old man gone.
O, father forsaken,
Forgive your son![2]

The second line refers to Joyce's father, the first to his grandson. Who is the father of the third line? If we assume it to be Joyce's father, Joyce is the "son" of line 4, a son quite close to the sleeping child of line 1.

In this poem, Joyce avails himself of the actual traumatic event constituted by John Joyce's death (December 29, 1931), closely and miraculously followed by the birth of his grandson,

Stephen Joyce (February 15, 1932), in order to act out his personal case: "Well, if the father who has not a son be not a father can the son who has not a father be a son?" (*U*, 9.864–65). In other words, if when a father loses his son he forfeits his right to be called a father, then when a "son" loses his father, he can no longer be called a son, but has to call himself a "father," not because he may happen to have a son, but because paternity has been handed down to him through this death: paternity as "mystical" and truer than the simple truth of a mother's love, since it can never be proven by the evidence of the senses and rests upon the superior truth of a purely "apostolic succession." This subjective sense of a succession bars the way to a feminine identification of an offspring and opens up the realm of the Symbolic–therefore, of literature: "When Rutlandbaconsouthamptonshakespeare or another poet of the same name in the comedy of errors wrote *Hamlet* he was not the father of his own son merely but, being no more a son, he was and felt himself the father of all his race, the father of his grandfather, the father of his unborn grandson who, by the same token, never was born, for nature, as Mr Magee understands her, abhors perfection" (*U*, 9.865–71).

It would seem, from a superficial glance at Joyce's family, that nature did not always abhor perfection: the famous photograph made by Gisèle Freund, showing "four generations of Joyces"[3] (Joyce's defunct father being adequately represented by his portrait, under which James, Giorgio, and Stephen Joyce are sitting, all gazing in different directions), would tend to testify to a fulfilment refused to Shakespeare. In that sense Joyce had clearly, to quote Nora Joyce's boastful summary of their literary rivalry, "got the better of" Shakespeare.[4]

But that would mean forgetting Lucia Joyce's tragic fate, a fate already symptomatically written by Joyce's theory of a purely male line of descendence. Lucia never married for lots of complicated reasons which literally brought her to psychosis, but her exclusion from the "four generations" and her barrenness had already, as it were, been textually programmed by her father's books. And when the allegorical photograph was taken, she was no longer with her family. Louis Gillet has very humanely and sensibly written about Joyce's despair and personal grievance, which underlie the pathos of many passages in *Finnegans Wake*, and compares Joyce to a Lear bearing Cordelia.[5] Indeed, Shakespeare, who perhaps had anticipated some of nature's most bitter dramatic ironies, had also written this scene in advance.

In "Ecce Puer," however, Joyce metaphorically becomes his own grandson in order to be able to address himself to his own father, asking for forgiveness. But the ethical force of such a prayer supposes that one link should have been forgotten: Joyce forgets his own real son in order to forgive and be forgiven. He can thus speak as his own grandson addressing himself to his grandfather, or himself, as in the silly riddle Bloom hears when looking at his own reflection in the mirror:

> Brothers and sister had he none,
> Yet that man's father was his grandfather's son.
>
> (*U*, 7.1353)

The detour through collapsible series of generations may well be the only way to get a close look at oneself. This is in any case how Joyce attempts to reach the core, the essence, the *je ne sais quoi* of his own insight into paternity, as vouchsafed by a passage from a letter, written just after his father's death, in which he sums up what his father has left him: "I got from him his portraits, his waistcoat ... but apart from these, something else I cannot define. But if an observer thought of my father and myself and my son too physically, though we are all very different, he could perhaps define it."[6] The mystical link has been replaced by the magical thread going through differences and tying them up in a knot; a knot which, to be perceived, supposes this imaginary fourth witness, gifted with a strong sense of psychic physiognomy.

Whereas atonement supposes the union of two persons, the process of redemption entails three or four generations in order to link transubstantiality with consubstantiality. Only at this level can Bloom and Stephen be linked, in the utopically perfect image of the artist as perverse God or complete "jewgreek," both incestuous and homosexual, laying down his law in the very movement of transgressing it. Besides, if Bloom is said to be the "only transubstantial heir of Rudolf Virag," while Stephen is the "eldest surviving male consubstantial heir of Simon Dedalus" (*U,* 17.534, 537), is it not because, apart from the fact that both Dedaluses are simultaneously alive, there has been a change, a transformation in the name of Virag, transubstantiated, metaphorized, into a disseminating Bloom?

Just as Christ had to promise that he would be followed by an intercessor, the Paraclete intervening after his death as a living memory or reminder of everything that he had uttered (an image mercilessly parodied by Bloom's vision of having "a gramophone in every grave" [*U,* 6.963]), the full force of literature comes for Joyce from its power to "redeem the times," but not as Eliot would have it: if a subject wants to create durable art that helps him to awake from the nightmare of history, he has to pursue the circle of his writing, returning not to his father, but to a displaced origin (or, more precisely, the displacing of origins in a movement of quest for ultimately wanting origins) that lies in language.

It is in this sense that Lacan argued in the seminar that he devoted to Joyce in 1975–76 that Joyce's writing was a symptomatic answer to his own father's absence: "*Ulysses* is a testimony of the way in which Joyce remains caught up, rooted in his father, while still disowning and denying him. This is precisely his symptom."[7] For Lacan, the radical "fault" of the father opens up a double deficiency: the insolvency of the father in his role as head of the family, which is allowed to go bankrupt; and a default in sexual relationships, which implies that for Joyce (just as for Lacan) "there can be no sexual rapport"—that is, sexuality can never be described as a balanced relation between two individuals. Both sexuality and paternity inscribe a lack of reciprocity that can be healed only by writing. It is, then, the purpose of the work of art to redeem this lack by a new artifice, the knot made up by the letters-litters.

Thus, in Lacan's reading, Joyce becomes the arch-"symptom" of literature, whose ambitions he sums up in his person; he has to be called *le Sinthome.* In this felicitous archaism that functions like a portmanteau word, one can hear *saint homme* ("saintly man," the saint of Catholic legends and of the "island of saints and sages") and *symptôme* ("symptom"), without excluding the echoes of "Saint Thomas" (Aquinas) and "sin." But if this sin adheres to the symptom as an epiphany of the lack of a relationship betrayed and healed by writing, then one may wonder which Saint Thomas is meant: when Joyce states that "the greatest power in holding people together" is doubt rather than faith, since "life is suspended in doubt like the world in the void," he gives a key that is valid both for *Exiles* and for *Ulysses*. In the play, what is at stake is the necessarily perverse structure of sexuality and love founded on the lack of a real sexual relationship, whereas the novel explores the bypasses of paternity, following the absence of the "real father" to its utmost logical conclusions. The Father of the church, Aquinas, is slowly being dispossessed by a more "original" witness, Thomas the apostle (which confirms the meaning of the previously discussed "apostolic succession"), and this chief doubter is of course Joyce's real patron.

Finnegans Wake attempts a rewriting of these two chains of questions, inextricably relating the doubt about the real father to a doubt putting his own sex (and sexuality in general) into question.[8] Paternity becomes dis-located in the *Wake*, in which we constantly hear of a *pater in se*, opposed to a relational father, linked to the son by subsistent relations and an ethical relationship, the *pater per se*. For *Per-se* O'Reilly becomes a French *perce-oreille*, an earwig, Earwicker as an insect, to show the *in-se* of incestuous tendencies. Those *in-se* and *per-se* fathers merge only in the name of Finn, a name that marks the end and the beginning of the cycles and the title of the book, leaving outside of its scope the *"Ding in idself"* (*FW*, 611.21), both the thing in itself of Kantian aesthetics and the irreducible difference and untranslatability of the *id* in the Unconscious.

It is only when language risks the double loss of meaning in attempting to cope with this *id* (about which no wiser sire can ask, "Which is id?") that writing may appear in the guise of this debased supplement, waste or litter(s), which nevertheless escapes the domination of the father's economy. Writing as a supplement becomes this imaginary father of himself, joining the split subject with a textual and historical Unconscious. Thus the fantasies of a spiral self-begetting are not restricted to Stephen Dedalus; we stop imagining him imagining a father, because he then appears as a fictive character and a springboard for our own fantasies. We do not know who Stephens's imaginary father would be because the very fact of imagining this catches us up in a process whereby our unconscious is superimposed on the textual unconscious created by Joyce in his books. And we are again led back to the transcendent, transubstantial, and transymbolic power of the name, predetermined by the indelible signature of a linguistic rejoicing. Paternity, thy name is Joyce.

> It is because the Unconscious needs the insistence of writing that critics err when they treat a written work in the same way as they treat the Unconscious. At every moment, any written work cannot but lend itself to interpretation in a psychoanalytic sense. But to subscribe to this, ever so slightly, implies that one supposes the work to be a forgery, since, inasmuch as it is written, it does not imitate the effects of the Unconscious. The work poses the equivalent of the Unconscious, an equivalent no less real than it, as the one forges the other in its curvature. . . . The literary work fails or succeeds, but this failure is not due to the imitating of the effects of the structure. The work only exists in that curvature which is that of the structure itself. We are left then with no mere analogy. The curvature mentioned here is no more a metaphor for the structure than the structure is a metaphor for the reality of the Unconscious. It is real, and, in this sense, the work imitates nothing. It is, as fiction, a truthful structure.
>
> Jacques Lacan, Foreword to Robert Georgin, Lacan

What is a father? Who is the father? What is common between my father, your father, me as a father, the man next door, the mailman, the commercial traveler, or He whom we picture walking in the clouds? A father as Viconian giant, thundering, farting, belching, castrating sons and daughters alike, with his pockets full of sweets to lure little girls astray, or cakewalking as the cake that you can both eat and have in his last triumphal march, just to provide critics with one of their great white whales? Thus, *Finnegans Wake:* a list of names, all dubious, corrupted by tradition and oral distortion, voluntary manglings, and unconscious censorship, all of which try to pin down the father to a definition or to a precise spot on earth. Among those, one appellation seems to offer a clue that might serve as a point of departure: "apersonal problem, a locative enigma" (*FW,* 135.26). This can lead to three sets of preliminary remarks. A father is not simply an "individual," but mainly a function; paternity is that place from which someone lays down a law, be it the law of sexual difference, the law of the prohibition of incest, or the laws of language. A father is not a person but the focal point where castration can be brought to bear on the structure of desire; as such, he is the knot binding the anarchic compound of drives and the realm of cultural codification. Next, a father is not a "problem," but a nexus of unresolved enigmas, all founded on the mysterious efficacy of a Name, which in itself remains a riddling cipher. And last, Joyce's formulation helps us to replace the question of designation by an exploration in positioning; if, as we shall see, a father is defined by his absence, paternity and patriarchy are set adrift in a world of substitutes, in which everybody is endlessly elsewhere.

Lacan's epigraph[9] should, rather, come as a warning not to apply Freudian hermeneutics to a text which already uses and makes fun of so many Freudian, Jungian, and Rankian tags. Lacan's statement could also suggest that a psychoanalytic interpretation, although now wary of unlocking the "author's psyche" behind his text, has its limits, to be found not in a textual uniqueness or irreducibility, but in the deliberate manipulation of uncertainties through which Joyce sought to infinitize the possibilities of language. If the unconscious works like a text, as a text, what Joyce may imitate of its effects in his "epical forged cheque" (*FW,* 181.16) of "many piously forged palimpsests"

(182.2) only bursts through at times as symptoms. And the symptoms do not so much betray Joyce himself as a state of language in its overdetermined and complex articulation with politics, sexuality, and history. In these language-symptoms, released and not simply created by Joyce, the role of paternity is perhaps not so ominous as one could be tempted to believe, yet surely more problematical, more elusive, and more perverse. As we move from *Ulysses*, which seems hinged to a careful delimitation of the various functions of fatherhood, to *Finnegans Wake*, where the father, struck dead or hidden, is slandered on every page, the nature of the link between the two sets of problems will have to be more explicit. Many mistaken assumptions arise from too strict an application of the overall pattern of *Ulysses* to the symbolic liquidation of the father that *Finnegans Wake* achieves.

Ulysses begins in the atmosphere of the pervading presence of the mother and ends with a hymn to femininity; the reader can even conjure up the unwritten text that would join Molly Bloom's final "yes" to Stephen's melancholy musings on his dead mother, if the circularity of *Finnegans Wake* could apply to *Ulysses*. It is fitting to remember that the concept of "atonement" is dropped like a brick upon Stephen's theory of paternity in *Hamlet* precisely by Haines, the usurping Englishman coming to rescue Mulligan the Irish usurper: "I read a theological interpretation of it somewhere he said bemused. The Father and the Son idea. The Son striving to be atoned with the Father" (*U*, 1.576–77). Despite the vagueness of the reference—an imprecision which Stephen would never allow, since he almost always quotes by name—this remark only then prompts Stephen's thoughts on the "consubstantiality of the Son with the Father." Now, the very origin of this "interpretation" ought to invite suspicion and prevent us from too glibly glossing over the text in the same way.

In "Ithaca," the term of "atonement" is given as a mock-religious description of Bloom's and Stephen's walk back to Eccles Street: "nocturnal perambulation to and from the cabman's shelter," as we have seen on page 52. This is listed as one of the various causes of "fatigue" recapitulated by Bloom before sleep. As the Archive shows, Joyce added the parentheses with the Jewish rituals at a very late stage. The proofs were returned on January 30, literally two days before publication. The margin also reveals that Joyce had put "(peace offering)" as the fifteenth rite, then crossed it out and replaced it with "(atonement)." This should not, however, be interpreted as a proof of the belatedness of such a motif. It shows, more precisely, that Joyce was faithful to his principle of cross-referencing, and lets the book reread and rewrite itself, applying the same terms to different context so as to stress their symbolic overdetermination.

The context tends to point out the parodic associations, since "atonement" is the last item in a series that begins with "burnt offerings" to evoke the breakfast and its burnt kidney, and seems a list of failures rather than of real achievements. Moreover, at the close of the book, the question of atonement is met with an offhand dismissal in the abortive conclusion to Bloom's proposal that Stephen (as Telemachus, who has found Ulysses at last) should spend the end of the night in his house. Bloom ponders on the difficulty he will have in keeping in touch with the young poet as he meditates on the "irreparability of the past" and remembers an incident which had taken place in a circus: "once . . . an intuitive particoloured clown in quest of paternity . . . had publicly declared to an exhilarated audience that he (Bloom) was his (the clown's) papa" (U, 17.975–79). The answer is the curtest of the sarcastic comebacks contained in the catechistic chapter of Ithaca: "Was the clown Bloom's son? / No." This little scene quite deftly sketches the whole structure of the book, placing Stephen as clown, jester, or fool, not too far from the laughing audience; it shows, by a kind of *reductio ad absurdum* of the basics of the theme of paternity, that the "fusion of Bloom and Stephen" which Joyce had contemplated, as the Linati scheme reveals, was at best temporary and bound to fail. Therefore, the claim to paternity on which the greater part of *Ulysses* seems founded is now challenged by the widening gap that sets "father" and "son," like Bloom and his notched coin, drifting further apart. "Had Bloom's coin returned? / Never" (17.987–88).

If the "possible, circuitous or direct, return" Bloom had hoped for never really occurs in *Ulysses*, this failure points to the scene of *Finnegans Wake*. I shall try to trace out the path opened by the concept of "atonement" in *Ulysses* to show how the shift from a living "impossible" father to a dead father, one reduced to his pure function, governs the basic unit of the family and generates a radically new orientation in the language of fiction. If the father is a "legal fiction" in *Ulysses*, in *Finnegans Wake* he opens the door to the laws of fiction as "truthful structure." True, at any rate, to the joy of naming.

THREE

THE FIGURES OF INCESTITUDE

One of the basic elements of *Ulysses* is the duplication of the father figure, and the relationship between the real father (Simon Dedalus) and the symbolic father (Bloom as Ulysses) is a first key to the function of paternity in the book. The dissociation is established progressively between the two, and at the start there seems to be a close link between Stephen and his father; at least, there is evidence for this link in the words of others as recalled by Stephen. Two physical motifs, the voice and the eyes, recur to stress this resemblance, so that a certain degree of "consubstantiality" seems to unite father and son in the flesh. The editor of the newspaper exclaims that Stephen is a "chip off the old block" (*U*, 7.899) when Stephen suggests a pause in a pub; likewise, Kevin Egan had told him in Paris, "You're your father's son. I know the voice" (*U*, 3.229). In the same way, when Bloom thinks about Rudy, his only son, who did not live, he mentions the two features: "If little Rudy had lived. See him grow up. Hear his voice in the house. . . . My son. Me in his eyes" (*U*, 6.75–76). Even quite late in the novel, towards the close of the *Walpurgisnacht* in the "Circe" chapter, Stephen, who tries to kill the "priest and king" in his mind, has not killed his father yet, for he still imitates his prodigal father by being consistently prodigal: "Play with your eyes shut. Imitate pa. Filling my belly with husks of swine. Too much of this. I will arise and go to my. . . . No voice. I am a most finished artist" (*U*, 15.2495–2508). Stephen imitates the mannerisms of his father when he sings, but in his drunken state, the blindness and the voicelessness alone reveal that Stephen is closest to his real father: he is about to return, although he represses the mention of his father. No voice, no eyes, a closed, opaque body—already caught up in the cycle of repetition in which failed artist and failed gentleman merge their shortcomings. In fact, for Joyce the voice and the eyes seem to have embodied the true clue to affiliation, since when he proudly announces Giorgio's birth to his family back in Dublin, he writes: "The child appears to have inherited his grandfather's and father's voices. He has dark blue eyes" (*Letters,* 2:101) and this is enough of a description.

These distinctive features loom out again when Stephen imagines the lovemaking of his parents. But, though his vampiric and necrophiliac fantasies revolve around his mother's corpse, they are blended with theological speculations on paternity, for Stephen identifies himself with a divine form, revealed in the likeness of physical characteristics (eyes, voice), a form which lends to this contingent existence the ineluctable necessity of a law. "Wombed in sin darkness I was too, made not begotten. By them, the man with my voice and my eyes and a ghostwoman with ashes on her breath" (*U*, 3.45–46). Stephen implies that he has not merely been generated in the flesh by his parents, but has been *made*, or willed eternally, by a divine Creator. The transmission of a pure form thus seems instrumental in canceling all reference to the sexual role of the mother, and the *lex eterna* of the father's law prepares the way for the assertion of a "divine substance wherein Father and Son are consubstantial" (3.49–50).

But Stephen is betrayed by the ambiguity of his images, as he feels locked in a post-mortem embrace with a mother who haunts him, and he refutes the Arian heresy only to fall into the trap of an unnamed heresy which would interpret the "substance" as the womb of imagination. If Stephen's first temptation is to rule out the Oedipal triangle so that he may enhance a dual relationship with his Maker, it then appears that he has never killed his mother and cannot take his father's place. For him, to kill the mother would mean to deny this substance without an origin which fascinates him and whose truth he ultimately discovers in the materiality of the act of writing: "Belly without blemish, bulging big, a buckler of taut vellum, no, whiteheaped corn, orient and immortal, standing from everlasting to everlasting. Womb of sin" (3.42–44). The white vellum or parchment is Eve's sin as well as the future blank page kept waiting for Stephen's traces and signs, "signs on a white field."

By a very telling shift in Stephen's reflections, which shows the ambivalency of the *lex eterna*, the imagined voice of Simon Dedalus proceeds with an attack, although oblique, on the incestuous potentialities of the family pattern. Just after these thoughts, Stephen wonders whether he will visit his aunt: "Here. Am I going to Aunt Sara's or not? My consubstantial father's voice." Stephen is deterred from such a visit by the sneers he has often heard: "Did you see anything of your artist brother Stephen lately? No? Sure he's not down in Strasburg terrace with his aunt Sally? . . . And and and and tell us Stephen, how is uncle Si? . . . and skeweyed Walter sirring his father, no less! Sir. Yes, sir. No, sir" (3.62–66). Through Simon's voice, we hear Uncle Richie's stammer and Walter's obsequious sirring. This voice conjures up a series of vivid pictures in a spirited ventriloquism which fuses with the rhythm of Stephen's musings. The "old artificer" even parodies the Daedalan myth in a sordid fall: "Couldn't he fly a bit higher than that, eh?" Such a flexible idiom lends itself perfectly to mimicry and abuse while it achieves its aim: the scene is so effectively reconstructed that Stephen, walking along the strand, passes the house and forgets to call on them. The father's voice has been powerful enough to shunt Stephen's thoughts to another track, and yet reveals even more of his incestuous link to his "in-laws," and by way of another detour, to Bloom's possible fosterage.

All this becomes clearer and more pointed when the same sequence recurs in a different context, during the funeral procession, as Bloom, Simon Dedalus, and friends are driving to the churchyard. Bloom tells Mr. Dedalus that he has just spotted Stephen, "your son and heir," walking on the beach, thus giving the cue for what seems to be one of Simon's clichés: "Down with his aunt Sally, I suppose, Mr Dedalus said, the Goulding faction, the drunken little costdrawer and Crissie, papa's little lump of dung, the wise child that knows her own father" (6.51–53).

Simon Dedalus no longer responds to Walter's servility but mocks Crissie's love, and his insinuations modify the previous remark made by Stephen about Crissie ("Papa's little bedpal. Lump of love" [*U*, 3.88]). Now the scatological abuse makes clear the incestuous relationship between Richie Goulding and his daughter. For Simon, this is what characterizes the mother's side of the family: it is a faction involved in a continuous intrigue, always plotting against the supremacy of the real head of the house. As such, it threatens the orthodoxy of the father's law; it questions the original atomic or adamic structure. The mother's family is a constant reminder of degradation ("O weeping God, the things I married into" [3.65]). When Stephen is tempted for a while by this possible shelter, he may well be looking for a temporary substitute home, by anticipation finding in his "fraction" of an old decaying unity the maternal and heretical shelter only Bloom can offer. The displacement of the incestuous nexus toward Bloom's paternal attitude is then made more obvious before reaching a climax in Molly's dreams of seducing a "sonhusband" (as *Finnegans Wake* neatly puts it in 627.1).

The specific meaning of *incest* entails a pun on blindness and insight contained in the verb to *know*. The phrase "wise child that knows her own father" echoes proverbially and also recalls *The Merchant of Venice*. Launcelot tells his blind father, who does not recognize him, "Nay indeed, if you had your eyes you might fail the knowing of me: it is a wise father that knows his own child" (2.2). But then adds confidently, "Murder cannot be hid long: a man's son may; but, in the end, truth will out." Bloom, who must be confusedly remembering those lines, distorts them as "The body to be exhumed. Murder will out" (*U*,

6.482). Bloom also has his skeleton in a cupboard, and through the associations with the Childs murder he is led to his own fifteen-year-old daughter Milly: "She mightn't like me to come that way without letting her know. Must be careful about women. Catch them once with their pants down. Never forgive you after. Fifteen" (6.483–85).[1] The equating of familial promiscuity with murder—soul-murder, as Schreber would say—is a typical feature of the Oedipal fantasies linked with the hallucinated primal scene. We shall see how this association determines the father and son relationship in *Finnegans Wake*, replacing the father and daughter relationship of *Ulysses*.

Bloom and Richie Goulding thus have been connected, for the reader at least, heaped together as they are by this "lump of love." This connection is emphasized by the parallelism of their situation in Sirens, when both are silently listening, enthralled by Simon's superb tenor voice; "married in silence" they talk a little.

> —A beautiful air, said Bloom lost Leopold. I know it well. Never in all his life had Richie Goulding.
> He knows it well too. Or he feels. Still harping on his daughter. Wise child that knows her father, Dedalus said. Me?
> (*U*, 11.642–45)

On the one side, there is a "Master's voice," the voice of a man "full of his son" (*U*, 6.74) and endowed with a rich voice all others admire; on the other side are two fathers who are hampered by their half-conscious incestuous wishes and who can only literally "harp" on that theme. Bloom is quite right to describe the "relations" of the two "brothers-in-law" with the musical simile: a rift in the lute (*U*, 11.1164). Thus, will it finally "make the music mute / And ever widening slowly silence all."[2]

The gap between the right lineage and the maternal line of descent already introduces the contrast between the symbolic order as defined by the law of the father and the prohibition of incest, and an imaginary realm where the fantasies of incest merely cover the wish to return to the womb. This contrast explains why a qualification needs to be made about Bloom's role as a symbolic father. To be a father, symbolically, does not imply merely a real paternity; on the contrary, it takes death, absence, and radical otherness into account. Bloom can be said to become Stephen's father only after they have parted; it is when they are closest that this relation is impossible. Contact is the reverse side of the coin of mystical fatherhood. Because of Bloom's offer and Stephen's subsequent refusal of hospitality, Stephen has to choose for himself in order to father himself: he accordingly begins the new cycle of dawn while Bloom is getting buried in his deep night (according to the Linati scheme).[3] A symbolic father is not simply the father of a son, as such can be left to the real father's function; a symbolic father is, as it were, the father of a father—a grandfather, in a way—who fades away to become increasingly identified with a pure name. But Stephen's new home can only be a text which he still has to sign as he incorporates Bloom's name to it.

The way to such a symbolic father can be discovered only if the refusal of any acknowledgment it implies is based on the ignorance of the real father. Stephen and Simon, in spite of their objective complicity, have to ignore their respective presence in the blind link which prevents them from knowing each other. Simon Dedalus fails to recognize his son several times, as for instance when Lenehan praises him with "Greetings from the famous son of a famous father" (U, 11.254). Simon's "Who may he be?" expresses his lack of concern, and after he has admitted his oversight ("I didn't recognize him for the moment"), he rapidly shifts the conversation to another subject. Stephen similarly does not aspire to have "a wise father who knows his own child": such would be the imaginary father as Bloom dreams of himself ("Now he is himself paternal and these about him might be his sons. Who can say? The wise father knows his own child" [U, 14.1062-63]). Stephen has had the opportunity to reflect earlier in life upon certain ambiguous expressions of his father's; for instance, the scene in the pub during the visit to his father's hometown in the *Portrait* showed the rivalry to be more apparent. Stephen would probably have failed by his father's standards and those of his friends: "Then he is not his father's son, said the little old man. —I don't know, I'm sure, said Mr

Dedalus, smiling complacently" (*P,* 94). What a wry remark on the dictum *Pater semper incertus!*

But this uncertainty cannot be pushed to its end in a denial of filial or paternal ties. And Stephen makes an interesting parallel between John Eglington (Magee) and himself when in *Ulysses* he accused Magee of "denying his kindred" (*U,* 9.817). Magee deals the most decisive blow to Stephen's theological and parapsychoanalytical theory of creation in Shakespeare when he says, "What do we care for his wife or father? I should say that only family poets have family lives" (9.814–15). Stephen's paradox lies precisely in the fact that he needs to present Shakespeare in the midst of family rivalries, usurpations, and treacheries in order to free paternity as creation from the power of the mother. Magee is in fact a sort of alter ego for Stephen, but is as yet unaware that he has had to deny his heritage in order to live on romantic and outdated principles. Stephen thinks: "He *knows* your old fellow. The widower. / Hurrying to her squalid deathlair from gay Paris on the quayside I touched his hand. The *voice,* new warmth, speaking. Dr. Bob Kenny is attending her. The *eyes* that wish me well. But do not *know* me" (9.824–27; italics mine). The widower refers to Stephen's father, and the phrase "He knows your old fellow" was said by Mulligan about Bloom, whom Mulligan jokingly suspects of pederasty ("He knows you. He knows your old fellow. O, I fear me, he is Greeker than the Greeks" [9.614–15]). Bloom is already the "jew-greek" combining incest with homosexuality.

It is only then that Stephen finds the courage to develop his theory with the famous statement "A father is a necessary evil." While Magee places Shakespeare as a creator alone in a mythic space, surrounded by the figures of Falstaff and others, Stephen sees him as the representative of paternity as artistic creation: this "mystical estate" can only be transmitted to a son; it cannot be made conscious. Thus, "fatherhood, in the sense of conscious begetting, is unknown to man" (837–38). The "mystery" of fatherhood is this unconscious begetting through which an artist feels the unconscious to exist. The consciousness is reserved to the mother: every man "knows" his mother and "does not know" his father, because his father himself is unaware of the nature of their link. Only a mother's love can mean truth, since the evidence of the senses proves the filiation and also since the son shares with the father the unmentionable privilege of having crossed in person, once at least, the threshold of her womb. "What links them in nature? An instant of *blind* rut" (9.859; italics added). *Amor matris,* a true "genitive" subjective and objective, but *Caecitas patribus,* an "ablative" plural: desire and castration, places and replacements. This blindness anticipates the full treatment of the incest theme. Stephen has already defined incest, following Saint Thomas, as "an avarice of emotion" (9.781) that he relates to the Jews, "the most given to intermarriage." Stephen still attempts to reach a definition of the "mystical father," and he gets lost in his self-contradictory developments; he finally locates the elusive relationship in a complete refusal of incest. For Stephen, if there can be no reconciliation without first a "sundering," the father and son are "sundered by a bodily shame so steadfast that the criminal annals of the world, stained with all other incests and bestialities, hardly record its breach" (9.850–52). Incest marks the negative limit of paternity, incest literally taken as the love between father and son. In the vast array of perversions, one taboo still holds, stronger than the forbidden yet tempting intercourse of the son with the mother. The "bodily" shame is confirmed by the common "transgression" of the mother's sex. Therefore, if the rapport between the mother and son is one of prohibition and transgression, the relation between father and son is what constitutes the essence of the law; it lies at the very core of the Oedipal pattern that introduces the subject to the symbolic realm of language. Without the mother, the son could not *not know* his father. But the mother by herself is unable to tell her son the way to his origins, or even his name.

The famous remark of Telémakhos to Athena in the first book of *The Odyssey* underlines all this discussion: "My mother tells me that I am his son [of Odysseus], but I know not, for no one knows his own father." Through language, a play of absence, difference, and incertitude are brought to bear upon one's own kinship. The mother's voice is not forceful enough to prove the truth of her motherhood: her love has to be true, since it can do without proof. Now, as soon as the subject attempts to define himself, he needs the symbolic order of language as conditioned by the absent father, so that he may wander through meaning in quest of a father. For Lacan, the acquisition of language is contemporary with the Oedipal stages.[4] When first I speak, I accept a symbolic castration in that I have to renounce my intense desire for fusion with the mother: as I learn the rules of language, I accept the externality of a symbolic code which existed prior to my unique connection with the other and even predetermined it. The church is for Stephen such a symbolic world of discourse and culture, which ought likewise to renounce the lure of a madonna "flung to the mob of Europe" (*U*, 9.840) in order to found its world "upon the void," "upon incertitude, upon unlikelihood." If the mother's self-sufficiency is denied, the father is not, for all that, a presence embodying the legitimate succession. Language is a system of differences, a power of death and absence in which he too is caught up. This paternal complicity explains the guilt lying within language's very foundation, the guilt of having to displace the mother and kill the father as presence. Hence, the shame which makes up the voice of the artist, "Shame's voice" as the voice of Shem the artist in *Finnegans Wake*.

Castration and incest thus are played off one another to define the symbolic order of the written text. Paternity is reduced to being a name, which can be separated from the bearer and transmitted to an heir, as Shakespeare did when he transferred his power to Hamlet, who was "disarmed of fatherhood, having devised that mystical estate upon his son" (*U*, 9.835–36). The divine procession of the Logos needs no virgin to encourage believers, but a name is necessary. It is then striking to notice that the first time Joyce wrote the phrase "legal fiction" to define fatherhood, he used it in connection with his own son's name: "The child has got no name yet, though he will be two months old on Thursday next. . . . I don't know who he's like. . . . I think a child should be allowed to take his father's or mother's name at will on coming of age. Paternity is a legal fiction."[5] The same expression sounds quite different in *Ulysses*, since Stephen has to ascertain at once the fiction of paternity and the ineluctable power of a name; this difference explains the shift to a modal phrase ("Paternity may be a legal fiction"): any "definition" of paternity has to be hypothetical. And the suspension of the imposition of the name cannot last very long, since a name implies this "mystical" function—a mystique without love or belief—binding heredity to the law. The name becomes a signifier, as Lacan expresses clearly: "The attribution of procreation to the father can only be the effect of a pure signifier, of a recognition, not of a real father, but of what religion has taught us to refer to as the Name-of-the-Father."[6]

Stephen does not really claim his name. It is imposed on him from the outside; even his listeners refer his subtle digressions back to his name: "Your own name is strange enough. I suppose it explains your fantastical humour" (*U*, 9.950). Although a name explains nothing in such a direct way, indeed its function is to raise the physical resemblances (eyes, voice) to the power of a symbolic signifier. Only a signifier can be related to a voice, in a pattern opposing name and bearer, inherited signifier and speaking subject. Stephen has then to choose a delicate balance between usurpation and right lineage. He says: "I am tired of my voice, the voice of Esau" (9.981). Thus, although he is really the first-born and seems hardly to care about his brother Maurice, he is both Esau and Jacob in his double role of actor and acted upon: as actor, he displaces both brothers and father; as acted upon, he obeys the mother's wishes ("Act. Be acted upon"). The course of his self-generation is a journey through writings, from the Bible to Shakespeare, in which he sets out to assume his father's name in full ("Dedalus"), after having passed the labyrinths of his own logics: "Lapwing. Icarus. *Pater, ait*. Seabedabbled, fallen, weltering. Lapwing you are" (9.954–55).

So the voice is less of a clue revealing one's descendance than a symptom of a division within the subject; it is less "his master's voice," as Paddy Dignam exclaims (*U*, 15.1247), than a cracked reproduction that splits asunder in the effort to maintain warring opposites in the same position of discourse. Just before Dignam's exclamation, Father Coffey's voice was heard: "Namine, Jacobs Vobiscuits. Amen," in a sacrilegious variation on Jacob's biscuits. The name-of-the-father as received must be written down to be efficacious as signifier, but in this very movement, the play of differences opens up and fastens the subject in a knot tying Jacob to Esau. Stephen had wondered: "What's in a name? That is what we ask ourselves in childhood when we *write* the name that we are *told* is ours" (*U,* 9.927–28; italics mine). This statement is a new departure from what Telémakhos said when he mentioned that no one knows his father by himself. No one knows for himself, but everyone, even a poor schoolboy, has a signature, a name that becomes a coat of arms, a personal emblem, or simply the illegible cipher of the most common signature: "a crooked signature with blind loops and a blot. Cyril Sargent: his name and seal" (*U,* 2.130). A name entails a writing, a hand reappropriating what another's voice says of it. This hand and voice are here locked together in the blind gaze of a signifier that has to reconcile the name-of-the-father with the mother's desire. Now, the voice of Esau is twice absent: a first time because it has been usurped by Jacob's voice, a second time because it has been replaced by his handwriting. When this problematic knot is linked to the creation of a text, the antagonistic elements are integrated into the machinery of sense that adequately uses the brothers' conflict to bring about the father's fall. Such a scenario adumbrates the nuclear organization of *Finnegans Wake.*

In *Finnegans Wake,* the story of Jacob and Esau, exploited to satiety, offers the model of a potent performative function of language, a paradigm even more interesting than the divine *fiat lux,* since it works with a deceived paternal namer. Isaac's name is already a pun ("laugh!"–"When is a pun not a pun?" asks the textbook in 307.1–2, with the answer "Isaac" in the margin, suggesting that the answer is "when it is a name"), and he cannot alter his benediction after he has realized Jacob's ruse. Now Esau stems from his father's side; he is the natural heir of patrilineal descent, while Jacob, the second-born, is his mother's favorite. The mother needs the paternal benediction to place Jacob at the head of the family: she needs the ritual power of a name. Jacob obeys his mother's *voice;* Rebecca tells him, "Only obey my voice" (Genesis 27:13). When, later, the blind father feels his son's body hidden beneath a goatskin, he seems to renew a sensual contact with his wife. His lyrical benediction takes the form of a fresh alliance with a feminine earth: *"See, the smell of my son is as the smell of a field which the Lord hath blessed."* In his blind vision, through the almost homosexual contact of a trembling hand with a son's fake skin, the old father turns back to the mother and her heir to bless the erotic gift of food and a body fetishistically identified by hair. All this is bartered against his name. In his voice, something is inexorably written, a signature which becomes a fate: *fari fatum.* Speech is a production entailing irreversible action as soon as it is undersigned by a name: "Speech, speech. But act. Act speech. They mock to try you. Act. Be acted on" (*U*, 9.978–99).

The same division between name and bearer reappears in Bloom's complex relationship with this father's name. This theme is introduced when Bloom remembers the words his father was fond of quoting: "Nathan's voice! His son's voice! I hear the voice of Nathan who left his father to die of grief and misery in my arms, who left the house of his father and left the God of his father. / Every word is so deep, Leopold" (*U*, 5.203–6). These lines from the play *Leah* are said by Abraham, a blind Jew who recognizes the voice of the villain, Nathan, a recanted Jew who changes his name and abjures his faith. He persecutes Leah (who bears the name of one of Jacob's wives in the Bible), a Jewess, as he attempts to erase his origins. The scene, vividly evoked by Bloom's father, recurs in Bloom's mind to mark his guilt when he thinks of his father's suicide. The coming anniversary of his death sends Bloom's thoughts spinning around his inheritance of a changed name, a name never exactly fitting nor properly placed. "Bloom" is a translation from the Hungarian name "Virag," which means flower. Hence Bloom's pen name of Henry Flower. In this exile from an origin, the name has suffered a certain degradation. This instability is enhanced by the absence of any male heir in Bloom's family. Throughout the book Bloom mourns both his father and his son, poised between a transcribed origin and a nameless issue. At this juncture, he can only imagine a substitute heir, like Stephen, and must also use pseudonyms. This prudence makes him unable to sign his own real name; that is confirmed by the gossip in a pub: "O Bloom has his good points. But there's one thing he'll never do. / His hand scrawled a dry pen signature beside his grog" (*U*, 8.984–86).

Whereas Stephen balances between a father's and a son's name, Bloom's own signifier is unstable, a prey to transformations: "Bloom" will never acquire the status of symbolic signifier. One relevant instance of that general distrust for his name— which, like the name of Odysseus, *Outis*, allows for all sorts of puns—lies in the obvious legal action which changed Virag to Bloom. Martin Cunningham explains the procedure to his drinking companions: "His name was Virag. The father's name that poisoned himself. He changed it by deedpoll, the father did" (*U*, 12.1639–41). The pub idiom ("father's name that") opens a significant ambiguity here, since the sentence could even imply that the name was poisoned by itself, or simply that the father's suicide could be due to a certain flaw in his name. The same type of idiotism occurs to question Bloom's ability to stand as a real father. A certain J. J. continues with: "Every male that's born they think it may be their Messiah. And every jew is in a tall state of excitement, I believe, till he knows if he's a father or a mother" (12.1646–48). Here, of course, father and mother refer to "father of a son" and "father of a daughter," but if we are to take this literally, Bloom is then only a mother, an insinuation which will be acted out in one of the most paroxysmal hallucinations of Circe, when he gives birth to eight children.

The transformation of the name and the suicide can then arise from similar causes; a suicide like that of Rudolph Bloom is a desperate act, committed in isolation, while the *deedpoll* that ratified his new name is a deed executed "by one party only." (It is quoted at *U*, 17.1869–72: "I Rudolph Virag . . . hereby give notice . . . at all times to be known by the name of Rudolph Bloom."). "To poll" means to cut off or to cut even, as with the sheet of paper for instance; this practice of polling the edge of the paper is opposed to the practice of indenting it, which supposes two parties at least and is meant to reconstitute the original sheet, "each section being later fitted if necessary to the sections having an exactly tallying edge as proof that the sections are parts of an original authentic document" (*Webster's Dictionary*). *Finnegans Wake* mentions, for instance, a certain Mr. Cockshott, "present holder by deedpoll and indenture of the swearing belt" (524.17) in a passage introducing the father's bisexuality. Since the change of names has been, in a way, unilateral, its symbolic function as name-of-the-father is more than problematical. The real *symbolon*—an object cut into halves that can be reconstituted as a token of identity—implies the dented edge that is lacking in the case of a deedpoll. "Cockshott" is here a signifier of the phallus; one of the most enigmatic recurrent names of *Finnegans Wake*, he unites the broken line of the symbol (indenture) and the clean edge of castration (deedpoll). It is no surprise then to see Bloom's grandfather, Leopold Virag, in one of the visions of Circe, holding a parchment roll, which among other things is the text of his son's deedpoll (he provides us with a hint when he exclaims "Pretty poll!" [*U*, 15.2412]). The old Virag, more than Rudolph Bloom, appears as Bloom's real father in this scene, since he at least is an authority on sexual matters: "(He taps his parchmentroll energetically.) This book tells you how to act with all descriptive particulars" (15.2342–44). He is also a master over his son's fate, and he toys with the anxieties of his grandson: "Consult index for agitated fear of aconite. . . . Virag is going to talk about amputation" (15.2395). Sex and death are reconciled in Virag's hysterical ramblings, and the sequence of the first names—Leopold, Rudolph, Leopold, Rudy—offers a pattern that goes beyond the change of surname. Virag, in fact, initiates the series of metamorphoses that affects the Blooms; Virag calls up the apparition of Henry Flower in person and is described aptly as "sloughing his skins, his multitudinous plumage moulting" (15.2623). As "Basilicogrammate," he is "Lord of letters"; like Thoth, the god of letters Stephen invokes, he welcomes all the travesties, transsexualisms, and metempsychoses of the book—all of which are rife in the "Circe" episode.

FOUR

CIRCE'S STAGECRAFT

The reader who enters Circe's den after having been swept away in the babel of mixed idioms heard at the close of "Oxen of the sun" immediately realizes that a new stage, a "Nother Scene," is now lying in wait: a theatrical staging that Joyce borrowed from Flaubert and Goethe reorganizes all the motifs centered around perversity in a huge masquerade. Voices are linked to gestures in a wild pantomime that generates the most delirious of hallucinations, while the themes developed by this staggering gesticulation body forth myriads of symptoms all produced by an unconscious, a very peculiar textual unconscious that can only be attributed to the preceding chapters of the novel.[1]

Stephen's first intervention in English in this episode (he has been chanting a Latin introit) drunkenly and bombastically asserts that gesture could pave the way to a "universal language," "the gift of tongues rendering visible not the lay sense but the first entelechy, the structural rhythm" (*U*, 15:106–7). This shows that Stephen does not merely want to replace language with gesture, but wants to generalize the notion of "gift of tongues"—a notion that, in the Trieste notebook, amounted to a definition of art: "Art has the gift of tongues"[2]—so as to take gesture and oral speech together into account. Language thus goes back to the formative *eidos* that determines the actualization of a power, to paraphrase Aristotle's definition of *entelechy* in his *De anima*. With this "so that," Stephen attempts to conclude the dialectical meditation on subjective permanence as "form of forms" he had undertaken in the library, a meditation to which we shall return in the last chapter. Besides, the fact that most theoretical pronouncements made by Stephen in this episode derive from the Trieste notebook (dated 1907–9) should inspire some prudence and perhaps imply that these statements reveal Stephen's immaturity rather than give a key to the episode.

Act would thus perhaps be a better term than *gesture* here, if by *act* we understand the performative power of language and its capacity to reveal the hidden motives of the unconscious—everything that belongs to the category of events created in or by language. *Finnegans Wake* will eventually radicalize this notion by preferring that of "gest" with reference to Jousse's theory and to the medieval *chanson de geste* ("In the beginning was the gest he jousstly says" [*FW,* 468.05]) but adds a feminine conclusion ("for the end is with woman") which should also evoke "Penelope."[3] "Circe" presents the textual unconscious in its "acting out" of all the potential fantasies contained in the book—this is the sense of "actualization" developed by "entelechy." Lacan's comments on the dangers of "acting out" fantasies in the practice of psychoanalysis can be useful here, all the more so as they also invoke Circe's charms:

> It is incredible that certain features, which have nevertheless always been obvious enough, of man's action as such should not have been illuminated here by analysis. I wish to speak about that by which this action of man is the *geste* that finds support in his *chanson.* This side of exploit, of performance, of outcome strangled by symbol, that which makes it symbolic therefore . . . , that Rubicon whose own desire is always concealed in the history to the benefit of its own success, all

that to which the experience of what the analyst calls "acting out," gives it a quasi-experimental access, since he shares in the entire artifice, the analyst reduces at best to a relapse of the subject, at worst to a fault on the part of the therapist. . . .

Here the very path by which he proceeds betrays him, when it is necessary for him to introduce himself into the very phantasy by way of that path, and offer himself as an imaginary victim to fictions in which a besotted desire proliferates—an unexpected Ulysses giving himself as food so that Circe's pigs may grow fat.[4]

This might find an equivalent in Stephen's more guarded statement about his own situation, when he says to himself: "Play with your eyes shut. Imitate pa. Filling my belly with husks of swine. Too much of this. I will arise and go to my. Expect this is the. Steve, thou art in a parlous way" (U, 15.2495–97). His unfinished sentences, which suggest that he is about to play the part of the prodigal son and return to this father's home, also betray his acute sense of derivativeness. He imitates the mannerisms of Simon Dedalus when singing and playing the piano, thus meeting him in spite of himself, thanks to a symptomatic and deliberately willed blindness.

To speak of "acting out" and of a "textual unconscious" that exhibits itself on a theatrical stage entails a modification both of what we generally mean by "unconscious" and of the actions that are performed in this way. The reader cannot, for instance, emphatically identify with the characters, cannot indulge in any transference with their sufferings or passions. A tragic catharsis seems to be impossible, since farce and parody constantly parasite the at times pathetic actions represented. But in fact, it is the modality of this representation that now has to be explored, a modality halfway between the visible and the audible, that of a truly "verbivocovisual presentment" (FW, 341.18).

The specificity of "Circe" lies first in its material presentation on the page: the convention of a theatrical layout of the text distinguishes between stage directions in italics and speeches attributed to characters, the speakers being identified by capitals. There is at first no major difference between this episode and the layout of *Exiles,* Joyce's only real play for the stage. Both begin with a description of the scenery, with all the details necessary to creating an atmosphere. Just as we learn that there is a "a framed crayon drawing of a young man" in Richard Rowan's study and that it "is a warm afternoon in June" at the outset of *Exiles,* so we discover in "Circe" the "Mabbot street entrance of nighttown" with its "skeleton tracks" of tram sidings, "rows of grimy houses," and strange "stunted men and women" in the background. In allowing objects and abstract entities to speak for themselves (the first "character" we hear is "The Call" of a whistle), "Circe" presents another variation on the *Tentation de saint Antoine* model, in which stage directions can become poetic narratives of their own. For instance, when Flaubert introduces his hermit in the desert, he lavishes color notations in order to create a sunset landscape curiously foreshadowing the conclusion of his text (the same vibration of light on the last page signals the return of the morning sun and marks the end of the hallucinations):

> Le ciel, dans le nord, est d'une teinte gris-perle, tandis qu'au zénith des nuages de pourpre, disposés comme les flocons d'une crinière gigantesque, s'allongent sur la voûte bleue. . . . et dans l'espace flotte une poudre d'or tellement menue qu'elle se confond avec la vibration de la lumière.
>
> ### SAINT ANTOINE
> qui a une longue barbe, de longs cheveux, et une tunique de peau de chèvre, est assis, jambe croisées, en train de faire des nattes. Dès que le soleil disparaît, il pousse un grand soupir, et regardant l'horizon:
>
> Encore un jour! un jour de passé![5]

Flaubert lets his smaller-type stage directions present the visual element of his monstrous evocations, while the speeches in normal type are left to the characters who can be headless Blemmyeas or Nisnas with only one half of the body. Joyce, it is true, goes one step further when he lets his stage directions be contaminated by the dialogues of the characters. When Stephen appears singing his *introit,* the parentheses can indicate the changes of his pitch in Latin—"(altius aliquantulum)" (*U,* 15.84) and "(triumphaliter)" (*U,* 15.98)—to suggest absolute mimicry. Such contamination destroys any division between inside and outside; everything gestures in this episode. Since the parentheses are thus often scenic, they tend to develop scenes generated by a chance word in a given speech. When Bloom quotes a passage from *Lallah Rookh,* his romantic declaration creates an oriental landscape with leaping gazelles, and the vision seems to stop him in the middle of a sentence:

BLOOM
(*forlornly*) I never loved a dear gazelle but it was sure to . . .

(*Gazelles are leaping, feeding on the mountains. Near are lakes.* . . .)

(*U,* 15.1322-24)

It is as if the suggestive power of words were undone by its own excess, the excess of actual embodiment of fantasies. The fantasy evoked in this case is typical of Bloom's oriental musings and dreams of Palestine (the scene is a fitting setting for the revelation that Zoe is Jewish and English). The reader hesitates between laughter and wonder, admiring the repeated display of stylistic virtuosity and taking pleasure in the remotivation of age-old clichés: "*It burns, the orient, a sky of sapphire, cleft by the bronze flight of eagles. Under it lies the womancity, nude, white, still, cool, in luxury. A fountain murmurs among damask roses. Mammoth roses murmur of scarlet winegrapes. A wine of shame, lust, blood exudes, strangely murmuring*" (*U,* 15.1326-30). Is the repetition of "murmuring" a sign of stylistic parody, Joyce taking off *fin de siècle* languor, or is it a sign of Bloom's bad taste? What is fundamentally stressed is the almost infinite power of language to mobilize literary and cultural associations; just as the word "gazelle" suggests an entire landscape, roses create grapes which in turn produce this allegorical wine of "shame, lust, blood."

At times, the stage directions entirely belie their appellation, as when, during the trial, they give an accelerated version of

Bloom's evidence. This is triggered by an echo ("cough") linking the parenthesis and the speech:

PROFESSOR MACHUGH
(*from the presstable, coughs and calls*) Cough it up, man. Get it out in bits.

> (*The crossexamination proceeds re Bloom and the bucket. A large bucket. Bloom himself. Bowel trouble. In Beaver street. Gripe, yes. Quite bad. A plasterer's bucket. By walking stiff-legged. Suffered untold misery. Deadly agony. About noon. Love or burgundy. Yes, some spinach. . .*)

(*U,* 15.927–31)

The same bucket (with *défense d'uriner* printed on it) will reappear at the end of the episode, this time carried by Edward VII (*U,* 15.4456). This is an incident in which the episode uses up the very material it presents, since the appearance of the bucket derives not from Bloom's day, but from a story overheard by Bloom while passing a "gaffer" talking to "loiterers" (*U,* 15.585–87). It is then grafted onto the fart which he blamed on the Burgundy wine at the end of "Sirens."

The semantization of gestures—jerks, twitches, hops, Saint Vitus's dances, spasms, contortions and convulsions—is accompanied by a language that keeps gesticulating to parade its mimicry. Mimetism is conveyed by an alliterative and paragrammatic writing constantly verging on poetry. This is enhanced by the varying speed of the hallucinations, which fade quickly into one another: Mrs. Breen "fades from [Bloom's] side" (*U,* 15.577); further on, "all recedes" while "Bloom plodges forward again through the sump" (*U,* 15.1267). The progressions have a dreamlike quality, both unnaturally swift and nightmarishly difficult. The dream occurs on the stage, as it were, without any conscious intervention from the characters.

The only logic is the hallucinatory blooming of fantasies: Bloom meets his parents; all his messianic and masochistic wishes come true with a vengeance; he becomes a woman, is prostituted, witnesses the love scene between Boylan and Molly. his political career is well documented; the universal utopia of his new Bloomusalem occupies several pages before its collapse. Each scene is marked off by changes of dress—the notes for "Circe" record "transformation scene"[6]—and puns. When Zoe asks for a cigarette, Bloom lewdly replies that "the mouth can be better engaged than with a cylinder of rank weed" (*U*, 15.1350); she retorts, "Make a stump speech out of it" (*U*, 15.1333). Then she is silent for the duration of the political hallucination, until she comes up again with "Talk away till you're black in the face," which could follow directly from his first retort, but in fact derives from the fact Bloom has become "mute, shrunken, carbonised" (*U*, 15.1956). Each time, a specific form of rhetoric is established and pours forth into a confined space, the demagogy of the social reformer giving way to the firm words of the paternalist leader, then to the wimperings of the betrayed and booed dictator.

This transformation scene, changing costumes and roles, permits an endless proliferation of the space of the stage, since, for example, the merest object can take the floor, giving rise to a bar of soap that sings, to a door that barks, and to kisses that coax and coo. Abstract entities come alive, Bloom's "halcyon days" are acted out by the schoolboys he knew; the "male brutes" who have slept with Zoe let out their roar of pleasure. The décor turns to delirious frenzy, and the tableau, far from being reassuring, flings out image after image, each one toppling over into the next. Language is pushed to the point of explosive hallucination: it only needs a prostitute to read in the newspaper that the end of the world is nigh, and we see her appear in the form of a two-headed octopus decked out in a kilt asking in a Scottish accent, "Wha'll dance the keel row, the keel row, the keel row?" (*U*, 15.2181).

Hence, in these hallucinations, the visual element is not totally predominant. Joyce described his technique in this chapter as "visione animata fino allo scopio,"[7] vision animated to the point where it explodes, which characterizes very well the dialectic of *stasis* and *dynamis* that takes hold of each scene. Each episode fixes a play on language which most of the time derives from the rest of the book; it exploits to the full its baroque potential before exploding and disappearing amid a display of fireworks. The laughter comes less from the surrealist aspect of this or that image than from the discrepancy between the initial context and the hallucinatory combination. The Scottish octopus absurdly embodies the esoteric prattling of Russell overheard by Bloom in the street, which the latter had already distorted. ("What was he saying? The ends of the world with a Scotch accent. Tentacles: octopus. Something occult; symbolism" [*U*, 8.529–30].) The grotesque allegory arises from the crossing of Bloom's wishes with those of a prostitute.

Such crossings abolish every property of the fantasies; the latter are exchanged one for the other, multiplying and merging with each other in the most absurd ways. The private languages, the idiolects of streams of consciousness, escape the control of the characters. We are in the realm of Circe, who transforms men into swine: in this case it is the entire text of *Ulysses* that is plundered and placed at the mercy of desires; the personification of the objects thrusts them onto the stage with a violent force, and the bringing to life of things entails a corresponding reification of desires and anxieties.

The "symbolism" Bloom acts out without being conscious of doing so is determined by fetishism, a key strategy in the technique of the episode. Bloom retrieves his potato from Zoe's clutches while Stephen uses his ashplant to bring about the final annihilation. These two major fetishes play the same role as that of Bella's fan, which triggers Bloom's feminization. The Fan speaks to Bloom while Bella's eyes "rest on Bloom with hard insistence" (*U*, 15.2751). The Fan blurs all personal pronouns in its speech ("Is me her was you dreamed before? Was then she him you us since knew? Am all them and the same now me?" [15.2768–69]). This prepares for Bloom's almost hypnotic trance facing Bella-Bello. The fetish has perverted grammatical categories; its "flirting" has managed to find the weak point in Bloom's sexual urges, the point where the fantasy comes into being and swells into a scenario. In fact, this place is revealed precisely by a fetish that approaches him in the form of a foot or a paw. As for Bella, she does not speak but simply beats her fan, letting her shoes be laced. She only really begins to speak after her masculine transformation into Bello, a sex change that simultaneously feminizes Bloom. When Bella turns into Bello, Bloom becomes a hound for a while (which remains a masculine subject until the dog is feminine: "*her eyes turned ... yaps*" [15.2851]). Bloom has tied the knot that hangs him by amorously lacing up Bella's boots; imprisoned by the reversal of roles and sexes, he becomes a swine, a prostitute, raped, violated, and auctioned off before a public who mock her because she has lost her "curly teapot." This is the only time the hallucinations appear to call up anger or frustration in Bloom; if he still enjoys being "buttocksmothered" (15.2939) under Bello's rump, he attempts to reassert his damaged dignity ("I was indecently treated, I . . . Inform the police" [15.3146]) and becomes almost frantic when he returns as Rip van Winkle to Eccles Street: "Let me go. I will return. I will prove" (15.3191). Pathos is indeed reached when he breaks down sobbing "tearlessly," but the sneers of Bello never let seriousness invade the scene: "Crybaby! Crocodile tears!" (15.3218). And after the moment has passed, the nymph embodies another fetish for Bloom, since she has witnessed most of his unspeakable practices (masturbation on soiled drawers, pleasure taken in reeling off dirty words, onanism on Molly's buttocks, lovemaking on the commode).

The theatricalization of the natural world, in which the objects have a stage turn at the expense of the "actors," gives fetishism the role of staging post in the crystallization of fantasies—fantasies of castration, transsexuality and prostitution. The fetish that captures Bloom by playing on his most secret sensual pleasures places him in the control of the implacable logic of a perverse discourse.

Like Bloom giving birth to several sons, each fetish produces a moving fantasy world, which exhausts the combinatory possibilities of the successive scenes. The fantasy thus decrees its own scenario, its voice becomes law, and its force of law derives from its power to actualize itself immediately in a reality whose only status is to serve as its place of incarnation. In this way we witness, helplessly paralyzed, the display of the absolute power, despotic but also unstable and ephemeral, of the fantasies, whose curve follows that of the political and orgasmic rise and fall. The unique character of each fetish opposes the systematic recurrences that make every scene the repeat of one or several previous elements. And it is precisely when that element returns that it acquires the power—at one and the same time baleful and salvation-giving—of the objects. For it is nearly always a name that becomes incarnate in a voice.

Thus, soon after having passed through "hellsgates" (*U*, 15.578), Bloom is questioned by two nightwatches who lay a hand on his shoulders and play on the declensions of his name: "Bloom. Of Bloom. For Bloom. Bloom" (15.678). Bloom tries to evade their inquiry by passing for his namesake, the dental surgeon. His alibi is that he was at Dignam's funeral, and he is finally saved by the evidence of Dignam's ghost:

PADDY DIGNAM

(*in a hollow voice*) It is true. It was my funeral. Doctor Finucane pronounced life extinct when I succumbed to the disease from natural causes.

(*He lifts his mutilated ashen face moonwards and bays lugubriously.*)

BLOOM

(*in triumph*) You hear?

PADDY DIGNAM

Bloom, I am Paddy Dignam's spirit. List, list, O list!

(15.1209–19)

The recall of the morning's burial blends with the Hamletian ghost still so present in Stephen's mind. Just as Father Conmee had punned on "Dignam" and *dignum* in "Wandering Rocks," just as Bloom had linked Coffey's name to a coffin in "Hades," now Dignam's metamorphosis into a dog underlines the bestialization of his name: he is a "name-digger," as it were, digging like the fox in Stephen's riddle, a ghostly and disembodied voice attached by metempsychosis to the memories of a name:

FATHER COFFEY

(*yawns, then chants with a hoarse croak*) Namine. Jacobs. Vobiscuits Amen.

JOHN O'CONNELL

(*foghorns stormily through his megaphone*) Dignam, Patrick T,
deceased.

PADDY DIGNAM

(*with pricked ears, winces*) Overtones. (*he wriggles forward
and places an ear to the ground*) My master's voice!

(15.1240–47)

The illustrious seated dog in the advertisement for Victrola
phonographs has realized Bloom's idea of putting a phonograph
in every grave. The "master" is not even Death but a chaplain at
Glasnevin cemetery who blesses the dead in mock-Latin derived
from the famous Dublin biscuits. When the Second Watch expresses his bafflement and asks how this may be possible, Paddy
Dignam answers, "By metempsychosis. Spooks" (15.1226). The
ghosts thus called up are nominal and linguistic spooks coming
back from the rest of the book, an actualization of names that
in real life could only be called psychosis. The mock psychosis
of "Circe" shows reality as made up of linguistic repetitions,
brackets off the characters' psychologies. (From what we know,
all the hallucinations happen on the stage, leaving no trace or
even memory in their minds.) Besides, these hallucinations
migrate from one consciousness to the other, without any attempt
at verisimilitude.[8] In Joyce's almost obsessive investment in this
episode (which he had to rewrite nine times) and in his recurrent
complaint at the time that the handling of the action was exact-
ing and difficult, we must recognize a theoretical need, a wish to
go beyond the previous limits of his novel, to push the exploration of perversity into another space of writing.

"Circe" seems, at first reading, to present a catalog of sexual
perversions, or at the very least a systematic exploration of the
sexual fantasies of Bloom first of all, and to a lesser extent of
Stephen. Stephen's Parisian "Parleyvoo" at the end of the episode manages to shock even Bello, who laughs at his pun on
Hamlet and omelette. In a typical obsession sex is connected
with religion ("Perfectly shocking terrific of religion's things
mockery" [15.3890]), but sexuality remains a dominant concern.
This is how Stanislaus Joyce read "Circe," although James

replied that the chapter did not tend to show the omnipresence of the sexual instinct. Stanislaus supposed that the aim of the chapter was to represent "the analogy between the imagination in the intellect and the sexual instinct in the body" (*Letters*, 3:104), which apparently was the *idée fixe* of Stanislaus himself. Joyce had replied in a letter since lost that "Circe" was not about the sexual instinct, but about the locomotor apparatus.[9] Actually, Stanislaus had made the error of taking seriously Bloom's remarks on the instinct governing human and animal expression: "Instinct rules the world. In life. In death" (*U*, 15.2457). This is not a serious statement, but a symptom of Bloom's mental exhaustion.

Joyce had also confided to Budgen that the rhythm of the chapter was that of "locomotor ataxy," a learned term that jars somewhat when uttered by one of the prostitutes (15.2592). The paralysis of the movements underscores the scenes; the organization of the tableaux is not entrusted to any one organ, as with other chapters, but to a system that reveals itself through its dysfunction, a system whose disorders and lack of coordination govern the fantasies. The articulations are tense and stiffened so that a theatricality acted out by a few voices and a few names arises from the painful freezing of cinematographic scenes that very rapidly dislocate themselves. Joyce attaches himself to language's infelicities, the cramps of the textual body, in constant metamorphosis. Sexuality provides no "release"; there is no joyful sexual organ that would complete the image of the body reflected in the rest of the book. Here, the sexual organ often serves as a lever to set in motion this great dislocation of sentences and motifs. The locomotor apparatus establishes a controlling network that lies beneath the ataxia of the chapter, but it is a frozen control that has no more credibility than the strawmen that are slashed open on stage.

As we have seen, the "Circe" pantomime unfolds outside the classical theatrical space of the catharsis through which the spectators purge their emotions. Bloom is not stoned to death "for real" in the course of his downward slide: *"All the people cast soft pantomime stones at Bloom"* (*U*, 15.1902). Similarly, Ellen Bloom, Leopold's mother, appears *"in pantomime dame's stringed mob-*

cap" (15.283). The pantomime refers in "Circe" to more than just a certain way of playacting, or even of staging fantasies beyond any psychology: rather, it pushes the text into the category of amusement park bric-a-brac, pornographic newspaper cuttings mixed up with artistic statues in plaster, and forgotten refrains that reemerge at the wrong moment. When Bloom sees again the chaste nymph to whom he opens his heart, she evokes the circumstances of the discovery:

THE NYMPH
Mortal! You found me in evil company, highkickers, coster picnicmakers, pugilists, popular generals, immoral panto boys in fleshtights and the nifty shimmy dancers, La Aurora and Karini . . .

(15.3244–47)

The teeming of apparently irrelevant particulars produces another type of literary uncertainty. Since the reading of the previous fourteen chapters functions as the text's particular "reality,"[10] and since such a reading is reeled off, to the dregs as it were, one is never sure how to interpret the recurrence of familiar elements. There are instances when the literary competence required of the reader goes beyond the boundaries of *Ulysses*, as when the mention of a "pandybat" by Lynch (*U*, 15.3666) triggers a scene in which Father Dolan appears for the first time in *Ulysses* and quotes from *A Portrait of the Artist as a Young Man* ("Any boy want flogging? Broke his glasses? Lazy idle schemer. See it in your eye"), whereas the scene has only been fleetingly evoked by Stephen in the library ("A child Conmee saved from pandies" [*U*, 9.211]).

But even when the recurrent elements remain within the confines of the book itself, their significance can be unclear. For instance, we have already been treated to a lush and exuberant description of Gerty's hair in "Nausicaa" (" . . . and a prettier, a daintier head of nutbrown tresses was never seen on a girl's shoulders" [*U*, 13.510]) and have met her as another whore at the outset of "Circe." When the sentence recurs (*"And a prettier, a daintier head of winsome curls was never seen on a whore's shoul-*

ders" [*U,* 15.2587–88]), it describes Kitty's hair, not Gerty's, which may imply that her very presence in Nighttown has not been because of a "real-life" occupation but a result of the general migration of textual motifs. Whereas Flaubert's *Tentation* diffracted a whole library through the prism of the saint's hallucinations, in "Circe" all the linguistic gestures of the text can be redistributed. The "Lestrygonians" episode is particularly plundered, but in some cases the text looks proleptically forward, as when Mrs. Breen anticipates Molly's final monologue with her "eager" "Yes, yes, yes, yes, yes, yes, yes" (*U,* 15.576).

What is definitively lost with the baroque dispersion of all the motifs is the notion of psychic economy. Bloom and Stephen do not gain anything in this scene; they do not learn any deeper truth about themselves and never mention their fantasies when dialoguing after the episode. The parody of catharsis implies another debunking; the destruction of a still Romantic image of the artist as a purger of Dublin, as a lonely stag flashing his antlers:

> Myself unto myself will give
> This name, Katharsis-Purgative.
> I, who dishevelled ways forsook
> To hold the poets' grammar-book,
> Bringing to tavern and to brothel
> The mind of witty Aristotle . . .
>
> . . . .
> I stand the self-doomed, unafraid,
> Unfellowed, friendless and alone,
> Indifferent as the herring-bone,
> Firm as the mountain-ridges where
> I flash my antlers in the air.[11]

The aim of the episode's "wit" is to collapse the two images—a failed catharsis and all-too-real antlers—which merge at the only moment when one can speak of a (specular or speculative) "atonement" of Bloom and Stephen.

For it may seem that "Circe" is after all going to disclose the major secret of the book, that which remains as a repressed weight on Bloom's mind all day, namely the lovemaking of

Molly and Boylan. As nothing can remain hidden on this stage, the scene finally takes place, with an exuberance that can only be attributed to the excess provoked by a renewal of perverseness. Bloom's connivance and subserviency as a cuckolded husband reaches a climax when he welcomes Boylan disguised as a flunkey and plays the role of hat rack: Boylan *"hangs his hat smartly on a peg of Bloom's antlered head"* (*U*, 15.3764). Bloom's compliance takes here the shape of a voyeuristic fantasy when he is allowed to "apply [his] eye to the keyhole" (15.3788) and finally erupts with these words: "Show! Hide! Show! Plough her! More! Shoot!" (15.3815)—a scene which will recur in the Wakean anecdote of the Russian general. It is no longer a desire to see without being seen, but a wish to see the essence of fantasy itself, its structure of evanescent and flickering glimpses. Being at last aware of his status of "bawd and cuckold," Bloom can be identified with Shakespeare, through the agency of a remark by Lenehan, who quotes *Hamlet's* "mirror up to nature":

> (*Stephen and Bloom gaze in the mirror. The face of William Shakespeare, beardless, appears there, rigid in facial paralysis, crowned by the reflection of the reindeer antlered hatrack in the hall.*)

SHAKESPEARE

(*in dignified ventriloquy*) 'Tis the loud laugh bespeaks the vacant mind. (*to Bloom*) Thou thoughtest as how thou wastest invisible. Gaze. (*he crows with a black capon's laugh*) Iagogo! How my Oldfellow chokit his Thursdaymornun. Iagogogo!

(15.3821–29)

A paralyzed Shakespeare unites Bloom's and Stephens' faces before looking again like Martin Cunningham, the other Dubliner whose wife is unfaithful. Shakespeare speaks only in quotations, as is normal, since they are associated in Bloom's mind: "Shakespeare said. Quotations every day in the year" (*U*, 11.905); his antiquated diction allows for a pun linking "thou wast" and "you waste," suggesting both Bloom's masturbatory frenzy and the "thrift" implied by Gertrude's hasty remarriage. Besides,

Othello's choking of Desdemona is superimposed onto an evocation of father and son (Bloom as "oldfather" of a young Stephen born on a Thursday, the same "today" as June 16, 1904, as we have just learned on *U*, 15.3685), as if their reunion could be achieved only by the perverse murder of woman, be she mother or bride or wife. (One never entirely forgets the ghostly presence of Mrs. Dedalus, "killed" by her pregnancies and her difficult life.) Stephen develops the potentialities of this theatrical situation, going back to his theory of a universal perversion of sexuality, which founds his notion of creative "incestitude": "Queens lay with prize bulls. . . . And Noah was drunk with wine. And his ark was open" (15.3865–69). Bella, however, mistakenly believes that he is hinting of homosexuality and replies: "None of that here. Come to the wrong shop" (15.3871).

Bloom and Stephen both seem caught up in the "mousetrap" Hamlet had prepared with the players in order to get a final proof of Claudius's guilt, but here Shakespeare can only mumble the words the Player Queen addressed to the audience: "None wed the second, but who kill'd the first" (*Hamlet* 3.2.190). The lovemaking of Molly and Boylan is presented as the parody of the luxurious royal couple in *Hamlet*, with *Othello* providing an example of impotent, deceived, and misguided jealous rage. The acting out of jealousy is frustrated in advance—it can only repeat empty formulae—whereas Stephen's artistic freedom is still encompassed within the frame of his paternal reverence. After he has shouted "*Pater!* Free!" (*U*, 15.3936), his actual father, Simon, appears as a buzzard swooping "uncertainly" through the air, before uttering dog's calls. No action is final, no gesture can be liberating enough to free Bloom or Stephen from the fetters of symbolic repetition.

The act becomes paralyzed when it passes through this booby-trapped echo chamber: Shakespeare says "ago" (I act) in order to discover the self (I), the eye; but the performative splits into two, divided between the agent and the actor of the act, between Othello and Iago; Iago must be repeated *à gogo* (ad libitum), reiterated in a derisory parody, "Iagogogo." Shakespeare is confirmed in the role of the son of his son given him by Stephen, and more than that, a voiceless son who rehearses only with difficulty the text of *Hamlet* and *Othello*. His mute rage underlines the limits of pure theatrical gestuality: the voice denounces a hindered gesture that does not show anything. The mirror, which is as abominable as paternity, according to Borges, only proffers a structure of misrecognition for which all paternal identifications are much of a muchness, since they are all equally destined to fail. In this ventriloquism the writing acts parasitically on the voice, rendering it more opaque by swelling it with quotations, which the distorted gesture invalidates. Shakespeare in his distorting mirror thus offers the epiphany of the perverse theatricality of "Circe," a mirror intended to deceive in the fullest sense any subject who gets caught in its imaginary network. It is the reader who is cuckolded by the text.

The looks and the voices here act out again an initial paralyzed gesture that had marked Bloom's entry into Nighttown. At the very moment that a monstrous sand cart comes down the road Bloom is crossing, he is handicapped by an attack of ankylosis, the aftereffect of the lengthy stop made on the rock opposite Gerty; as the cart only just misses him, the driver throws an insult at him: "Hey shitbreeches, are you doing the hattrick?" (*U*, 15.195). This "hattrick," which Bloom transforms immediately into a "shoes trick" consists in covering a dog's turd with a hat and getting some innocent person to guard it under the pretext that it is a bird, until he verifies the nature of the object. The cramp, the spasm, the stitch here become the "hattrick"; the anality of "shitbreeches" combines with the hat that conceals a stiff erection (Bloom recalls "that awful cramp in Lad Lane" [15.207], a highly eroticized place): Bloom's body is perched hatlike atop its own excreta. The driver has hit the nail on the head, for Bloom comments, "True word spoken in jest" (15.207). The trickery normally referred to by this "hattrick" also serves Stephen in his moving from Catholic Ireland, symbolized by Saint Patrick (invoked on *U*, 15.4576), in the fight with Private Carr, alongside Hamlet), to the perpetual shifting between the three persons of the Trinity: "The hat trick! Where's the third person of the Blesed Trinity?" (15.4590–91). Stephen's rebellion against his mother land is expressed through the absence of the third hypostasis—in other words, the Holy

Spirit. The absent Spirit is also, of course, the missing ghost from *Hamlet,* who does not cease to incite his son to commit murder. But the "hattrick" also refers to three consecutive winning strokes with the bat (in cricket), or three winning horses at the races: the fateful repetition of the three blows joins with the conjurer's trick to bring the paralyzed ithyphallism back within the restrictive framework of the mirror surrounding the horned "hatrack." This signifier-fetish returns later on used by Molly, when she compares the masculine appendage and its paltry dimensions to her breasts: "are they so beautiful of course compared with what a man looks like with his two bags full and his other thing hanging down out of him or sticking up at you like a hatrack" (18.541–44).

Molly's typical derision of all phallic attributes is a welcome return to reality after the wild verbal dances of "Circe." This movement is prefigured at the end of the long episode, when the "actings out" are multiplied: Stephen shatters the lamp with his ashplant and abandons his stick on the floor; then he goes out to get knocked out by the British soldier. Bloom has picked up the stick and rushes after him; seeing that he cannot ward off the brawl by himself, he attempts to enlist Lynch, who dismisses him with "He likes dialectic, the universal language" (*U,* 15.4726) before retreating abjectly. But Stephen refuses the stick Bloom wants to give; he does not need any weapon, since he has already shouted "Nothung!" in the brothel to indicate that he has not been hung like the Croppy Boy of the Irish song, that he calls upon Siegfried's sword to defend himself, but also that this sword will be invisible and imponderable, like the defense of Bertha's soul and body in the notes to *Exiles.*[12] Stephen's last "dialectical" gesture lies in his deliberate passivity in the face of violence, a passivity that enables him to see this last struggle as a "feast of pure reason" (15.4735). This ultimate rationalist appeal comes at the close of the long *ridda,* the frenzied saraband of the episode.[13] *Finnegans Wake* will then radicalize the questioning of reality in the dance of words and languages: "And roll away the reel world, the reel world, the reel world!" (*FW,* 64.25–26). This is what one hears when the End of the World speaks as an octopus dressed in a kilt and singing with a Scotch accent.

FIVE

SPINNING MOLLY'S YARN

Reading is carried out in the wake of the symptoms it flushes out and stirs up; it produces the traces of which it had always already been made up. Its "ineluctable modality," moreover, presupposes the audible alongside the visible, since "to speak is not to see," as Maurice Blanchot remarks.[1] We have just danced; why not sing now, as the ant said to the grasshopper in the famous fable. What if reading were this silent song, a song which, according to Kafka's masterful inversion of Homeric legend, derives all its power from its being inaudible? Blanchot glosses Kafka's tale in these terms:

> True enough, Ulysses was really sailing and one day, at a certain moment, he met the enigmatic song. He can then say: now, this happens now. But what happened now? The presence of a song still to come. And what did he touch in the present? Not the event of presence becoming present, but the opening of this infinite movement which is the encounter

itself, and which is always at a distance from the place and time where it is affirmed, for it is this very distance, *this imaginary distance through which absence is actualized and at the end of which the event only starts happening:* a point in which the truth of the encounter is accomplished, and from which at any rate the speech which utters it wishes to be generated.[2]

The ineluctable silence of an imaginary event that we are forced to see and hear resounds through the pages of *Ulysses.*

Will we really, then, remain in the ineluctable? And to start with, what does this term mean? What we call "ineluctable" is that which cannot be overcome through struggle, struggle representing that physical, material, and sensory hand-to-hand combat in which are invested an eye, an ear, affects and fantasies through which the reader hopes to endow the text with a throat, a voice, a sound, and a meaning. The bodily struggle with Proteus that opens Stephen's chapter on the beach can take on an emblematic value.

Let us recall the story: Menelaus tells Telemachus how Proteus's daughter has advised him to overcome the sea god by trickery. Menelaus disguises himself as a seal with two of his companions and waits for the god to rest on a rock so that he can seize hold of him bodily without allowing himself to be intimidated by his myriad metamorphoses, of which he has, of course, been warned. Finally, the exhausted god tells him what is in store for him and reveals what was obstructing his return. Menelaus is then able to carry out the sacrifices and make it back to his home without any mishaps. The feminine wile, almost Circean in nature, caught in a parricide tension, lends support to the heroic journeying.

A little earlier in the same book of the *Odyssey,* Menelaus, who henceforth lives in harmony with the spouse he has found again, evokes a curious incident that could have fallen within the *Iliad.* He is only seeking to give Telemachus an example of Ulysses's cool-headedness, the latter having managed to foil one of the most insidious ruses of the same Helen, who is present. While the Greek warriors are inside the horse already brought by the Trojans within the city walls, Helen, prompted by an involuntary perversity, begins to sound out its sides, suspecting the trick, and she summons all the chiefs, first by their names, then imitating the voices of their wives. Ulysses alone resists the temptation, even going so far as to muzzle the jaws of one of his companions with his hands. A complex struggle with a metaphorical divinity, a compromise with silence, blindness, and deception: silence, exile, and cunning—these are to be the first arms against a text that forces us, the readers, into an exhausting struggle with its own strategies in order that it may continue still to speak to us. Should this be taken as a sound piece of advice, or rather as disorienting guidance: silent and cunning reader, never think you have arrived safe and sound at your destination. You have danced, you have sung; would you now have to plug your ears and close your eyes?

We can go back to the scene I have already commented upon in Chapter 3, in which Bloom and Goulding are "married" by a common listening attitude in the Sirens' bar. Bloom twines a rubber band around his fingers ("Bloom wound a skein round four forkfingers, stretched it, relaxed, and wound it round his troubled double, fourfold, in octave, guved them fast" [U, 11.682–84]), which is a metaphor for the knot tying him to his ship's mast. He turns the elastic just as the echo could turn back his musical motives in a memory of bird songs a page earlier. The Sirens, Bérard had revealed to Joyce, were above all birds and binders, who sang a song of grace and fascination (a word in which the same etymology of "binding fast" can be heard). As birds perhaps related to the cormorants, they belong to a series linking them to Circe, the hawk-owl; to Calypso, a nocturnal bird of prey; and finally to Penelope, the teal, daughter of Ikarios, the partridge.[3] All these female birds inhabit a curious "echoland" in which mirrors offer a visual equivalent of echoings. For the barmaids, Miss Kennedy and Miss Douce, at first refuse to hear, plug their ears at the beginning of the episode, and they do not sing themselves; only men are heard singing and playing the piano, Ben Dollard and Simon Dedalus soon replacing the Sirens at their song. Besides, the division of the Ormond Hotel rooms—with a saloon in which the men sing, a central bar in which the Sirens serve drinks, and a dining room in which Bloom eats and then writes a letter to Martha—helps to allegorize the repartition of functions: there are two opposite sides separated by a sort of hymen—tympanum, eardrum, shell, or gilded mirror of femininity. On the one side is the "voice production" of male singers, and on the other, the "restrospective arrangement" of male listeners, to take up the two phrases coined by Tom Kernan, concepts that create much mirth among his friends but can nevertheless qualify the curious musical setting of the "Sirens" episode.

For in the place of "retrospective arrangement," we find Bloom, who looks at the barmaids in order to imagine the sound they hear when they listen to a shell: "He heard more faintly that that they heard, each for herself alone, then each for other, hearing the plash of waves, loudly, a silent roar" (11.935-36). The ear becomes a shell, too, conjuring up an imaginary song well expressed by the oxymoric "silent roar." Finally, Bloom's Homeric ruse amounts precisely to this: he asks the waiter to leave the door open so that he can hear the songs while looking at the fascinated and fascinating barmaids. He sees their ears in order to hear the songs without falling prey to the power of music, uses this visual mirror as a relay between emission and reception. If he misses the vision of the singers' faces, the distance allows for a better audition: "Wish I could see his face, though. Explain better. Why the barber in Drago's always looked my face when I spoke his face in the glass. Still hear it better here than in the bar though farther" (11.721-23). The barber when addressed looks at his customer's mouth, while the customer speaks to his reflection in the mirror; otherwise the latter would risk nicks on his cheeks or ears. This structural disalignment is similar to the complex apparatus that enables Bloom to look and hear without being seen or heard, to enjoy himself without being trapped.

The other mast Bloom remains tied to is that of the table on which he is writing; writing functions as the major antidote against the potential threat of song.[4] When Bloom finally leaves, having asserted the supremacy of writing (a writing that even destroys music, thanks to this diffracted, echolalic silence), he thinks: "Time to be shoving. Looked enough" (11.1074). The final resolution of the fugue is, as we know, Bloom's fart in the street, a parodic blending of gas and language, of emanations from food and drink, a mixture of words and mute bodily language, which, intertwined as it is with a patriotic quotation, finally asserts, in another oxymoric paroxysm, the identity of *pianissimo* and *fortissimo.* "Pprrpffrrppffff. / *Done*" (II.1293–94).

> *First you will come to the Sirens, who bewitch every one who comes near them . . . Go on past that place, and do not let the men hear; you must knead a good lump of wax and plug their ears with pellets. if you wish to hear them yourself, make the men tie up your hands and feet and fasten your body tight to the mast, and then you can enjoy the song as much as you like. Tell them that if you shout out and command them to let you loose, they must tie you tighter with a few more ropes.*
>
> Homer, Odyssey, trans. Rouse

Who is this time playing the role once played by the daughter of Proteus in warning Ulysses of the danger of the Sirens, a Ulysses who, left to himself, would probably succumb to the temptation? The reader who is accustomed to Joyce's text will be hard-pressed to answer this question, for he will forget that it is Circe, the sorceress, who says this to Ulysses. Unlike Pound, who acknowledges the Circean nature of the *nekuia* ("Circe's this craft"),[5] Joyce carries out a strange inversion of the sequence of episodes in Homer which focus on Circe. In the *Odyssey* Ulysses first of all has the *moly* given him by Hermes, the plant that will protect him from the drugs that would otherwise transform him into a swine; then he overcomes Circe and thanks to her clears the Sirens' reefs. In *Ulysses* we follow Bloom into the Sirens' pub in chapter 11, then we meet him with Stephen in the Circean brothel of chapter 15, and it is in chapter 18 that the real Molly-moly, and not the potato fetish that Bloom carries on him, affixes the "countersign" of her voice on the hero's "passport to eternity." That fulsome and even voice that spins around in time with the revolutions of the earth has no equivalent in *Finnegans Wake,* which breaks up and mixes the tones, modes, and vocalizations, probably because Joyce shows less confidence in the salvation-bringing good faith of the sorceress who nevertheless permits the voyage among the dead. In the *Wake* there is no antidote to the feminine charm of the sonorities, for everything suggests a final ruse on the part of Circe, a ruse to which the heroism of the *nostos* of a Spirit returning home would succumb.

Moreover, this last enchantment is surely not yet over. For if it is the sorceress who devises the complicated setup with the ropes and the wax plugs in order to arrange for Ulysses a forbidden pleasure, there remains the possibility that the hero might have let himself be led into a trap: wouldn't he have been bewitched at the last moment if he had not been saved by the intervention of the author? Indeed, how do the sailors know that the ship is out of range of the fatal song if they really can hear nothing and if Ulysses cannot move? Are we not, we poor and excessively Cartesian readers, obsessed with the confused drone hidden by this piece of wax, deceived by a cunning imp of the perverse, so that we still remain chained, whether to the rowing bench or up against the mast, all slaves in a galley the hull of which resounds with the babbling of all languages?

In fact, the resolution of the critical aporia comes from the way the sailors, at least in the *Odyssey*, and perhaps also in *Ulysses*, open their eyes wide and see; they even judge by seeing— that is to say, by struggling in their turn with this ineluctable modality. Within the struggle of prestige between the divine and the heroic in which the imagination revels and which, moreover, rapidly reaches its limit, in that there is scarcely any real risk for Ulysses—who will take his pleasure unscathed—there appears the necessity of a constant fight for meaning. For the sailors see, and they have to take bets, they take risks. Ulysses no longer writhes in the ecstasy of that supreme pleasure bordering on suffering; the Sirens' rock seems out of sight; a choice must be made, and without stopping rowing, a sailor—the first one to do so—unstops his ears. If he is not the real hero, at least he can represent the first reader, and his rejuvenated ears will buzz with the void of the echo when he hears Molly Bloom instead of the Sirens. This mechanism with three terms or three positions setting out the interaction between the heroic subject ready to do anything to realize his perverse pleasure, a cunning, seductive, but destructive feminine voice, and finally a glance from the rower who is productive and critical despite himself, governs the action of the reading; in this scheme alone could the auditive or visual fascination of the perverse text be thwarted, which supposes that the parting of the ways between sight and hearing would be perpetuated—a chiasmus that *Finnegans Wake* attempts precisely to reduce. But the explosions of the word will there commit the text to a disconnecting with no return.

Between the stratified mass of *Ulysses* and the new Summa, there still remains to be discovered another type of music articulating definitively the relations between paternity and maternity, and a voice, the voice of a singer who no longer sings, but talks to herself, almost as an extra, after the collapse of the book. Joyce thought his novel was finished but not completed after "Ithaca" and was duty-bound to append Molly's signature at the bottom of his logbook. One last visa before the wandering, the revolutions of the heavenly bodies.

In "Circe," as we have seen, a very drunk Stephen plays the piano and thereby attempts to revert to his problematic positioning as son. He plays a series of "empty fifths" in a hesitant rendering of a psalm by Benedetto Marcello and comments:

> The reason is because the fundamental and the dominant are separated by the greatest possible interval which. . . . Interval which. Is the greatest possible ellipse. Consistent with. The ultimate return. The octave. Which. . . . What went forth to the ends of the world to traverse not itself, God, the sun, Shakespeare, a commercial traveller, having itself traversed in reality itself becomes that self. Self which it itself was ineluctably preconditioned to become. *Ecco!*
>
> (*U,* 15.2105–21)

Stephen mixes up, in his "Pornosophical philotheology" (15.109), definitions about the relationship between the fundamental and the dominant, the prime and the fifth tone in the octave. Father and son are compared to the fundamental and the dominant (and, indeed, the one "begets" the other in musical theory), and they are separated by "the greatest possible interval . . . consistent with the ultimate return." In the musical analogy developed by Stephen, the father and the son remain Sabellian modes of the self, a self that must go to the end of the world to find its truth. "Ellipsis" then transcribes the musical metaphor in a cosmic analogon; the distance compatible with harmony is identical to the course of the sun around the earth.

It is no coincidence that Stephen plays the psalm *Coela enarrant gloriam Domini*, since it presents the sun as an emblem of God's justice. In Psalm 19, one finds a systematic parallelism between the words praising God's "handiwork" and the sun: "Their line is gone out through all the earth, and their words to the end of the world. In them hath he set a tabernacle for the sun. . . . His going forth is from the end of the heaven, and his circuit unto the ends of it" (Psalm 19:3–6, authorized version). In the Latin Vulgate version of the psalm, which Stephen is using, the course of the sun goes clearly "a summo coelo egressio ejus" to "occursus ejus usque ad summum ejus" (Vulgate, Psalm 18), and thereby testifies to God's *Lex aeterna*.

In a typical fashion, Stephen conflates the two meanings of "ellipse," the geometrical figure accomplished by the sun's course around the planets, and the ellipsis of linguistic avoidance, the omission of the repressed in the longest detour before a return home. A father is "what went forth to the ends of the world to traverse not itself": the avoidance of self brings about the circuit through which otherness preconditions the safe return. As in the psalm, the circuit of the sun rests on the assumption of God's absolute otherness, manifest in His Law as written. Even if Stephen seems rather impatient of that "noise in the street," he still adheres to the scholastic structure of thought that impels the subjective drift of a purely male dialectic of self-realization. But there is a tension between the two metaphors: in the geometric paradigm, the sun represents God's law, whereas in the linguistic sense of *ellipsis*, what is repressed in Stephen's almost Hegelian dialectics is the centrality of femininity. The center of the geometrical ellipsis will therefore be the earth and not the sun, an earth that will be embodied in Molly Bloom's foreign and yet welcoming curves.

Bloom, who has learned the essentials of paternity through his repeated absences, obeys the drift towards the earth, whereas Stephen feels propelled towards the sun. In that sense, *Ulysses* keeps repeating the mythic paradigm of father and son as Icarus and Dedalus projected in *A Portrait*.

It is not because Stephen and Bloom are not really father and son that they fail to "atone," for Stephen sees even less of his father during Bloomsday; it is because Stephen is the son-type in the process of fathering himself, approaching the creative stage, at least one hopes, and Bloom is the imperfect father in the process of husbanding all his forces to find himself. Bloom's absence from home, his Homeric pilgrimage, has started in 1893, at the time when he had his last complete sexual intercourse (i.e., coitus non interruptus) with Molly; his physical and intellectual absence has increased ten years later, in 1903, since his daughter Milly's puberty. The wider frame of Absence covers the minor "temporary absences" in which Bloom feels his freedom inhibited by the female alliance of Molly and Milly. The nine months and one day that have come between the "consummation" of her puberty and the date of 16 June 1904 indicate that Molly's adultery with Boylan is nothing but the natural outcome of the symbolic incest that both links and separates Bloom and his daughter. So the different triangles overlap and displace each other successively. We shift from Molly–Bloom–Rudy, the early Oedipal triangle ended by the death of Rudy, to Molly–Bloom–Milly, the familial triangle, and to Molly–Bloom–Boylan, the triangle of adultery. The next triangle would, of course, be Molly–Bloom–Stephen, a triangle that would be both incestuous and adulterous, since "the way to daughter led through mother, the way to mother through daughter" (*U,* 17.963–66). Molly, who entertains thoughts of seducing Stephen, could still be a foster mother for him; by the possible offer of her daughter, she would become Stephen's mother-in-law, thus finding a new point of return to her husband, freed at last from his Oedipal infatuation with his daughter. Hence the impossible superimposition of the two basic triangles, Molly–Boylan–Bloom and Molly–Bloom–Stephen, ideally would give rise to the one stable lozenge,

Molly—Milly—Bloom—Stephen. But this superimposition does not happen.

Such a combination would bring about the ideal fusion of the contradictory "French triangles" Stephen had discovered in Shakespeare's life and creation. "You are a delusion, said roundly John Eglinton to Stephen. you have brought us all this way to show us a French triangle" (*U*, 9.1064-65). Their fusion would build one of the *French lozenges* which are passed around in Bella's brothel: "No objection to French lozenges?" (*U*, 15.2710). This pattern will, in turn, be included in the expanding sex of the mother whom *Finnegans Wake* presents with "the no niggard spot of her safety vulve, first of all usquiluteral threeingles" (297.26-27): she is drawn as A.L.P / παλ (293), and her figure sums up the different possible positions in the family: "It will be lozenge to me all my lauffe" (299.28, with a note referring to a sigla of the family).

In the *Portrait*, the young Stephen, who still has to "encounter" experience, denies family ties as well as all triangular relationships. He seems to be a victim of the delusions of grandeur that, according to Freud, accompany those family romances most children evolve around their origins. Stephen stands aloof and in proud isolation, cut off from his relatives despite his father's awkward attempts at intimacy with him: "I treat you as your grandfather treated me when I was a young chap. We were more like brothers than father and son" (*P*, 91). Typically, Stephen sees himself as the foster child of Irish lore: "He felt he was hardly of the one blood with them but stood to them rather in the mystical kinship of fosterage, fosterchild and fosterbrother" (*P*, 98). His vocation of artist, which is yet a pure promise, implies a severing of the most immediate ties, and this process goes on well into *Ulysses*. But in the *Portrait* this romantic attitude is left without any complementary positive father figure, and his temporary hope to "save" his family from chaos, thus becoming too slackly his parent's father, is undermined by parodic economic metaphors, much in the same way as the image of a "cash-register" comes to debunk the masturbatory enthusiasm of his first creative act, the composition of his villanelle.

Stephen then tries to use his family as a secure bolt-hole from which he could define himself, in spite of its evident frailty. The values embodied by the family could have served as a "bulwark" or a "mole" against the mounting "tides" of desire that threatened to overcome him, but the only effective check to his impulses can come from religion. Stephen generously places the money he got from his school prizes at the disposal of his family, hoping to give a new vitality to their life "by rules of conduct and active interests and new filial relations" (P, 98). But as soon as the money is spent, "the commonwealth fell, the loan bank closed its coffers and its books on a sensible loss"; Stephen is no longer able to resist the call of Nighttown. The latent ironical tone of some of the sentences stressing his wish to promote quasi-usurious practices—all in a noble cause, of course—shows Stephen "press[ing] loans on willing borrowers so that he might have the pleasure of making out receipts and reckoning the interests on the sums lent" (P, 98). This situation is paralleled in *Ulysses* as the hesitation between squandering and lending at interest takes on heightened significance when Stephen explains in the library that for Saint Thomas incest is a kind of usury of emotions. The "breakwater of order and elegance" Stephen wants to erect is a desperate attempt at limiting the circulation of desire to the little microcosm of the family, and when it crumbles for want of money, he measures his failure in terms of a renewed sundering of ties: "He had not gone one step nearer the lives he had sought to approach nor bridged the *restless shame* and rancour that had divided him from mother and brother and sister" (P, 98). The single difference is that here, the "shame" does not apply to his relationship with the father. In *Ulysses,* a physical shame dividing father and son gives them both the impetus to travel to the ends of the world in order to avoid meeting the other with the same voice and eyes.

The ellipsis of sexual intercourse conditions the heavenly and terrestrial ellipse centered on Gea-Tellus, Molly as *ewig weibliche.* And Molly, who is perhaps the only "present" character in a text woven by the apparitions and fade-outs of various absent males, can rightly pun on Bloom's omissions and her own emission. At one point, she remembers the doctor who was to cure her venereal disease that was contracted during her too frequent masturbations due to Bloom's inspired erotic letters: "that doctor one guinea please and asking me had I frequent omissions" (*U*, 18.1169–70). She still thinks he had guessed the cause of her ailment, which she of course "omits" ("and I said I hadnt are you sure O yes I said I am quite sure"). When she later considers diverse ways of seducing Bloom, she imagines his discharge on her drawers: "then Ill wipe him off me just like a business his omission then Ill go out" (18.1538). Bloom, the "commercial traveller" who follows his son in his wanderings, has perhaps chosen the longest loop around sexual commerce; but if this "wiping out" is by no means an "atonement," if it is no more than a promise of a fulfilled and generative sexuality, it can tentatively point to an issue. After all, to cancel an omission may asymptotically approach the shortest route to a direct statement.

This is precisely what Molly achieves, in an idiom that keeps contradicting itself in order to assert her supreme "indifference."[6] She can, for instance, criticize Bloom's meanness when he obliges her to do the work of a maid, and denounce his erotic interest in Mary Driscoll, the former female servant of the Blooms, who occasionally stole from them, according to Molly. Each statement in her "monologue" can find its negative counterpart somewhere else, and this provides the linguistic equivalent of the slow rotation of the earth on itself: any point will, in turn, be above and under, while borne along in the flow of life. Molly's monologue proves that "the same roturns" (*FW*, 18.5) in this "ourth of years." However, Molly "concludes" a text that seemed to have exhausted its possibilities as she subverts its written status by an unexpected return to oral discourse. And for her, literature is at best a titillating fiction, if not a direct lie. The truth of life apparently contradicts the spurious nature of textuality.

Thus, she dismisses jointly Rabelais and pornographic novels so as to debunk both Stephen's mediaevalism and Bloom's prurient fantasies:

cant be true a thing like that like some of those books he brings me the works of Master Francois Somebody supposed to be a priest about a child born out of her ear because her bumgut fell out nice word for any priest to write and her a——e as if any fool wouldnt know what that meant I hate pretending of all things with that old blackguard face on him anybody can see its not true and that Ruby and Fair Tyrants he brought me that twice I remember when I came to page 50 the part about where she hangs him up out of a hook with a cord flagellate sure theres nothing for a woman in that all invention made up

(*U,* 18.487–95)

Molly refuses the ellipsis of censorship which changes "arse" into "a——e", and although she expresses her irony at seeing a priest writing dubious prose, she seems to require direct expression. The Virgin's conception by the ear, which was the butt of Rabelais's satire, is identified with "pretending" and with a purely male imagination. However, as absolutely every statement is negated in another part of her monologue, one can verify that she allows her thoughts to be contaminated by the cheap sadomasochistic novels brought by her husband: "Id like to have tattered them down off him before all the people and give him what that one calls flagellate till he was black and blue" (18.961–63). In short, even if she debunks the theological abstrusities of self-conception, her speech itself has been fabricated in part by literary reminiscences.

In fact, Molly does not reject the idea of literature or of poetry; she likes to imagine that Bloom when young looked like Byron, and some of her fantasies revolve around Stephen Dedalus, whom she sees as a Romantic poet who would immortalize her in his verses:

I always like poetry . . . they all write about some woman in their poetry well I suppose he wont find many like me where softly sighs of love the light guitar where poetry is in the air . . . Ill sing that for him theyre my eyes if hes anything of a poet two eyes as darkly bright as loves own star arent those

beautiful words as loves young star itll be a change the Lord
knows to have an intelligent person to talk to about yourself
(18.1323-41)

It is clear that she too is looking for a "change," a new type of
otherness in order to redefine herself by talking, and that such
a new relationship can take the form of literary and physical
love at the same time. For Molly, too, alterity and authority are
intricately connected: Stephen is identified as a "son" and an
"author" above all ("I wonder what sort is his son he says hes an
author" [18.1300–1301]). The scene of seduction she makes up is
quite detailed in her mind, not forgetting fellatio and various
positions, yet it remains strangely stereotyped: "Im sure itll be
grand if I can get in with a handsome poet at my age . . . then
hell write about me lover and mistress publicly too with our 2
photographs in all the papers when he becomes famous" (18.1358–
66). Her misconstruction of Stephen as a young athlete "standing up in the sun naked like a God or something and then plung-
ing into the sea" (18.1347–48) blends trivialization and idealiza-
tion in another type of ellipsis, a necessary omission of the
other men in her life, Boylan and Bloom. It is impossible to
know whether she refers to the former or the latter when she
adds: "O but then what am I going to do about him though"
(18.1366). If Boylan is indeed the topic of the next and last sentence, which begins just after this break, it implies that Boylan
has been "killed," dispatched by the young poet. For Molly still
resents Boylan's lack of manners when he slapped her behind in
guise of a leavetaking, and her speech adds up negative forms
that prepare for the yesses of the finale: "no thats no way for
him has he no manners nor no refinement nor no nothing in
his nature slapping us behind like that on my bottom because
I didnt call him Hugh the ignoramus that doesnt know poetry
from a cabbage" (18.1368–71). If it is Bloom she means, then it
implies, rather, that she cannot forget the real husband for the
imaginary son and lover and that Bloom has already begun to
take charge of her unconscious, since she never denies Bloom a
certain knowledge ("still he knows a lot of mixedup things

especially about the body and the inside" [18.179–80]). Toward the end of her monologue, Molly has definitely acknowledged her husband as a synthesis of a young lover and older sage: "yes he said I was a flower of the mountains yes so we are flowers all a womans body yes that was one true thing he said in his life and the sun shines for you today yes that was why I liked him because I saw he understood or felt what a woman is" (18.1576–78).

When Molly remembers the books she has been given, she notices that she hates those that refer to her name ("Lord Lytton Eugene Aram Molly bawn she gave me by Mrs Hungerford on account of the name I dont like books with a Molly in them" [18.656–58]). On the other hand, she uses the mediation of print script to realize that her name has changed after her marriage ("I never thought that would be my name Bloom when I used to write it in print to see how it looked on a visiting card or practising for the butcher and oblige M Bloom" [18.840–42]). She seems to have no qualms about being called Mrs. Bloom and sees this as a turn for the better; she even enjoys the facile puns her friends cannot resist making ("youre looking blooming Josie used to say after I married him well its better than Breen or Briggs does brig or those awful names with bottom in them . . . my mother whoever she was might have given me a nicer name" [18.843–47]). Although she contemplates then the possibility of divorce and of becoming Mrs. Boylan, all this prepares in fact for her final metamorphosis into a blooming "flower" of the mountains at the end of the episode. Yet this shows that she shares with Bloom an awareness of bearing a modified or borrowed name: the rather exotic names Virag and Laredo have managed to be tied up together in their flowering substitutes. After all, *bloom* is etymologically linked with *blow* in the basic sense of "inflate, swell," which in its turn is close to *phallos*, a phallus which is described at the end of "Lotus Eaters" as Bloom's "languid floating flower" (5.571–72). However, this does not point to any "phallic symbol" but rather to the lability of the changes underwritten by an absent phallus.[7]

If Bloom's uncertainty as the status of his own name reenacts symbolically his uncertainty as a deceived husband, it is through his name that he carries off a definitive victory over all rivals, real or imaginary. In a sense he signs Molly's text, dominating its imaginary world not by bringing into play the power of the conquering male, like Boylan, but by acting parasitically upon the flowers of her rhetoric through the bloom of his name: his name is diffracted and disseminated into a multiplicity of signifiers.

It seems as if these signifiers themselves may have brought about the meeting between Bloom and Molly. She explains that at the time of her flirtation with Mulvey, her first sweetheart, she claimed to be engaged to a rich Spaniard, Don Miguel de la Flora, and she comments: "theres many a true word spoken in jest there is a flower that bloometh" (*U*, 18.775). This name becomes very logically "Don Poldo de la Flora" (18.1428). Hence Bloom, who thought he was the umpteenth in a series of suitors begun with Mulvey, a series that goes beyond him to include Boylan and possibly Stephen, finds himself well placed in Molly's imaginary world, which he had invested in advance with his name. His victory over Boylan does not depend on his having "more spunk" than the other, but on his name's ability to be combined, translated, and inverted and to frolic with complete liberty in the voice which accepts it: "I like flowers" she repeats, which also means "I like flows" and everything that flows.

The music of the "Sirens" finds itself overcome in the following chapters; it abolishes itself as a particular technique and becomes a means of structuring, an architectonics. In "Circe" the transmigration of textual atoms deriving from the book as a whole carries the words along in a revealing as well as concealing movement, in an eclipse of rationality; this occultation of barriers causes the last vague impulses of psychological plausibility to disappear. But the drift of the successive appearances and disappearances is subsumed in the cosmic flux of "Ithaca." The two centers of the ellipsis make Bloom and Stephen orbit around a Molly who is herself spinning. Now when that earth begins to move into a new ellipse, the Copernican decentering is itself displaced in an infinite spiral of misunderstandings and substitutions. Molly alone is capable of jumping outside the circle, and through her affirmation of the fluxes and of the "oceanic," she gives the book the maternal complement it was lacking; without her playing the "good mother," her countersignatures, which keep countering all the book's signs, surpass all anxieties and enable the enjoyment of breathings and voices.

Ulysses opens with two closely linked paradoxes: Stephen, whose mother has just died and who still has a father, is supposedly in search of a father ("Japhet in search of a father" [*U*, 1.561]), not of a mother; but the mother haunts Stephen's consciousness much more than the living father. The dead mother is alive; the living father is dead. Fathers in Joyce's work keep repeating that they are not yet dead, in a denegation which gradually loses all credibility as it echoes from the *Portrait* to *Finnegans Wake*. The shifting perspective Joyce offers on those successive dead fathers can be read as a very simple play on pronouns. In the *Portrait*, Mr. Dedalus's asseverations encompass Stephen's fate in the damned circle of his degradation: "*We're* not dead yet, sonny. No, by the Lord Jesus (God forgive me) not *half* dead" (*P*, 66; italics mine). Stephen will have to take up the cue, distinguishing a living half from a dying half within the composite entity that juxtaposes father and son. The use of a first person plural is quite deliberate; it departs from the original words as transcribed with probably more accuracy and hate by Stanislaus Joyce: "Just *you* wait. *I'm* not dead yet. No, by god, not half dead. Who-op! What do *you* think?"[8]

In *Ulysses*, one section of the "Wandering Rocks" presents Simon Dedalus trying to dodge past his daughter Dilly, who has come to demand some money to feed the family before he drinks it away; in his vividly mocking and mimicking voice, Simon parallels his own future death to that of his wife: "An insolent pack of little bitches since your poor mother died. But wait awhile. . . . I am going to get rid of you. Wouldn't care if I was stretched out stiff. *He's* dead. The man upstairs is dead" (*U*, 10.682–85; italics mine). Although he has played a part in "killing" his wife, as has Stephen, to him her memory is now sacred, even as her death marks the end of the libidinal and economic balance of drives in the family. Simon then perceives quite rightly in Dilly's cold rage at his irresponsible squandering a desire to see him dead—Dilly voices earlier the terrible "our father who art not in heaven" (10.291) – and Simon projects his own wake in a mourning fantasy: he is a corpse, stretched upstairs like Father Flynn's body in "The Sisters." Through his projected death, he can get rid of those who want to get rid of him, since he already is a third person, an absent reminder of the past in the impending future of a symbolic threat. The father will fit, therefore, in his role of dummy in the game; he will elude and escape, while remaining the stabilizer of a symbolic order defined by his name.

In *Finnegans Wake*, the father never really speaks in person; for instance, he never exactly utters the original words said by Tim Finnegan in the famous ballad: "D'ye think I'm dead?" The initiative always belongs to the others, to the collective cries of the mourners: "Macool, Macool, orra whyi deed ye diie?" (*FW*, 6.13); and the father always speaks as the object of their wishes (he would say: "D'ye think *me* dead?") not as a subject: "Anam muck an dhoul! Did ye drink me doornail?" (24.15).

And as soon as the mourners see Finn about to resuscitate, they persuade him to lie back, and they eventually force him to stay in his bier: "lie quiet and repose your honour's lordship! Hold him here, Ezechiel Irons" (27.22–23). The conclusion is straightforward: "Repose you! Finn no more!" (28.35). They go on to explain that he can rest in peace, since a substitute has already been found, for now comes Earwicker the publican, Finn's "namesake" and "randy" substitute: "For, be that samesake sibsubstitute of a hooky salmon, there's already a big rody ram lad at random on the premises of his haunt of the hungred bordles" (28.35–29.1). Finn is the dead giant whose dreams spin universal history; he is buried in a landscape limited to Phoenix Park and the outskirts of Dublin, and Anna Livia flows on to the sea with her continuous feminine prattle.

So it seems at first that the pattern of *Ulysses* can be applied to *Finnegans Wake*: a split between a real and a symbolic father contrasts the dead father identified with the law against a living father whose shortcomings, failures, and perversions are the talk of the town. In fact, the relation between Finn and his substitutes (for they are perhaps more than one) is never quite clear, as nothing is clear in this dream book of a language merging into a night of all languages; but we already can state that the archetypal father is not "consubstantial" with his sons or substitutes. *Finnegans Wake* leaves a logic of substances to enter one of relations, which means that the principle of "incestitude" is now operating at the very level of language. The language is in such a perpetual confusion and hesitation about its own objects that everything is moving in a reversible world centered on a mysterious guilt. Even if the father appears to be the origin of the guilt, he is not a Christlike persona; he is no host of "corpus meum." His first function is to bequeath a symbolic debt inside language to the community.

Like Louis XV, about whom Freud cites an anecdote, the father is never the "subject" but always the "object" of the jokes of others: "The king is no subject."[9] The father becomes the shifting ground of an absence made good by the empty discourses that always fall short of his debt; the object of discourses, he requires a specific form of writing, which he helps to produce with the aid of the mother. This complex strategy will be analyzed in terms of *idiolect* and family ideology: the voices and the names will have to be incarnated in a new language.

"Circe" holds up a deceptive mirror, not to nature, but to what I have called the Unconscious of the text, in a pantomime that animates the writing with considerable force. The writing involves the question of the Unconscious, especially in the last chapter, where everything is exposed, set out, and seems to present Molly's dreams, fears, and loves in a uniform light, as if, in order to have her play her role of dark continent all the more effectively, Joyce had in a sense stripped her of the mystery that is generally associated with the unconscious. Molly's voice, however, sets out the problem of an overflowing of the Unconscious of the text, which has held sway until this point. For Bloom and Stephen believe in an Unconscious, of which Stephen tries to construct the theory and which Bloom seeks in his para-scientific approaches to a cosmos he believes can be reduced to deterministic laws. Joyce made extensive use of Jung's little book *Die Bedeutung des Vaters für das Schicksal des Einzelnen,* which he owned, to develop a conception of paternity linked to the Unconscious. Jung uses a phrase that cannot fail to have attracted Joyce's attention: "Die Unbewusstheit ist das *peccatum originale*"[10]—the Unconscious (or more precisely, unconsciousness) is the original sin. Jung analyzes cases of tyrannical and incestuous parents whose desire is seemingly to obey a myth of absolute power, and whose neurosis models in advance the psychoses of their children. "Without knowing what they are doing," to quote Jung, they enslave their sons and daughters to this legacy of servitude, which becomes their unconscious. Jung's terminology, which is not here absolutely Freudian, enables one to elucidate Stephen's main attitude, which is still hesitating between "Unconsciousness" and "the Unconscious." For him, original sin is lived out in the connection between "womb" and "tomb" and "wound": "wombed in sin darkness" (*U*, 3.45), "Our souls, shamewounded by our sins, cling to us yet more, a woman to her lover clinging" (3.421–23).

Original sin arises as a result of an obscure gestation in the belly of a woman; Stephen wants to close his eyes to this darkness in order to rediscover in the blindness the intangible link with the symbolic father. In this way Stephen would be able to distinguish between the Unconscious that ties him to the mother and Unconsciousness that would deliver up the secret of the mystical filiation: fundamentally, he dreams of an immaculate conception. Molly puts an end to these fictions, not only because she makes fun of them with Rabelais, but above all because, through her voice, through the affirmation of her desires, she cuts all these semblances down to size, in the same way that she deflates the windbag Boylan, the ithyphallic suitor. Stephen, having become the reader of the idiolect, will learn to write on this maternal belly in a creative "doublecrossing" of the womb, as Dylan Thomas put it with reference to Christ's passion.[11]

Bloom believes in a more cunning Unconscious, one that does not fall into the snares of the imaginary and thrives in the proximity of written signs; it is thus that, among his numerous projects for sensational advertisements, one in particular attracts our attention: Bloom had suggested to his former boss, Wisdom Hely, whose sandwich men pass through the streets at all moments of the day, that he use young girls in a cart as an advertisement for the stationery. "I suggested to him about a transparent showcart with two smart girls sitting inside writing letters, copybooks, envelopes, blottingpaper. I bet that would have caught on. Smart girls writing something catch the eye at once. Everyone dying to know what she's writing. Get twenty of them round you if you stare at nothing" (*U*, 8.131–35). Writing is reduced to pure gesture, with no other aim than having people gaze: its aim is a "nothing," a blank titillating the rather voyeuristic desire of the passersby. The trick of this stage setting (with a transparent cart, paper, blotting paper) seeks to grab the reader's gaze, with the reader seeing only a void upon which he superimposes his own fantasies, rather like the mirror in which Shakespeare appears. And the memory of the time when Bloom worked at Hely's reminds him of the happy days, of his father and his photographic studio, of the flow of life, and leads to a curious slip of the tongue; Bloom has noticed in the *Journal* that Nanetti, the foreman of the composition room, had forgotten Monks's name, the "dayfather." He himself cannot now recall the name of Major Penrose (which he remembers a few minutes later [8.1114]): "Pen something. Pendennis? My memory is getting. Pen . . . ? Of course it's years ago. Noise of the trams probably. Well if he couldn't remember the dayfather's name that he sees everyday" (8.178–80). The play on *pen* and *penis*, relayed by the allusion to Thackery, leads the writing over towards the name of the dead father; writing amounts to a continued manipulation of the fetish, in forgetfulness of the name.

These two quotations are important insofar as they merge in "Ithaca" at the moment when Bloom's unconscious is scarcely distinguishable anymore from Stephen's, shortly before the separation. Stephen, to whom Bloom has explained his advertising project, imagines a hotel, a room, a young lady writing, sighing, falling silent, while a young man comes to read what she has written. She has written in every direction ("in sloping, upright and backhand" [*U*, 17.619]) "Queen's Hotel," the name of the hotel at Ennis in which Bloom's father had poisoned himself. Bloom prefers to attribute the homonymy to a "coincidence" (17.635). In fact, this term, "coincidence," will refer in *Finnegans Wake* to the junction between homophonies, the structural system of superimposing characters, and the distortions that constantly rewrite in a new way the name of the father. *Finnegans Wake* begins as a sort of sequel to *Ulysses*, just as Molly, having become "adult" for the first time through adultery, delights in her name, which she writes in her imaginary works, and just as Bloom frees himself from the paternal metaphor. The relationship between writings and languages will in this way shift the question of the "author" and of interpretation; perversity will mark a stage in the relation between the text and the reader.

SIX

IDIOLECTS, IDIOLEX

The most frequent reproach leveled at Joyce concerns his "illegibility." When Pound, for example, denounces the loss of communication brought about by the displays of verbal audacity in *Finnegans Wake*, he criticizes the disproportionate demands of a work that constructs its own codes, determines its own reading protocol, and asks the reader less for knowledge and erudition than for an active participation in the deciphering of a language whose autonomy is already affirmed in *Ulysses*. So when *Finnegans Wake* develops not only its own code, but also a language that spills over the frontiers of English in order to establish this new schema of reading, the textual system may seem to shut itself within a closed world, restricted to initiates, like a trap that allows the reader to enter only in order to devour him and absorb him in its language games. *Finnegans Wake:* a polyphemic text, a very Polyphemus itself, whose eye must be blinded so as to escape its domination, a book against which all acts of trickery and treachery are permitted and even justified, since it is a question of discovering the lever with which to turn it upside down, to set its enormous mass back on its feet, and finally make visible the real, the light, and values perhaps.

If the closure of the book is referred to a deceptive system of values, to an ultimately ideological perversity, the criticisms that one comes across practically everywhere imply a narrow logical connection between two terms that I shall endeavor to explain, *idiolect* and *ideology*. From this arises the possibility of understanding the links between perverse writing and languages or history. I hope to bring out a central problematics in Joyce's work and lead to the fundamental questioning of a language linked to the question of the nation, political strategies, and verbal creation.

Every text probably falls in between the absolute, utopian objective of total communication of its elements—in short, a code—and the creation of an individual language that is not to be found anywhere else—in other words, an idiom. Caught between these two extremes, the so-called "modern" text tends to tighten the bonds between the code and the idiom in order to establish the inner necessity justifying all its presuppositions; it is the road to the idiomatic code—that is to say, the idiolect. The monstrous idiolect of *Finnegans Wake* intensifies that endeavor, by offering itself as a universal history exploiting family ideologies, since for Joyce the family appears as the source *par excellence* of idiom production.

This leads, then, to a dialectic of language and idiom on the one hand, and of mother language and foreign languages on the other. How does the "matricide" of Joyce's writing bring it initially to re-endow with all its rights a mother language oppressed by an imperialist cultural idiom? This is the type of question that can arise after reading *Ulysses*, and it, in turns, opens onto the more general problematics of the refusal to assimilate the mother tongue to a living speech dominating all other languages. The questioning then widens to embrace the constitution of the Babel-like idiolect of *Finnegans Wake*.

From a certain point of view, every work of art offers itself as an idiolect, if one admits that every work forms a system and imposes its own law on a language it fabricates. Such is, for example, the thesis of Umberto Eco: he defines *idiolect* as the specific code of a work, broadening to the domain of literary semiotics a linguistic concept that designates the private and individual code of each speaker.[1] The text thus becomes a "class with a single member," which sets up a homologous structure at every level of its code. In a rather different way, according to Norman Page,[2] every character in a novel possesses an individual language, and each time he opens his mouth the novelist systematizes a series of stylistic traits that pin him down as surely as a description: Dickens provides a great many examples of this type of emblematic discourse. In fact, every time someone speaks, that person uses language in his or her own way, and that usage gives away as many clues as the voice or fingerprints. On one level, therefore, the idiolect of the book is the sum of the idiomatic traits of the characters.

This is how Joyce and Stuart Gilbert understood the term, when, collaborating so as to take stock of the various stylistic figures of the "Aeolus" chapter, they identify Bloom's expression "Citronlemon" (*U,* 7.226) as an "idiotism (Bloomism)."[3] In fact, the choice of the examples requires a few clarifications: the "idiotism" is clearly attributed to a character; it takes the form of a portmanteau word, simple enough to be understood but with a complex determination. Bloom has just recalled a telephone number through an habitual mnemonic device, his association with the address of a former neighbor in Saint Kevin's parade, J. Citron. He next takes out his handkerchief, and then says "Citronlemon?" because of the lemon smell of the soap he has previously bought ("sweet lemony wax" [5.512]). The proper name meets the common noun in an assemblage that can be read either as a translation (for example, from English into French) or as an etymological game (on the name of the plant *Citrus limon*) juxtaposing near-synonyms. The evocation of a happier past with Molly, who had asked him to call in at the chemist's, integrates this idiotism into Bloom's subsequent meditations, up until its transformation into "melon" to describe Molly's buttocks (17.2243). This portmanteau word, however, does not yet have the flexibility of the complex distortions of the *Wake:* the idiotism next acquires a wider significance.

"Idiotism" is not synonymous with "idiomatic phrase." In any given language, what is generally called "idiomatic" is what resists translation. Bloom's "idiotism" is a condensation relying on the presence of two linguistic stocks in English. The term "idiotism" recurs in *Finnegans Wake*, in a footnote commenting on the appearance of two famous orators, Hamilton and O'Hagan ("We like Simperspreach Hammeltones to fellow Selvertunes O'Haggans" [*FW*, 299.22–23]). The third footnote adds: "Pure chingchong idiotism with any way words all in one soluble. Gee each owe tea eye smells fish. That's U" (299, F 3). Hamilton, who had delivered a brilliant maiden speech in the Parliament, had thereafter remained silent, whereas the nationalist O'Hagan was to sell out to the British. The silvery tones of Irish orators and betrayers turns into an enigmatic and chiming ditty that parodies patriotism.

The note points to the presence of an "idiotism," but in which language? The word "chingchong" echoes with other Chinese words on the same page ("Vely lovely entilely! Like a yang-sheepslang with the tsifengtse." [299.25–26]). The shift to oriental pronunciation (*l* for *r*) creates another type of "slang," and the note may allude to another orator, Eglington, whom Mulligan had mischievously nicknamed "Chin Chon Eg Lin Ton" in *Ulysses* (*U*, 9.1129). Joyce's notebooks confirm this allusion, since we find in VI.B.46 a list of jottings about Chinese, probably taken from a French grammar of the language. This is why "ideotism" precedes "ü fish", "ts (mot)," and "iang (sheep)."[4] The term *ideography* is generally used in French to describe characters such as *ü* or 㒑, which represents a fish by its stylized bones. The same page of the notebook contains a reference to the change of *r* to *l*, pronounced backwards in Chinese.

However, the footnote does not limit itself to Chinese. It plays on English "ideotisms" by alluding to the well-known joke of G. B. Shaw, who declared that G-H-O-T-I could spell "fish" using the pronounciations in "enou*gh*", "w*o*men," and "na*ti*on." The idiocy of Irish politicians who are willing to speak in another language redoubles the absurdity of the English spelling system. The detour through Chinese, with its particular system of characters (whose poetic potential had been stressed by

Pound and Fenollosa), send us back to the perverse relationship uniting speech and writing. This relationship offers a mirror to the reader ("That's you!") and points to the dangers posed by a Universal English (U English). The singularity of exact references to two figures of Irish politics evades the abstract universality of such a language and brings the reader closer to the specificity of an awkward position. For the reading will always be hesitating, trapped by slips of the pen and misprints. The idiolect of the book retranslates constantly the idiotisms of languages: "you" know in advance that your reading will fail, will misconstrue, will miss something. "Spells" has similarly been turned into "smells"; the text cries "stinking fish"; it shows that Irish betrayals smell fishy, even if one needs an Irish writer (Shaw, who was not exactly a friend of Joyce) to see the inconsistencies of the language he uses. What is attacked, beyond politicians, is the ideology of proper usage, an ideology that is of course underwritten by nationalism. Joyce seems, on the contrary, to plead for a "solubility" of all the words, which may melt into each other and thus produce the "hundredletterwords" that punctuate his book. In order to reach this ambitious aim, Joyce needs to play with alphabets and dictionaries, so that any new reader, Chinese, Bantu, or Basque, may start rereading his text and find associations he himself had not foreseen, had not planned.

For Joyce, therefore, "idiom" has to be restricted to particular expressions found only in certain languages. For instance, he writes that "for in the ersebest idiom I have done it equals I so shall do" (*FW*, 253.1–2). In Irish, *tà sè dèanta agam* is used to promise something when it means "I have done it," "it is as well as done." The tenses of "Erse" suggest a certain timelessness with their undecidable statements. The fundamental "idiom" of *Finnegans Wake* is thus Anglo-Irish (in terms of grammar above all), this *English as We Speak It in Ireland*, whose inventory had been made by a namesake of Joyce at the turn of the century.[5] Those who speak such an idiom can be attracted by the purity of a "hard and guttural tongue," as Joyce would describe it for his Triestine readers. His acutely felt incompetence in Gaelic may explain the allusion to a "fish" in the footnote: "The League organizes concerts, debates, and socials at which the speaker of *beurla* (that is, English) feels like a fish out of the water, confused in the midst of a crowd that chatters in a harsh and guttural tongue."[6] Even when he could appreciate the parallels between the Irish nationalist movements and the Triestine Irredentists, Joyce never believed in the possibility of a Gaelic revival and was in favor of complete bilingualism: what he favored was "a bilingual, republican, self-centred, and enterprising island with is own commercial fleet."[7] Bilingualism derives from the acceptance of a state of affairs and not from a deception as to possible returns to the origins. The language must nevertheless remain double, for it is made up of the same stuff as history—long lists of martyrs and betrayed leaders—so that no "native" speaker will be able to forget an inherited duplicity.

Joyce's exile takes its meaning from its own duplicity: a self-imposed exile, it was also conditioned by the reactionary dreams of the nationalists. He wrote to his brother in 1906: "If the Irish programme did not insist on the Irish language I suppose I could call myself a nationalist. As it is, I am content to recognise myself an exile: and, prophetically, a repudiated one. . . . If it is not far-fetched to say that my action, and that of men like Ibsen &c, is a virtual intellectual strike I would call such people as Gogarty and Yeats and Colm the blacklegs of literature" (*Letters*, 2:187). The last sentence may sound very unjust toward Yeats, who, after all, managed to be active on all fronts; yet the evolution of his politics in the nationalist camp bear out the validity of Joyce's remark. Language thus places a wedge between the artist and his country; it forces him to remain abroad, the unacknowledged legislator of *his* world.[8]

In *Ulysses*, Joyce is careful to distinguish between Griffith, who is said to have derived some ideas from Bloom's Hungarian models, and the citizen in the pub, who embodies jingoism and anti-Semitism in its worst aspects. True, he insists on "self-centeredness," but it is an autarky with the results described by Vico in his *Scienza Nuova:* for Vico, the Cyclops represents the first stage of civil society, just after the bestial state of nature. His inhumanity, isolation in caves, and lack of mutual aid finally dooms him; this is how Ulysses can triumph over Polyphemus (*SN*, §§365–905). Having at least two languages, he can see with both eyes, as it were, and thus blind the one-eyed giant. He pierces the Cyclops' eye just as in the *Wake* the earwicker is reputed to pierce eardrums. But when one shifts from Bloom as Homeric Outis to Earwicker as Persse O'Reilly, the patriots of the Easter Rising seem to have managed to sneak back into Joyce's verbal agglomerations. We shall see that this implies no condoning of the politics of Padraic Pearse: he has indeed become a hero, supporter of doomed politics, aware that his only chance will be the epic transformation of an impossible coup. In *Finnegans Wake*, "Nobodyatall" as "*Per Se*" will have to be destroyed and dismembered in linguistic juggernaut subverting any monolinguism.

In the *Wake*, the problematics of the idiolect becomes more complicated and resolutely locates itself amidst paradox. If Joyce establishes an autonomous language, "invented" from start to finish as a totality of language, he is refusing a certain tradition, a certain solely cultural heritage: the Latin idiom as Dante understood it, or again, the idea of French as an imperialist language that seduced Brunetto Latini when he wrote his *Livre du trésor*.[9] The irreducible singularity of this original place, Dublin, authorizes all betrayals. To write with the idiolect amounts to constant betrayal of the cultural (Shakespearean) tradition, by "going back over" an attachment to an idiom evoked by rhythms, accents, and names. This return provides the occasion for a new plundering, a new ransacking of the hated and idolized ties—in short, to betray the living betrayal of a mother language already sold to the enemy since it comes from the enemy, without seeking to be *naturalized* elsewhere. A process of "denaturalization" is under way, breaking up the taxonomy of the other languages, constituting a language above and beyond the various tongues, retaining the voices of each idiom according to that idiom's technical capacities, rather in the manner of the *De Vulgari Eloquentia*, which selects the distinctive characteristics and properties of each Italian idiom before analyzing the qualities of the sounds themselves. Joyce said, "I'd like a language which is above all languages, a language to which all will do service. I cannot express myself in English without enclosing myself in a tradition."[10] The idiolect leads to the idea of a language of pure technical mastery, to a language conceived of as a totalizing of all possible effects. Usage transformed into service ensures that the only way not to be a slave to language is to subjugate it for one's own purposes. The idiolect constructed by the piling up of neologisms rebuilds a place that is unique, but the dynamics of this local belonging is transformed into a machine of all languages.

I have hitherto distinguished between idiom, idiotism, and idiolect; I would like now to draw a contrast between what one can with Joyce call his "idioglossary" and idiolect properly speaking. Joyce worked for seventeen years on this special language, which irritated certain of his friends and which overspilled the limits of *Finnegans Wake*. In this text he multiplies the allusions to his idiolect, and Shem is accused by Shaun of writing an incomprehensible language with words stolen from others, this being *Shemish* (a new avatar of "Bloomism"), the "idioglossary he invented" (423.9). "Idioglossary" refers to the constitution of a particular vocabulary, and the expression can be applied to texts other than *Finnegans Wake* to designate all those parallel fragments written in a style recalling that of the *Wake*.

Joyce took some pleasure in writing pastiches of his own new style, first by sending a letter of insult ("A litter") to "mister Germ's Choice."[11] He laments his oncoming blindness in a few moving lines devoted to Swift ("Twilight of Blindness Madness Descends on Swift").[12] He praises wildly an Irish tenor, John Sullivan, in a purple patch that incorporates the names of most famous opera singers.[13] In fact, the "idioglossary" of these separate pieces appears simpler than that of *Finnegans Wake* and would correspond to the earlier stages of his chapters, as for instance the first version of "Anna Livia Plurabelle." The "translations" given by the author are generally simple explanations of puns and soon reproduce a sentence in normal English, with simple portmanteau words ("glowcoma" is glossed as "fireside and repose" plus "glaucoma" in *Letters*, 1:274) and a few forays into exotic vocabularies. The only exotic word in Burmese given by Stuart Gilbert is not used in the short text, which relies on Greek, Latin, English, French, German, Spanish, and Irish – quite an impressive list, but if one adds Italian, Dutch, and Norwegian, this is the sum of the languages Joyce knew well enough to use them more than decoratively. The difference between the "idioglossary" and the "idiolect" of the *Wake* lies in the fact that the piece on Swift gains an added significance when read in the context of the Swift and Sterne network of the book, while as such it remains in the plaintive mode of empathy, the two Irish writers being identified by a common plague. In the book, each character's speech possesses idiosyncratic features that first help us to recognize them (Earwicker stutters, Issy lisps, Shaun betrays his urges by slips of the tongue, the twelve customers are always announced by twelve abstract words, and so on) and then build up into a coherent polyphony.

This is why each sentence in the book can become a mirror of the whole book and prove the "solubility" of its words: they do not so much dissolve as disseminate along lines that guide the reading. When Joyce glosses his own text, the situation changes significantly. A letter published only in 1975 gives a few indications to a rather bewildered Miss Weaver (*Selected Letters*, 326). Joyce explains the meanings of nine words – "L'Arcs en His Cieling Flee Chinx on the Flur" (*FW*, 104.13-14) – which generate seven different translations. The second "meaning" would in itself have sufficed if we had been reading one independent piece; here it is:

> 2) The Rainbow is in the sky (arc-en-ciel) the Chinese (Chinks) live tranquilly on the Chinese meadowplane (China alone almost of the old continent[s] has no record of a Deluge. Flur in this sense is German. It suggests also Flut (flood) and Fluss (river) and could even be used poetically for the expanse of a waterflood. Flee = free).
>
> (*Selected Letters*, 326)

One may of course marvel at Joyce's ingenuity in the subtle unfolding of dense meanings. Soon after, one may wonder why only these seven meanings? For instance, Joyce does not account for the x at the end of "Chinx" (all the interpretations he gives are consistent with "Chinks" as he writes the word in the parenthesis). Should we admit that there is at least an eighth gloss, which would for example start from "jinx" and lead to "Fluch" ("malediction" in German)? But then should it be taken to mean that the divine rainbow destroys bad luck, or, on the contrary, that God's curses pour from heaven along with his benediction?

However, even if these speculations are possible, and perhaps also manipulated by Joyce, an associative logic seems to preside over his glosses, much more than linguistic cleverness. One meets always the same elements, first the Bible and, within it, a few archetypal stories (Noah's ark, the animals, and the three sons Shem, Ham, and Japhet, to whom I shall soon return), then the history of civilizations (China presenting a paradigm of otherness that is crucial for the blending of perspectives, and Irish history always in the background, with the sad fate of King Roderick O'Connor depicted here as typical of Irish isolation), and finally a few anecdotes centering on an Irish family: this is the home of H.C.E. identified by his siglum in the letter, with a restricted set of allegorical places, such as the city of Dublin and its suburbs, Phoenix Park and Chapelizod, the pub (here a "gin palace") and above it the parents' bedroom, whose ceiling is cracked.

What is, of course, more mindboggling is the awareness that the sentence is lifted from a list of about one hundred and thirty similar titles (it is at times not so easy to decide when a new title begins), all of which must also possess at least seven senses, which altogether should yield more than nine hundred little stories in less than three pages! But if the list is virtually infinite, it nevertheless bases its parataxis on the grid of limiting recurrences. Moreover, what matters most is that each phrase, title, or sentence can be understood in at least two opposite meanings, as in the case with the rainbow that can herald peace or war, destruction or reunion, loss or gain, amusement or mourning. God, who seems to enjoy his covenant with the world, also laughs at Noah's dismay when the patriarch realizes that his birds have fled. And finally all these proliferating stories crisscross and intersect at strategic points that are defined by the names provisionally lent to the different actors. Each actor is identified by a siglum and can pick, almost at random, an identity in a wide although finite set.[14] In that sentence, Joyce admits that the story primarily concerns E, or Earwicker; but one may note that only *H* and *C* can be discovered among the capitalized initials, whereas *L* and *A,* which begin the sentence, might evoke Anna Livia with as much strength. Thus, if the structural family becomes the only real "character" of the book, it will be crucial to understand how this nexus structures the interpretation of the text while demarcating and situating its idiolect.

The idiolect sums up the discourses of the little world constituted by the archetypal family—a family whose adventures can be made to condense universal civilization. The connection between the "idiolect" and the sigla should not be too arbitrary, since the footnote following Issy's remark on "chingchong idiotism" introduces the "Doodles family" with their nicely drawn sigla (299. F 4). This comes as a note to the "lozenge" we have already met when talking about familial triangles in *Ulysses*. From the five letters, *G, H, O, T, I,* one moves to seven sigla, which add the city or the book (symbolized by a square) and the Four Irish historians (symbolized by a cross)—but not, for instance, the twelve customers or apostles. The place of the action and the interpretation of the events (this is the main function of the Four annalists or Analysts) are part and parcel of the family, a family whose name also derives from the "secret" of the book—a secret which, as we know, Joyce was able to protect long enough—that is, its title. Let us now see how the familiar idiolect can be said to derive its several levels of meaning from the name of the dead father, Earwicker or Finnegan.

Finn seems to be equated with a place, Phoenix Park, whose name can be superimposed onto the title of the book—the spark of the embers consuming the Phoenix negates (*nix* in German) the end (*finis, fin*): Fin-negans, Wake! If such a majestic father lies at the root of all history, he can be expected to inform it in some way, to offer some kind of vital source, some heroic blood through a continuous transubstantiation. But what a close analysis of the text reveals is that no communion is ever possible because the origin disintegrates under the inquisitive eye of seekers and followers alike. Finn's body seems to be arrayed for its consumption in a parodic last supper; the mourners even say grace before eating it: "Grace before Glutton. For what are we, gifs à gross if we are, about to believe. So pool the begg and pass the kish for crawsake. Omen" (*FW,* 7.6–8). Fittingly enough, the parts of his body seem about to turn into bread and ale, "But, lo, as you would quaffoff his fraudstuff and sink teeth through that pyth of a flowerwhite bodey behold of him as behemoth for he is noewhemoe. Finiche!" (7.2–15). The sacred salmon of divine wisdom becomes a "behemoth," a gigantic monster fading away in the landscape, as white whale swallowing everything and everybody—Noah as well!—yet remaining invisible. This absent father is of course the *Wake* itself, both the ritual that is going on with its disappointed mourners and the bulk of the book, which must also frustrate the efforts of the readers: "He is smolten in our mist, woebecanned and packt away. So that meal's dead off for summan, schlook, schlice and goodridhirring" (7.17–19). The "salmosalar" is now a canned herring, destined to be exported rather than eaten on the spot: the textual metamorphosis thus evaporates the text, referring each sentence back to all the others. The meal is ended before it started, and the baffled revelers only say "good riddance" to the lure of this "red herring." The text parades its eucharistic nature only to expose it as illusion; the "someone" who might have been exhibited to us is nothing but a "sum-man," an addition, a combination of all past sins. As the communion can never be achieved, the sense is lacking, and the mythic totality can never be (re)constituted.

Whatever the exact degree of "inconsubstantiality" between Finnegan and Earwicker may be, they share the uncomfortable privilege of having committed a misdemeanor: both are implied in the endless trial that sets out to determine the reason of their "fall" and to ascertain the extent of the guilt that stains everybody else: "What then agentlike brought about that tragoady thundersday this municipal sin business?" (5.13–14). From the start, Finnegan's fall from a wall "in erection" epitomizes an original sin's having a collective and political significance. The whole book is just an immense reiteration of the manifold interpretations of such a transgression. Since the guilt is collective, the absence of the dead father prepares the scene for what appears to be a symbolic debt.

We have seen how Stephen had attempted to cancel his filial debt, beforehand as it were, by setting up his family's lending bank; in *Ulysses* his strategy of irresponsibility makes him insolvent and unable to relive the evident bankruptcy of his "house of decay." In *Finnegans Wake*, everything is bolted around the very name of the dead father, Finn. The dead Finn becomes "finis," the end, and also the beginning of the father's symbolic life: "Finn is." Thus, he becomes his family, transformed as he is into the Irish clan or *Fine*. The Fine was not limited to a nuclear family; it included several septs.[15] The sept itself is a further stage before the nexus of the Oedipal family; indeed, the sept as punned by Joyce into the French "sept" or "seven," and the basic family in the *Wake*, is made up of seven characters, the parents, three children, and two servants, Joe and Kate. The title of the book could well be "URGES AND WIDERURGES IN A PRIMITIVE SEPT" (267 R). The Fine includes the larger family, with the twelve customers in the pub, and the four old men. For instance, the Irish Brehon Law acknowledged the solidarity of all the members of a Fine; everyone is responsible for each other's crime. It also fixed a price for all offenses; the legislation stipulated a fine for murder, theft, etc., so that in this system the family is determined by a system of obligations and mutual responsibility. This collective commitment renders all the members of the Fine "sinnfinners" (36.26): they pay the fine for the sin, and as they acknowledge their kinship, they stand as politically subversive, at least in the eyes of the other law, the imposed English law. But since they pay their fine, they soon become accusers, and this is why the father has to answer for his offenses to his parents first; Earwicker says this exactly: "I am woowoo willing . . . to make my hoath to my sinnfinners." The Sinn Feiners are now sin finders.

Moreover, Earwicker's name is often traced back to "Eric," the Scandinavian name; when the inquirers search for the possible origins of the father, they list "the Earwickers of Sidlesham . . . offsprount of vikings who had founded wapentake and seddled hem in Herrick or Eric" (30.7-10). An *Eric* is precisely the price one has to pay for an offense; one paid a murder-eric, a theft-eric, etc. *Finnegans Wake* echoes this many times; "I will pay my pretty decent trade price . . . the legal eric for infelicitous conduict" (537.12-13), declares Earwicker as repentant sinner. Hence, the price the clan has to pay for the father's murder is the murder-eric, which places Earwicker in the following dynastic succession:

Finn (the dead father)
FINE (the family and familial debt)
Eric as Earwicker, substitute and scapegoat.

The family's origins are linked to the primal murder of the old ancestor who with his name countersigns the symbolic debt without which there could be no offspring. Shem likewise praises his father: "his farfamed *fine* Poppamore, Mr Humhum, whom history, climate and entertainment made the first of his *sept* and always up to *debt*" (173.22-24; italics mine). We now understand better why every time the buried hero offers to stand up, the crowd taunts him with derisive jeers: "Hahahaha, Mister Funn, you're going to be fined again!" (5.12). A father never can be defined, just as the book's end (*finis*) can never be reached.

For Joyce, as for Vico, the family is the basic unit of civilization. In the family lie the seeds of the *polis* and the political order, yet the historical passage to the system of families is marked by a return to particularism and even to autarky. For example, Vico's theory posits a certain catastrophe at the source of history, a catastrophe connected with the biblical Flood. According to Vico, the early giants, who indulged in unrestrained copulation in the open, were frightened by the thunder, which they took for a divine remonstrance; they then went into caves and there founded the rites and customs, such as religion, decency, moral laws, the prohibition of incest, that make up the family.

Subsequently, every family possesses "its own religion, its language, its territories, its matrimonial ceremonies, its name, its weapons, its government and its laws" (*SN,* §630). Joyce uses this independence to build an autonomous language, a sort of idiolect of the family. Vico's analysis of the familial organization anticipates in many ways Freud's theory of the primal herd in *Totem and Taboo,* as Vico sees in the father's law a despotic power: law and legacy are intrinsically connected; and using this right to leave a legacy, the father has often transformed the system of heredity into despotism, which can range from ordinary paternalism to absolute tyranny. Jupiter, as "Jus-Pater," represents the absolute authority of the fathers during the age of families. The first families also extend their limits; those "gentes" shelter clients (*famuli*), or runaway slaves, along with the nuclear family. Vico's analysis of the *Roman Twelve laws* is fascinating because it displays an awareness of the link between names, inherited from the symbolic father, the prohibition of incest, and the dialectics of revolt against the father's law. The family is soon cleft by struggling parties; the rebel slaves are joined by the sons, who are not much better treated and fight against the autocratic rule of the father. This rebellion breaks down the old unit and brings about the birth of a political state. Kings are chosen by the *patres* to subdue the rebellious *famuli,* replacing thereby the domestic authority by the civil one; the state, in place of the family, then controls property.

The case of the Roman plebeians is typical: they rebelled not to claim more political power, but simply to be granted the right to marry "like the Fathers" ("connubia patrum" and not "connubia cum patribus," stresses Vico, [*SN,* §598]). Without the rites of the fathers, marriage was not sacred, and the plebeians could not *name* their father, "non poterant nomine ciere patrem"; they could not prove their heredity, nor could they be part of a symbolic order. Vico clearly relates the lack of a name to the impending risk of committing incest: "The plebeians . . . who could not prove the legitimate ties which linked them to their fathers . . . incurred the risk of engaging, like animals, in incestuous relationships with their mothers or their daughters" (*SN,* §567). If we can generalize from this case in point, we may then notice that the sons react violently against a paternal tyranny that comes near to imposing a potential incest upon them. But by so doing—and this is where *Finnegans Wake* goes a little further than either Freud or Vico—the sons who finally defeat the father—if they do—unwittingly violate the most prohibited of the incest taboos: when they murder him, strangle him, shoot him, they are in a way having sexual intercourse with him. To bear this out in details, I will now turn to *Finnegans Wake* and the exemplary story of Buckley and the Russian General.

SEVEN

LANGUAGE OF EARSE

The essentials of the story are simple enough: Buckley, an Irish soldier fighting against the Russians at Sebastopol during the Crimean War, one day catches sight of a Russian general alone in a field. He is about to shoot him, but when he realizes that the general simply wants to defecate, he falters; then the general wipes himself with some grass, and Buckley, disgusted, braces himself and shoots.[1] The story is enacted with slapstick effects by Butt and Taff, appearing on a television screen in a pub. Joyce, who had heard this story narrated by his father, had enormous difficulties in inserting it in the *Wake*, despite the straightforward relevance of the classical Freudian themes. He could only include it after Beckett had given him a nationalist key to its conclusion: Buckley shoots the general because he wipes himself with a "sod of turf," offering "another insult to Ireland." The political theme is then grafted onto the Oedipal sequence of provocation and ritual murder. Earwicker is the incestuous father *par excellence;* an "earwig," he is also an "insect," and insects that can connote incest abound: "Insects appalling, low hum clang sin!" (*FW,* 339.22). The general seduces Butt's beloved sister ("odious the fly fly flurtation of his him and hers!" [352.7]), and this brings about the final insurrection: "We insurrectioned . . . I shuttm" (352.13–14).

The father's sacramental aura is what prevents the sons from murdering him at once. They try to come nearer to a sacred space and to "divulge" it: "Divulge!" (340.31) shouts Taff to his brother. They are both involved in an "interpretation," since, according to Vico's false etymology, *interpretatio* derives from *interpatrari,* which means "to penetrate [the designs of] the father": "The first interpretation applied to the divine laws and was made by means of auspices, earning thus the name of inter-patratio" (*SN,* §448).

The sons' interpretation does not render them intrepid: "And may he be too an intrepidation of our dreams which we foregot at wiking when the morn hath razed out limpalove and the bleak-frost chilled our ravery!" (338.29–31). Their "trepidation" wishes the father to be only a nightmare, a pure fantasy produced by their own guilty unconscious. The father as "necessary evil" is nevertheless part of the "nightmare of history" from which the sons hope they will awake in the morning. And when the day comes, near the end of the book, the mother uses similar words to calm a dreaming child: "Hear are no phanthares in the room at all, avikkeen. No bald bold faathern, dear one. Opop opop capallo, muy malinchily malchik" (565.19–21). The Russian phrase ("my little boy") calls up the Russian context of the story of Buckley, while the general has become the panther of Haine's nightmare in *Ulysses* ("the black panther was himself the ghost of his own father" (*U,* 14.1033]). He is also the Roman centurion who "polluted" Mary in the revised catechism expounded by Virag in "Circe." Any father is but the ghost of himself; he conditions the myth and the unconscious of the sons by his name. To forget the father means to hope for a mute awakening in the sad detumescence of a chilly morning. But happily for us, there is no waking out of the Wake, no place unaffected by the power of the name; and when the sun "raises out his lump of love," he also castrates the night's wet dreams. The father is the tribal totem, the bear ("urssian," 352.01; "Ussur Ursussen," 353.12, blending *U.S.S.R.* with an Irish bear, not bull) attacked by a pack of hounds. These dogs shout, "Bog carsse" (339.6)—*Bog* is "God" in Russian—meaning the curse of God/Dogs, but also the curse of the bogs, of peat and turf. As old bear, this father "reveals" himself and exposes himself to the interpretation in that he "bears/bares" his name: "Of the first was he to bare arms and a name" (5.06); he is thus a "forbear" who bares his body, his arse especially, inviting his own immolation.

Butt, though, repeatedly acknowledges that he had not the courage to shoot, and Taff pushes him along. To underscore this ideological block, Taff relies on the very machinery of the story itself, and a title is enough to suggest that something must have happened somewhere, and the recurrence of titles is as great as that of proper names. They all play the same role: "Since you are on for versingrhetorish say your piece! How Buccleuch shocked the rosing girnirilles" (346.18-20). Once Butt has been convinced that he must act, he becomes confident, garrulous even, while the general starts accusing himself of all the sins in the world, and Taff seems more and more reserved about the revolution. And when Butt tells the audience that he finally shot the general (the problem is never to know whether the action actually takes place or not; what matters is that he has been brought to express himself), Taff appears critical of his brother and aware that he is merely attempting to replace the father:

> TAFF (*camelsensing that sonce they have given bron a nuhlan the volkar boastsung is heading to sea vermelhion but too well-bred not to ignore the umzemlianess of his rifal's preceedings ... effaces himself in favour of the idiology alwise behounding his lumpy hump of homosodalism which means that if he has lain amain to lolly his liking—cabronne!—he may pops lilly like a young one to his herth—combrune—*)
>
> (352.16-22)

The revolution is going to triumph, and the boatmen of the Volga are heading to sea under a red flag, but this Easter rising is merely a boast by the vulgar, the people (*Volk*), and Taff poses now as the aristocratic liberator (Yeats) who does not know what to do with his gunmen. Taff "effaces himself" in favor of the ideology: he must blot out all the signs marking his difference. The new state that will replace the old will have as totalitarian an ideology as the former, with its insistence on a state religion (Butt is seen in the next paragraph with "his bigotes bristling" [352.27]); Butt has simply taken his father's place, and Taff uses the same title when he congratulates him: "And Oho byllyclaver of ye, bragadore-gunneral!" (352.23). Taff's indulgence for the past links him to his father, whose sins he shares ("homosodalism," for instance); like his father, he erases himself and disappears. As Shem the Penman, he will incur the same reproaches and insults, while his brother refuses the guilt that he yet betrays by constant slips of the tongue.

The "ideology" is the linguistic process uniting the two brothers in one person: "Butt and Taff (*desprot slave wager and foeman feodal unsheckled, now one and the same person* ...)" (cf. 354.7–8). The desperate wage slave and the feudal yeoman represent the alliance of the proletariat with the small landowners in an "ideal reconstitution" (355.01). But if the father's death may well have taken place in the reality defined by the confluence of their fantasies, the father still lives at the symbolic level of myth: their victory is "umbraged by the shadow of Old Erssia's magisquammythical mulattomilitiaman" (354.9–10). The general was only another disguise for Finn, the dead hero who survives by bequeathing his inheritance of guilt and debt: "As to whom the major guiltfeather pertained it was Hercushicupps' care to educe. . . . and the law's own libel lifts and lames the low with the lofty" (355.11–2). This ideology will be even more perverted in the next cycle, when the freed slaves are reduced to the role of victims or accomplices of the Nazi terror: "Forwards! One bully son growing the goff and his twinger read out by the Nazi priers. You fought as how they'd never woxen up, did you, crucket? It will wecker your *earse*, that it will!" (375.16–20; italics mine).

Beckett's suggestion gave Joyce a convenient relay, enabling him to move from the murder of the mythical ancestor to a wider interrogation about a role and place of the mother in language. Not only does Joyce fully "nationalize" the story,[2] but he also universalizes the national problem and shows its relation to idiom, idiolect, and ideology. Even the systematic opposition between anal and phallic elements thread through all the languages that really contribute to burst the mother's tongue. The most obvious symbols paraded in this story reveal that it re-enacts the struggle between phallic and anal drives. Butt with his gun is also called "Bod" ("penis" in Gaelic), and he taunts the father's "jupes": "Come alleyou jupes of Wymmington . . . !" (339.26). This correspondence points to the father's transvestism and feminizes his arse (*zhopa* means "arse" in Russian). Similarly, Stephen had been struck by the expression "les jupes," used by a Jesuit to refer to the Capucin dress, and he associates the priests' garments with "the delicate and sinful perfume" of the "names of articles of dress worn by women" (*P*, 155). The brothers' several attempts at insurrection are all failed uprisings against the tsar, or "Sur of all Russers" (340.35; *ser* means "shit" in Slavonic languages, and *sur* is "tsar" in Russian),[3] and though Butt's fly is unbuttoned ("and your flup is unbu . . . " [341.02]), he needs no less than three pauses and numerous exhortations before the actual shot. Taff's entreaties are unequivocal: "Whor dor the pene lie, Mer Pencho? Ist dramhead countmortial or gonorrhal stab?" (349.1–2). His venereal diseases should not prevent Butt's "ramhead" from butting into the father's arse. Yet, in spite of this abundance of anal/phallic themes, the role of the mother cannot be neglected, and indeed it affords a key for comprehending the shift from the different initial positions of the sons and father.

During one pause in the duet of Butt and Taff, a news report gives a clue to the interpretation of the overdetermined relation between all members of the family. The news ends with a horse race in which the father has the lead as *Emancipator, the Creman Hunter* (342.19)—we recognize the reversed initials of H.C.E., Earwicker as Here Comes Everybody—followed by *"three buy geldings,"* while two young mares (*"too early spring dabbles"*) are *"showing a clean pairofhids to Immensipater"* (342.25–26). The incestuous position of the Emancipator/Immense pater is blatant: he emancipates his doubled daughter (or his wife plus his daughter) just to abuse them, and he conversely castrates the sons who are mere "geldings." They, in turn, have only one alternative: to castrate or to be castrated. When the father seems about to get the upper hand, the horrified crowd witnesses an exhibition of incestuous relations and their associated perversions: *"Sinkathinks to oppen here! To this virgin's tuft, on this golden of evens! I never sought of sinkathink"* (342.26–28). This disclosure of the virgin's pubic hairs is another hint about the perverse nature of H.C.E., who perpetrates the same insult as the offense to the "Virgin Soil" (the title of a book by Turgenev that Joyce had in his library) of Ireland.[4] Butt and Taff cannot bear to have the family's secret revealed, so they fall back on the pretext of an insult to a virgin sister or a mother to enable themselves to shoot the father. The alliance of symbolic castration of a penis and patriotism in order to defend a phallic mother constitutes what Joyce calls ideology. The "virgin's tuft" will then have to be transformed into the "sob of tunf" with which the father wipes himself, "beheaving up that sob of tunf for to claimhis" (353.16).

As he wipes himself, the father claims the soil of the country as his; he soils it and makes a "s.o.b." of each son in this perverting action. The insult against national values and national honor—the customers shout "For Ehren, boys, gobrawl!" (338.3), joining *Ehre*, "honor in German, and "Erin go bragh"—can be reversed, turned back onto the father: he himself becomes a "son of a bitch." Taff thus exclaims: "The lyewdsky so so sewn of a fitchid!" (340.1). He is not uninhibited enough to say "The lewd son of a bitch" outright, and his guilt makes him stutter ("so so sewn"); he also disguises his statement as Russian, and translated in Russian, the sentence equates the general with mankind (*lyudskoi,* "human"). Through this piece of abuse, the father shrinks to the stinking role of a son of a polecat ("polecad" in 341.1), and "son" is rewritten as "sewn" because in Russian *sewn* is pronounced "shiti," which contributes also to "fitchid." The general is "sewn" with children; he is the "monad," or unity, about to disseminate its fragments of go(l)d ("scutterer of guld") in a golden rain that multiplies him by twenty (*fichid* in Gaelic).[5] The multifaceted complexity of a father's persona is literally made up by his sons. Hence, the primary sin is to stand in the relation of father and son: "son" in Russian (CGH) is said "Sin"; "sewn of sons" and "soiled by shit" are almost synonymous. The father has to pay the penalty for his own paternity, while the son can only wash away the sin of sense through this murder, which yet links him more closely to the shameful reproduction and incarnation of his father. "Shit" must then be replaced by "shoot," as the extremes meet when phallic becomes anal and anal phallic; in the process of "atonement" is no redeeming value but the simple reproduction of the father's ideology.

We now enter the matrix of the *Wake,* this nexus of transformations that constantly turn the tables on the father and his sons, since their libidinal places are interchanged; the brothers attack the father's anal perversions in the name of the mother's honor, only to repeat the same shift from orality (Shaun) to anality (Shem). When the general makes his confession shortly before the shot, we read: "*He wollops his mouther with a sword of tusk in as because that he confesses how opten he used to be obening her howonton he used to be undering her*" (349.30–32). He wallops his mother as he wipes his mouth with the famous sod of turf, which implies a whole inversion of the passage between mouth and anus, all this related to a mother tongue. "Mouth" replaces "arse" because it is linked to a maternal language, but the phallic connotations of "sword of tusk" nevertheless show that the general's sin is to make love as often underneath his wife as on top of her. His corruption of the mother language lies in this creation, since he "lowers" it when he perverts it in his obscene writing, open to all aberrations. Bisexuality is a necessary element in his nature—we learn, for example, that he is "smooking his scandleloose at bot thends of him" (343.24–25). But while bisexuality is part of the general's polymorphous perverse disposition, homosexuality, because it has been repressed from the ideology of "normalcy," contaminates the brothers' struggle for liberation. Butt is at one point identified with

Wilde, one of the archetypal figures of inversion in *Finnegans Wake*, and he takes his cue from the mention of *"pedarrests"* (349.33). What is meant simply by Wilde's pederasty is onanism in the biblical sense: "the whyfe of his bothem was the very lad's thing to elter his mehind" (350.14–15). This passage does not refer simply to the fact that his wife was no obstacle to Wilde's homosexuality: the text says that the "wife of his brother" was the "very last thing to enter his mind." Classical homosexuality (bottom, behind) is related to Onan's sin, the refusal to afford a posterity to a sister-in-law after the brother's decease. Onan spills his seed to the ground, refusing to raise the house of his brother: he does not want to be a father in his brother's name. And Joyce knew the medieval correlation established between onanism, contraception, and sin. What is more relevant is the confusion some theologians made between "parricide" and "sodomy." John T. Noonan sums up the whole issue in this way: "Thus Lactantius treats homosexuals as parricides: his implication is that they destroy potential human beings. It is entirely in keeping with this approach to treat the users of contraceptives and abortifacients as parricides or homicides."[6] Joyce does not treat homosexuals as parricides, but parricides (and who has not dreamed of killing his father?) as homosexuals. Women, spurned or raped, are the only fixed or stable points of reference in this reversible universe: but they are merely exchanged, taken as a pretext of the perverse male struggle for power.

At this level, the general lays the archetypal function of the drunken patriarch, Noah, who exhibits his arse, not his sons, "sham! hem! or chaffit!" (351.26). The drunkenness is another form of paternal blindness, while the open and deserted ark, after the flood has subsided, is now Noah's own anus. Stephen had already punned on this possibility in Circe: "And Noah was drunk with wine. And his ark was open" (*U*, 15.3868–69); the sentence follows a recall of his theory of incest—"Queens lay with prize bulls" (*U*, 15.3865; cf. *U*, 9.854). Noah must be covered by a son walking backwards; the similar perversions of the general and of the tsarist times ("those thusengaged slavey generales . . in sunpictorsbok" [*FW*, 351.22–24]) are inverted once more by the new puritanical order: "I did not care . . . for any feelings from my lifeprivates on their reptrograd leanins" (351.26–28). The renaming of St. Petersburg as Leningrad is part of the devious strategy focused on the obscene arse of the father. "Reptrograd leanins"; walking backwards with retrograde leanings toward the father. Noah's ark becomes Joyce's Trojan Horse, or Wellington's "big wide harse" (10.21), since we shift easily from *horse* to *arse* to *ark,* and then to *aerse* or *erse.*[7]

The father who exposes himself cannot be reduced to anality alone. When he is represented "expousing his old skinful self tail-tottom" (344.16), he is not only exhibiting himself, but also masturbating and mixing the different levels, top, tail, and bottom, all the while tempting the peeping Tom with is tail; then follows a surprising declaration of love from Butt: "as I love our Deer Dirouchy" (344.32), *ushi* meaning father in Russian. The love for the father is finally defeated by the alliance with the mother, so that, through the father's actual death, his name may live. Thus can he be invoked under the name of "*Old Erssia's magisquammythical mulattomilitiaman*" (354.10).

All this tends to imply that Erse, the grand old forgotten language the Citizen extolls in his pub, plays in *Finnegans Wake* the role of a "father-tongue": it appears as the metamorphosis of a native language, voiced and soiled by the father, returning to the materiality of loam or humus. Only then can it really fertilize the earth. When the father has completed the irrevocable outrage, he intones a song, "an exitous erseroyal *Deo Jupto*" (353.18). His royal arse, which is offered to be kissed—"he can kiss my royal Irish arse" (*U,* 7.991)—is a new "King's English" in which the proximity of the paternal arse displaces the mother tongue.

The mythic giants Vico places at the origin of history stem directly from Cham, Shem, and Japhet (*SN,* §369), but their exact genesis is not so "patrilinear"; it is referred to the neglect of their own mothers, who abandoned them, "let them roll naked in their own filth," in the post-diluvian primal forest. Left to themselves, "living in the midst of their excrement, the nitric salts of which constituted an excellent fertilizer for the earth," they then attempted to clear a way through the forests, "without any fear of gods, fathers or maters" (ibid.). Here, the mixture of earth and manure, with the added dimension of onanistic pollution, contributes to the mythic origins of civilization: it creates a new language, one blended with body products, that amalgamates "humus" and "human nature" in a type of very special "humor." Shem inherits this language from his father (although he derives his inspiration from his mother and his subjects from his sister), and this explains why he threatens to wipe the English language off the face of the earth: "he would wipe alley english spoken, multaphoniaksically spuking, off the face of the erse" (*FW*, 178.6–7). Shem will use all the other languages to break down the English rule; English will become a spook through the action of his spuking and diarrhea. *Arse* and *Erse* allied to a multinational *earth* both effect the murder of the mother language. The murder of the father is in fact only a dialectical climax in this indefinite struggle.

Such an unsteady blend of language and substances asserts nothing but its own regenerative power to live and die when it explodes the overgreat proximity of a native tongue. Accordingly, *Finnegans Wake* never ceases commenting on its own material appearance of living printed letters scurrying across a white page: "Owlet's eegs .. are here, creakish from age and all now quite epsilene, and oldwolldy wobblewers, haudworth a wipe o grass" (*FW*, 19.9–12). The sacred *terra firma* that would come as an ideal synthesis never wipes out the sexual and textual "hesitancy":[8] the epicene neutralization of sexual differences applies to the moments when ideology is about to triumph— the fusion of Butt and Taff, or the coalescence of Burrous, Caseous, and Anthony after the regicide, or the victory of Saint Patrick over the Druid who stands for the whole book, as Joyce said.[9] The text stages there its own defeat when the language of ideology blurs the differences; but the text thrives on defeat paradoxically, for the adverse criticism triumphs only after it has produced a piece of synthetic tissue in order to wipe the text afresh: "wipenmeselps gnosegates a handcaughtscheaf of synthetic shammyrag" (612.24–25). *Aerse* as a language is no synthesis, but rather a *coincidentia oppositorum*, playing as often as not the ambiguities of the written word of anal production against the

multiple puns afforded by spoken dialects and distorted pronun-
ciations; from *aerse* to *earse*, it turns to the root of P-earse
O'Reilly's ear and pierced eardrum.

The theme of the *aerse* as a father language is to be paralleled
with what Stanislaus reveals in his *Dublin Diary* when he
notices the frequency with which the word *arse* crops us in his
brother's mouth:

> Pappie has been drunk for the last days. He has been shout-
> ing about getting Jim's arse kicked. Always the one word. . . .
> I am sick of it, sick of it. I have a disposition like a woman,
> and I am sick of his brutal insistence on indignity. I writhe
> under it. I try to regard [it] as drunken, drivelling lip-
> excrement, but it is too strong for me. Ugh! It is a word that
> is scarcely ever out of Jim's mouth. He has been remarked
> for it and *playfully* accused of being a bugger because of the
> way he pronounces it.
>
> (*DD*, 49–50)

James and his father seem already linked in an ambivalent inheritance of anal abuse, while Stanislaus, instead of being accused
of homosexuality, stresses his own femininity. But the most telling detail is this: "Jim's criticisms of these notes of mine are characteristic. One of them is this: 'An' do ye be sittin' up here,
scratchin' your arse, an' writin' thim things.' He pronounces
'arse' something like 'aerse'" (*DD*, 148). Expressing his virtuous
contempt for the objective complicity of his idol, James, with
his tyrant, their father, Stanislaus pins down the characteristic
symptom with accuracy and reveals too that he does not want
to have anything to do with "aerse." Stanislaus voices his loath-
ing for his father because his father is Irish ("*Irish*, that word
that epitomizes all that is loathsome to me" [*DD*, 23]), and he
almost reproaches James for being too indulgent, as if he felt
that Jim had in fact kept the inheritance of gift and guilt left by
his father: "And towards Pappie, who, too, represents feudalism
to [Jim], his mind works perversely. But his sense of filial
honour, as of all honour, is quite humoursome" (*DD*, 55). For
Stanislaus, his brother is placed in the same perverse attitude

when confronting the church, the country, and the father: a delicate mixture of respect and contempt, of rejection and imitation, is at work in his mind, revealing a pattern which imposes its own duplication. The cunning debunking of the father who nevertheless is idolized defines a complex stance, parodic and patristic simultaneously; this is the position of "patriody," whose symptoms show in the pronunciation of "aerse."

These symptoms do not tend to betray new biographical aspects; they matter as the seeds of a future textual scene that will appear in full only with the episode of Butt and Taff. The notes of Stanislaus are relevant as literature, for we know that Joyce kept reading them and used many details in his later fiction from *Dubliners* to *Finnegans Wake*. It is no accident, for instance, that Stanislaus claims the paternity of interior monologue, since he experiments with it in his diary (*DD*, 167), a technique he himself imitates from Tolstoi's rendering of the thoughts of a dying officer in his *Sebastopol Sketches*. Joyce finally may have acknowledged his "debt" when he placed the scene of Buckley's shot near Sebastopol. Stanislaus is of course only part of the elusive figure of Butt, yet what remains of him in the character is his keen eye for easy justifications and escape in his brother's strategy, an escape James Joyce finally achieves through the multiplication of an English rooted in an Irish soil, with the added force of all other possible idioms: "Jim is thought to be very frank, about himself, but his style is such that it might be contended that he confesses in a foreign language—an easier confession than in the vulgar tongue" (*DD*, 110). And this was written in 1904!

In his "foreign" language, Joyce makes the crudest of all confessions, as he recognizes his "perverse" filiation to a despot who cannot be done away with simply and safely. Unlike Stanislaus's blunt rejection, Joyce's exile brings him back, after the journey through the languages, to a place where words are buried alive to be exhumed again and again. Aerse as language destroys what would be on a first level an enslaved mother tongue obeying the dictates of Rome and London. One of the first ironies of *Ulysses* is the attempt made by Haines, the Englishman, to reappropriate a language that the old Irish peasant cannot even understand: she mistakes his Gaelic for French. "Aerse," nevertheless, is not a thing of the past as Gaelic appeared to Joyce: it opens the individual discourses to a historical dimension. Taff expresses this possibility when he exhorts Butt: "Ath yetheredayth noth endeth, hay? *Vaerse*good!" (*FW*, 346.23; italics mine). Yesterday, which will be this today (yet here today), is not finished yet. The assent to this dynamic drive in which past and present exchange their qualities and properties means a release of all the historical dramas that show how the father's murder is equated with an incestuous sharing of perverse anality. Even castration, as a symbolic weapon wielded by the father, or as imaginary retaliation of the sons, participates in this *soiling* of a soil, "To the dirtiment of the curtailment of his all of man?" (353.4). Uncivility abounds on both sides, yet it is this desperate fight that gives birth to cities and civilizations.

When Taff is absorbed by the "son-ideology" that will replace the "father-ideology,"[10] he notes the "umzemlianess" of his rivals' "preceedings" (352.18)—that is to say, the "unseemliness" or else the appeal to the spirit of a maternal earth: *um* means "spirit," "intelligence," in Russian, and *zemlia*, the "earth." But in the next sentence, even the distinctions between father and mother get blurred, for Taff calls God his "maikar" ("*wiz the healps of gosh and his bluzzid maikar*" [352.34–6); "help" is written so as to let A.L.P., or Anna's initials, come to the fore, and "maikar" unites maker and mother in Bulgarian *maikar*. The foreign writings lay waste what would be paternal propriety or maternal place. Playing the game of "patriody," Joyce never criticizes perversion; he simply shows its comic or parodic fallout, inasmuch as it affects the father figure. And with this anal or analogical writing, endlessly multiplying the definitions that constitute the propriety of a language, he frees the words from their frozen meanings; he thereby short-circuits the illusion that there can be a mastery over meaning, a mastery that would correspond to a fixed position of the subject in his discourse and in society. Such a language woven with writings resembles a Penelopean tapestry to be pieced together by the reader, for it sets the names adrift, spins the codes around, while it continues to mime a historical process. History becomes equated with a cyclical process of renaming, the laws of history being easily reduced by Joyce to the laws of language. "The only difference," he said to Jacques Mercanton, "is that as with the dream, I perform in a few minutes what it sometimes took whole centuries to produce."[11]

Joyce considers his breakthrough in literature an insurrection and often sees himself in a state of war; his numerous comparisons prove it: "What the language will look like when I have finished I don't know. But having declared war I shall go on *jusqu'au bout*" (*Letters*, 1:237). This war is indeed a war against English, against a mother tongue used to the limit, mimed, mimicked, exploded, ruined. This scorched-earth policy—the earth being the still, maternal soil of words—has to be complemented by the anal fertilization of all the litters, fragments of works, pieces of mythologies, literary odds and ends which are left to proliferate in the text. When, at the conclusion of "*Exiles*," Richard, the artist, feels a "deep wound of doubt" arising from the agonizing incertitude over his wife's fidelity, when Stephen declares that paternity is the mystery of the void, and when Shem refuses to join the Irish Easter Rising because he "pray[s] to the cloud Incertitude" (*FW*, 178.31), they all reproduce the same pattern, a pattern constituting a feminine receptacle of language through the acceptance of a symbolic wound "which can never be healed." The fusion of womb and wound creates the only possible link between tomb and womb: in its unstable fusion, the father's perversity and the mother's constancy are merging, bridging the gap between the feminine flux of liquids, rain, water, urine, menstrual flood, and the anal idiom of aerse with all its litters and letters.

This self-canceling "idiolect" sets out to reveal an unknowable original sin in a quest without end or aim even, since what Joyce demonstrates is that original sin is the sin of sense as believed to be an origin: this "since" recurs in the *Wake* to date the barred origin, "since the flood. . . ." Stanislaus was then entitled to say later that "original sin . . . was to be the subject of *Finnegans Wake*."[12] Whether origins are alternatively identified with the father's law or with the dual relation to the mother, the fall has already separated the text from the hallucinated meaning. There is no devouring of the host, no communion, in a word, that is not a prey to the convoluted circuit of the father's bowels. If, as Atherton writes, original sin is for Joyce God's creation of the world,[13] this creation is marked off from the start by a certain failure, a miscarriage, a collapse. The happy fall (*felix culpa*) is acknowledged, but the doubt about its origins can never be raised fully. It may be phallic as well as anal; we never really know as we get lost among the seemingly haphazard digressions of the speakers at the *Wake*. "It may half been a missfired *brick*, as some *say*, or it mought have been due to a collupsus of his *back promises*, as others looked at it" (5.26–28; italics mine). Once more, though, the vocal emission is connected with the penis (prick), while the eye is connected with the arse.

Joyce's aim is to prick the bubble of narcissistic self-sufficiency, but not merely by a manic abandonment of the subject to the untamed flows of desire. He prefers to present the father in his symbolic role of dead ancestor casting his blessing on a realm of names and to use this mythical figure as a basis for diverse replacements; with all the surrogate figures, Joyce exhibits what wounds, what hurts. With the Russian general, killed or castrated by the sons uniting against him, Joyce demonstrates "the itch in his egondoom" (343.26): not only the painful preservative that prevents full conception and generation, but also the *id* inside the kingdom of the *ego*. As Freud phrases it, "Wo Es war, soll Ich werden." The different fathers can be placed on a descending scale that would seem to parody Vico's stratification between gods, heroes, and men: Zeus, Polyphemus, and Ulysses are thus seen on a descending scale. Zeus, like Finn, is the absent father whose powerful name can only be invoked, and often in vain; the fact that he castrated his own father must be repressed from consciousness. Polyphemus, the Cyclops, is the real father who transgresses all the laws and breaks the code of hospitality. This "impossible" father has to be overturned time and again by the sons whose fusion builds up the unstable figure of the imaginary father: this place where Stephen's and Bloom's unconsciouses were supposed to intersect appears now as the moment of the ritual murder, which, in the last analysis, aims not so much at a displacement of the father's guilt as it aims at the complete recasting of the mother tongue.

To say that we never know whether the father's sin was anal or genital means that one cannot ascertain the priority between his attempt to seduce his daughter or to exhibit his "white arse" to the buggering sons-soldiers, although the biblical pattern would tend to imply that Earwicker, like Lot, is seduced by his daughter(s), whereas he rather provokes his sons like the drunken Noah. This distinction concerns the "real" father as Earwicker the publican; if we now consider the divine "Loud" of creation who thunders among the clouds, his creative sin must have been anal; there is no doubt here for Joyce, and it echoes in the repeated hundred-letter thunder-words. This Lord is like the God of Moses who showed his "back parts" to him instead of his face.[14] In many respects, the Russian general is like Moses, the man Moses of Freud's last "historical novel." When the sons shoot him, they both shoot the tyrannic and monotheist leader and destroy their awe-inspiring idols. Butt says, "I shuttm" (352.14) to call up Shittim, the place where Moses is supposed to have been murdered, according to Freud and to Sellin.[15] Like Noah, Moses is related to an ark, or two arks rather, the first being the ark of bulrushes where he was miraculously found, and the second the ark of alliance with God, this ark of "Shittim wood." From the obscure legend that tends to preserve the purity of his Jewish origins to the empty ark containing the text of the law, we there find in a nutshell the dialectics of mystical fatherhood. Moses, too, is a father who founds paternity upon the void, upon a cloud of incertitude that hides his own God, upon the living doubt which abhors material or maternal representations.

To forbid the adoration of visible forms is a way of barring the way back to the mother, back to a feminine goddess of sexual fertility. Thus, the law of the father is asserted against the sensible evidence of the mother's hieroglyphics. It is probable that, like the Russian general, Moses is killed because of an "insult to the mother" and that, like him, he is at the source of the written character. Freud mentions that the invention of the alphabet may have been derived from the scribes of Moses, who, "being subject to the prohibition against pictures," "would even have had a motive for abandoning the hieroglyphic picture-writing while adapting its written characters to expressing a new language."[16]

Moses, like Earwicker, stuttered—Moses, according to Freud's version of the biblical legend, because he was in fact an Egyptian who spoke Hebrew with difficulty. Earwicker is a Norseman, a Viking invader who tries to speak Irish. As such, both are foreign invaders: "The unnamed nonirishblooder that becomes a Greenislender overnight!" (378.10–11). Nevertheless, their patrilineal rule will in the end "give omen name" (279.5), give a name to everything—the ominous and the numinous having been approached at last.

We started with the initial paradox of *Ulysses* in which the dead mother is living and the living father is dead. *Finnegans Wake* asserts the primary function of a dead symbolic father who allows for all the substitutions around his name, his "normative letters" (32.18), H.C.E. The living mother Liffey flows, on the contrary, toward her "bitter ending" when she finally meets Death in the form of her oceanic father at the close of the book. Since the mother in *Finnegans Wake* is the "only true thing in life," she too is undeniable; she feeds, condones, preserves. The father is constantly denied, dethroned, negated, but also reestablished for a new cycle, to prepare a new fall. He is absent in such a way that he generates the falls, flights, and flourishes of fiction. The legal fiction has really become the law of fiction, linking the performative power of language to the serial signatures of collapsible fathers.

Joyce's patrilineal fervor always was determining, even when he decided to explore the limitations of the father's function. As far as his own life was concerned, he even tried to rewrite his biography to put his father in a more favorable light. When Gorman wrote in the draft of Joyce's biography the very rhetorical question, "Of whom was he the spiritual son, and where would he find the Mystical Father?" Joyce abruptly inserted the following rejoinder: "His spiritual father is Europe, to which his natural father constantly urged him to go."[17] By the time Joyce was writing *Finnegans Wake*, his exile had to be considered a flight from a motherland of bondage and into a new country still to be created. Yet, Joyce needed the assent of his real father (his "grandoldgrossfather" [*U*, 15.3866]) in the new fiction of a biography, acknowledging his debt of paternity even if doing so meant a slight distortion of the facts.[18] Thus could he attempt to become his own spiritual father's father: he can still appear today as the absent father of much that is being written in Europe and elsewhere, in spite of some of our "bulldozers" (to quote the ending of Donald Barthelme's *The Dead Father*) pouring not earth, but tons and tons of printed matter on his Babelic burial mound. We could perhaps simply repeat Lucia's exclamation when she was told of her father's death: "What is he doing under the ground, that idiot? When will he decide to come out? He's watching us all the time."[19]

EIGHT

A PORTRAIT OF THE AUTHOR
AS A BOGEYMAN

Is it possible to recapitulate and to detail the stages of this voyage in search of the subject in the text and in history? The question of the author may well turn out to be only a decoy, yet it should be asked in order to overcome the aporias of consubstantiality and transubstantiality, aporias that reenact the interplay between the paternal and maternal figures, in the endeavor to think out a total text that would escape the closure of totality through perversity. To move towards the definition of the status of the author does not mean, then, that one identifies oneself with the "father" or the "mother" of the text, in the text, but that the recurrent question in *Ulysses* and *Finnegans Wake*— "Who the hell could have written all that?"—is interlinked with the problematics of reading itself.

Subjects read and write: they establish meaning in the transcendence of an aim which is never adequate to itself, which is always resituated in the immanence of a textual web, a historical rhythm. I would suggest that this transcendence through immanence is accomplished through the recognition of a debt, between the neutrality of a verbal knot and the loftiness of an authority. Hence, only the reader-writer will be able to tie himself up as a subject, thanks to the agency of the Other.

Any comprehensive account of the evolution of Joyce's writing, from juvenile attempts at artistic autobiography to the mature intricacies of a bewildering "chaosmos," requires at one stage or another the elaboration of a concept of the author of and in the text. Text is here understood both as the web of signifiers which can migrate from book to book and as the complete apparatus one usually identifies with literature, including reader, printed page, and the series of more or less godlike mediations ascending towards Creation as such. The concept of the author cannot be reduced to the measure of ironies willed or not by a narrator who often indulges in silently tripping up his characters. Nor can it be tantamount to adding up the textual devices mounted against whole provinces of culture by the cunning "arranger" of the episodes of *Ulysses*. Yet, although the question of the authority one can ascribe to an author may turn out to be as deceptive as the categories of transubstantiality and consubstantiality Stephen Dedalus applies to literary and cosmological creation alike, when the text keeps referring to its own problematic origins, the reader turned critic has either to invoke another writer or critic as an instance of authority or to produce his own theory of authority.

In the famous article already discussed in the Introduction, Roland Barthes heralds the "death of the author," dismissing the very notion of authority as another metaphysical bogey left over from the times when "the man and the works" could sum up the concerns of criticism. For Barthes, the modern text opens up to pure writing and attacks any "voice or origin." This opening is also latent in the more subtle cracks and hesitations of so-called classic or realist texts.[1]

Through this concept of writing, the author meets his own death on the page. This is emphatically true of the modern text, characterized by openness and subversion, deploying a meaning that has not been calculated by the old ghost within the machine of textuality, or by the author. Meaning lies on the page, waiting to be reinvented by the reader, who has as creative a role as the writer: "The birth of the reader must be at the cost of the death of the author."[2] Such is the concluding sentence of Barthes's article, which starts, interestingly, with a meditation on the question of the *neuter* space of writing.[3]

Finnegans Wake may well have remained outside the literary canon of Barthes; it nevertheless retains all the claims to such a stance: a heterogeneous "writing," into which the body of its "writer" dissolved, even during his lifetime (as can be evinced from many remarks made to friends by Joyce), staging the neutrality of a bisexual and irretrievably divided body of text. The naive question posed by existentialist anthropology–"Who writes, and for whom?"–loses its Sartrean candor only to be fed back into the mechanism whereby neutrality corrodes subjectivity; and when the same question occurs–and recurs, inevitably– in the dizzying rotation of roles initiated by Joyce at his own *Wake,* the meaning is totally different: "Say, baroun lousadoor, who in hallhagal wrote the durn thing anyhow? Erect, beseated, mountback, against a partywall, below freezigrade, by the use of quill or style, with turbid or pellucid mind, accompanied or the reverse by matication, interrupted by visit of seer to scribe or of scribe to site, atwixt two showers or atosst of a trike, rained upon or blown around, by a rightdown regular racer from the soil or by a too pained whittlewit laden with the loot of learning?" (*FW,* 107.36–108.7).

If we agree with Barthes that Joyce writes for a reader asked to become one of the "anticollaborators" of a writing in progress, the reader, lost in the maze of words, slowly understands that the progress (or process) teaches him the price to pay for the death of the author. Joyce's apparent paradox would then be that such a birth of the reader-as-writer can only be founded on a philosophy of authority.

To help us follow this track, the hidden reference to Hegel (in "hallhagal") may cast some light: Hegel would stand as Joyce's direct ancestor, and Joyce would start precisely where Hegel had desisted, retracing the steps of a widening totality. Such is, among others, Jacques Derrida's perspective when he calls Joyce "the most Hegelian of writers." The choice of plurivocity enacted literally in the *Wake* is the parallel and contradiction of a Husserlian reduction of ambiguity: Joyce's phenomenology of the mind repeats and mimes the totality of empirical culture, a gesture which, for Husserlian phenomenology, still smacks of empiricism and of historicism. In that sense, Joyce might well stand as our last author in the sense of *auctor,* the one who augments, adds to: he has clearly enlarged our notion of literary totality, a notion which, it might be recalled, is never too far from that of the monstrous.[4] A writer who pretends to dispossess himself of his traditional prerogatives in order to leave the burden of debt and sin to his reader is a notion rather familiar to Joyceans, and I would like to explore the figure of such an absent or dead author, the *dio boia* of his creation, "all in all," and thus coming back like a bogeyman to scare critics and readers; last parodic avatar of the "bog-man," the Irish bog-trotter scatologically returning like the cloacal repression of the English language finally exposed, flaunted, and splashed about; ultimate perversion of the god-dog of *Ulysses,* a Minervian owl wearing the rags of a scarecrow, pacing up and down the "enchained" labyrinth of culture.

We are now, thanks to Jacques Aubert's efforts, more aware of Joyce's connection with Hegelianism, and can balance the overrated influence of Aquinas with the added emphasis given to it by Bosanquet's neo-Hegelian grid.[5] Hegel proposes a model of totalizing encyclopedia which may have fascinated Joyce; but when Derrida called Joyce a Hegelian writer, he was not then in dialogue with Husserl, as in *The Origin of Geometry*; he was engaged in a friendly contest with Levinas, a philosopher who insists on rediscovering a Jewish relationship to the Other prior to any Greek—or, for that matter, German—philosophy. Let us quote Derrida's very words, for they can serve as an introduction to the problematic of "authority" already sketched: "Are we Greeks? Are we Jews? We live in the difference between the Jew and the Greek, which could be the unity of what we call history. . . . And can the strange dialogue between the Jew and the Greek, or peace itself, take the shape of Hegel's absolute speculative logic, a living logic *reconciling* formal tautology and empirical heterology? . . . What is the legitimacy, what is the meaning of the *copula* in this statement by the most Hegelian, *perhaps*, of modern novelists: *Jewgreek is Greekjew. Extremes meet?*"[6]

Derrida acknowledges in a footnote that Joyce's sentence offers only a "neutral" point of view of the "reconciliation of contraries," with a neutrality that could not be palatable to Levinas's radical otherness of subjectivity. For Levinas, Joyce would be the most Hegelian—*for sure*—of writers, sealing himself off from the violence of an act that opens up the realm of ethnics and precludes the smug totalities of conceptual systems: "The notion of action entails an essential violence, that of a transitivity lacking from the transcendence of thought, locked in itself, in spite of all its adventures, all finally imaginary or enacted by an Ulysses, merely to come back home."[7] If we were to ascribe to Joyce a statement which, in the Circe episode, is uttered by Lynch's cap—and which begins with the more ominous words "Woman's reason" and ends with "Death is the highest form of life" (*U*, 15.2097-98)—and which distorts other thoughts passing through Bloom's mind when he visits the graveyard, he would then certainly be accused of Hegelianism. *Accused* is not too strong a word in Levinas's case, since Hegel gives the pattern for all attempts at systematic totality, whereas to speak of an act of thought implies that thought thinks more than itself, in a movement which exceeds totality, decenters it, and confronts the infinity contained in the Other's face, in a text, in the statement of the Law.

On the one hand, a neutralization of all differences in the circle of reason; on the other, a declivity, an abruptness, a towering height. On the one hand, the Author, on the other, the Other: is the alternative too simple? The chiming juxtaposition adequately translates the French rhyme of *auteur* and *hauteur* (author and height). There can then be no "in between" along the lines of Levinas's polarized argument that would not be accused of false synthesis. The only way of understanding Derrida's qualification—his "perhaps"—or of situating the statement of strict equivalence of the contraries (Jewgreek is Greekjew) in a more disquieting "woman's reason" would be to trace the knot binding the subject to totality. In other words, to understand how the writer—not an author yet—has to acknowledge his debt to the Other prior to any self-authorization. And to do so, we shall have to return to the figure of Stephen in *Ulysses.*

It is, after all, in the episode devoted to Shakespeare and to literature that Joyce approaches most closely his concept of an author's authority, as a kind of transcendence immanent to his creation. The "Scylla and Charybdis" chapter is the last to leave free play to Stephen's musings, since he is afterward heard only in conjunction with Bloom or his friends in the hospital. The crossing between philosophico-theological ratiocination and the cunning of practical reason, or between Bloom and Stephen married in the mystical couple uniting Father and Son, is a move that may well have been intended at one stage by Joyce—his plans and schemes testify to this—but one not fully "authorized" by his text. Besides, this episode is crucial in that its "science" is "literature" in the Linati scheme, while the "technic" is "dialectic" in the Gorman-Gilbert plan. Joyce could only simplify the actual wanderings of Odysseus, who in the *Odyssey* leaves Circe's den, passes by the Sirens, arrives in front of Scylla and Charybdis, chooses Scylla, the monster who devours a part of his crew, and reaches the island of the Sun, where the slaughter of the sacred cattle brings him back to square one; he then opts for Charybdis, the whirlpool, loses all his companions, and manages to recover his raft. The deliberate interpolation of this episode in the narrative scheme of *Ulysses* breaks with a relatively straightforward adaptation of Homeric structures in the first part of the book. The episode focuses on Shakespeare, who is taken as a pretext for all types of conceptual and discursive whirlpools, which do not limit themselves to proving by algebra that "Hamlet's grandson is Shakespeare's grandfather and that he himself is the ghost of his own father" (*U,*1.555–57). Here, a new map is superimposed on the Homeric periplus, with striking emblematic correspondence:

The Rock—Aristotle, Dogma, Stratford
The Whirlpool—Plato, Mysticism, London
Ulysses—Socrates, Jesus, Shakespeare[8]

In the episode, both Bloom and Stephen play the part of an Odysseus, who comes back and forth—Stephen in his speech, Bloom physically in the library. London and Stratford become the imaginary counterparts of the opposition between scholasticism and mysticism. Stephen vividly depicts Shakespeare's household, his domineering wife, his unfaithful brothers, and the gaudy world of theatrical triumphs punctuated by mercenary or perverted lovemaking. The movement back and forth does not yet figure the full return home of Odysseus, especially as it was already performed by Stephen when he took his return ticket to Dublin after his stay in Paris. Have we to learn, along with Stephen, how to choose the lesser of two evils? And if the father is a "necessary evil," are there better or worse fathers? Should we, like Haines, pause and ponder on the sea, gaze at the Dublin bay and enjoy the sight of "a sail tacking by the Muglins" (*U,* 1.576) or get acquainted with the art of taking intellectual tacks? Is dialectics a synonym for scheming, maneuvering, cunningly shifting tracks?

Philosophy is conspicuously absent from Joyce's own "schemes." Nowhere is it labeled in his great table of correspondences, and it is probably in this episode that we experience a philosophical demonstration—the names of Plato and Socrates would tend to prove it—in the guise of literary disquisition. But we enter into the realm of a proper "woman's reason" in this episode—and this may be why philosophy cannot be named as such—since the real linking thread is not a dialogical or communal discovery of essences along the lines of Socrates' technique, but the more feminine principle of maieutics:

> What useful discovery did Socrates learn from Xanthippe?
> —Dialectic, Stephen answers: and from his mother how to bring thoughts into the world.
>
> (*U,* 9.233-36)

A shrew's tongue-lashing might therefore have been the prime incentive to the Socratic method of letting truth appear in dialogic agreement! At the same time, Stephen's brooding, his peculiar mode of introspective dialects, may owe its style to the guilt he still feels about his mother's death, whose ghost haunts him much more than any desired foster father. And then, Stephen has just been dealt a hard blow by Russell's apparently sound objection: "I mean, we have the plays. I mean when we read the poetry of *King Lear* what is it to us how the poet lived?" (*U*, 9.184–85). Russell is far from Stephen's own scholastic "composition of place," and his "idealism" or "spiritualism" is summed up in his peremptory declaration, "Art has to reveal to us ideas, formless spiritual essences." (*U*, 9.48–49). In Joyce's close reasoning, a formalism that concentrates on a "pure" text, without any consideration of the author of it *and* in it, is but a variety of Platonism—which does not entail that his theory of the author will necessarily have to be a scholastic theory of authority. It will have to examine the question, discarded by Platonism, of the poet's debts, of his legacies or wills: actual legal steps, endorsed by documents or historical records, which alone can enable one to gain a fresh insight into "Will's will." In such a repartition of roles, it is no accident that Russell, alias AE, should invite to his party the gay mocker Buck Mulligan, whose blasphemy and derision merely comfort the complacent spiritualism of those Dublin aesthetes, but not Stephen. Thus, Stephen's only weapon, other than his wild erudition and quaint phrases, remains his insistence on debt, on an actual and a symbolic debt; this is also why, in this episode, Mulligan reads the telegram sent to him by Stephen as his "papal bull": "*The sentimentalist is he who would enjoy without incurring the immense debtorship for a thing done*" (*U*, 9.551–52). The papal bull, Stephen's perverse variation on the Irish bull, is meant not so much as a means of excommunicating Buck Mulligan as of excommunicating Stephen himself. This is perhaps the only way to reach the full admission of guilt in an acknowledgment of debt.

But the motif of debt introduces another paradox: Stephen faces AE, who has lent him money, and although we know that Stephen has been paid by Mr. Deasy, he has no intention of paying back what he owes:

Do you intend to pay it back?

O, yes.

When? Now?

Well . . . No.

When, then?

I paid my way. I paid my way.

Steady on. He's from beyant Boyne water. The northeast corner. You owe it.

Wait. Five months. Molecules all change. I am other I now. Other I got pound.

Buzz. Buzz.

But I, entelechy, form of forms, am I by memory because under everchanging forms.

I that sinned and prayed and fasted.

A child Conmee saved from pandies.

I, I and I. I.

A. E. I. O. U.

(*U*, 9.197–213)

A first symbolic debt is being paid off by Joyce here, since he is probably pointing out what he initially owned to Russell's *Irish Homestead*, for which he wrote the first stories of *Dubliners*. Stephen, being aware both of the debt and of his unwillingness to pay, plays the part of a Till Eulenspiegel who merely agrees to *say* that he owes money, never feeling compelled to pay: *agenbite of inwit*, as Stephen notes, the bite of the unconscious starts with the perpetual debt, a debt that triggers the enunciation of subjectivity.

Enunciation is the only theoretical tool available for Stephen if he wants to overcome the facile Hamletic posture that still hinders him. And the utterance of the debt, albeit an interior utterance, a word pronounced by the mind's mouth for the mind's ear, constitutes the main proof of the self's permanence. For, if the ego is barely made up of molecules, which sooner or later are replaced by others, then the debt can be refused by a subject who cannot be held responsible for another's expenditures. And if the self has a purely spiritual nature, how could it be bound by gross material and economical encroachments? Stephen thus supposes that his ego is a ghost, neither hypostasis nor substance, but a trace of an image, a residue of divine projection into a text: in other words, an author, if by *author* we agree to understand an essential absence which nevertheless ensures its transcendence in immanence.[9] "As we, or mother Dana, weave and unweave our bodies, Stephen said, from day to day, their molecules shuttled to and fro, so does the artist weave and unweave his image. And as the mole on my right breast is where it was when I was born, though all my body has been woven of new stuff time after time, so through the ghost of the unquiet father the image of the unliving son looks forth" (*U,* 9.376–81). In *Hamlet,* Shakespeare, who played the part of the ghost of the murdered king, was not projecting himself in the "hero" of the play, as Mr. Best would have it, but in his father, so that his own lost son, Hamnet Shakespeare, who died at the age of eleven in Stratford, should live again as literature.

Stephen is entitled to a mixture of fiction and actual life of this kind because he has just uttered for himself the "A. E. I. O. U.," the IOU addressed to AE, in which one recognizes a real performative, enacting more than a promise, performing here the entire affirmation of a subjectivity. What is at stake, then, is not the real payment or its endless postponement, but the admission itself, an avowal that takes into account the whole of Irish history, linking AE with Mr. Deasy, since both come from Ulster, and therefore with Shakespeare, whose financial balance and usurious practices may be more relevant to literature than it first appeared. Just as Mr. Deasy misconstrued Shakespeare when quoting, "*Put but money in thy purse*" (*U,* 2.239), apparently forgetting that Iago is deluding Roderigo and professing cynicism at the same time (whereas Stephen wearily and guardedly answers just "Iago," an answer that recurs in "Circe" when Shakespeare, afflicted with facial paralysis, crows "Iagogogo" as we have seen in chapter 4), here Stephen underwrites his own birth–his performative maieutics–by a formula equivalent to an "I owe therefore am." Between the activity contained in "I + ago" and its parody in "Iagogogo," Stephen discovers the dialectics of subjectivity, in a move through language requiring its play with absence and difference. His "egowe" can thus rightly be written by a string of letters, the series of the vowels all repeating "ergo sum."

I had to imply this "ergo" in order to stabilize the interplay between letters written and pronounced, whereas the self-positioning of the subject requires no such logical intermediary. But what is gained is that the subject is aware of its function by becoming the grammatical subject of the "I. O. U." Joyce takes pains to show that the place of such a subjectivity cannot be reduced to the stability of a psychological center, not to the psychic substance of mentalism, when he has Stephen refuse to admit that he "believes" his own theory. He is not just deftly juggling with paradoxes, as Eglington thinks, but is attempting to free himself from all "nets," even theoretical speculations, thereby attempting to "create" himself, so to speak: "I believe, O Lord, help my unbelief. That is, help me to believe or help me to unbelieve? Who helps to believe? *Egomen.* Who to unbelieve? Other chap" (*U*, 9.1078–80). *Egomen* is the emphatic form of ego, and Stephen seems to situate "belief" on the side of illusion and deception, a misconstruction deriving from "myself" or the enclosed subjectivity—besides the rather improbable allusion to the *Egoist*[10]—while "unbelief," or more mature insight into imaginary constructions, comes from alterity, the others, not yet related to pure otherness by writing in this context.

The logical syllogism proving an "ego" as the concluding statement is opened to the function of the Other. Could the author be this "other chap" who authorizes me to speak in my transcendence, without being bound by the illusion of an immanent meaning? This implies a recourse to another type of authority, of a more traditional genre: not only to Russell's pseudonym of AE, but also, through him, to the authority of Dante, or rather, to Dante's conception of authority. For thanks to the felicitous reunion of an IOU and Russell's pen name, Joyce manages to quote from an author he almost knew by heart, Dante.[11] In book 4 of his *Convivio,* Dante explains that he wishes to develop a parallel between imperial and philosophic "authority" and therefore needs a sound definition of authority: "It must therefore be known that authority is nothing else than the activity proper to an author. This word (namely, *auctor,* without its third letter *c*) may be derived from two sources. The one is a verb, which has generally dropped out of use in Latin, and signifies much the same as the tying of words together, viz, A E I O U."[12]

Dante follows the tradition of medieval dictionaries, which distinguished between two words, first *autore* or *aucteur*, derived from the Latin of *augeo, auctor*, and then *autor* or *author/autheur*, which could either be referred to the Latin verb *avieo* ("I tie, I bind," *a + vieo*) or to the Greek form of *autentin* (rendered by Dante as "worthy of trust and obedience"). Let us then examine how he glosses the Latin verb:

> And if one carefully considers the verb in the first person present, he will see plainly that the word itself declares its own meaning, for it is made up solely of the ties of words, that is, of the five vowels alone, which are, as it were, the soul and tie of every word [*anima e legame d'ogni parole*]. And it is composed of these by the method of transposition, so as to present the likeness of a tie [*per modo volubile, a figurare imagine di legame*]. For beginning with A it turns back to U, and then proceeds straight through I to E; thence it turns back and reverts to O, so that in truth the vowels shape themselves into this figure A E I O U, which is the figure of a tie. And so far as the word "author" comes and is derived from the verb AUIEO, it is applied only to poets who have tied their words together with the art of the muse.[13]

The long development concerns only the poetic sense of *authority*, leaving aside kings and philosophers, and Dante explains that he wants to concentrate on the second derivation. I wish to underline a strange denegation, which tends to omit that we start with a trinity—poets, kings, and philosophers—a trinity, moreover, that would never have been gathered, tied together, without the intervention of a poet. Dante seems to forget the first definition and hurries on to the second, with which he deals much more rapidly, once he has stated the derivation from *autentin:*

> And the "*author*," which is derived from this word, is used for any person who deserves to be trusted and obeyed. And from "*author*" comes the word of which we are now treating, namely "authority"; whence it can be seen that authority is

that activity to which trust and obedience are due.

It is manifest that Aristotle is most worthy of trust and obedience: and that his words are the supreme and highest authority may thus be proved.[14]

Dante's hurry, doubled with a strange modesty, may stem from the too high claims he feared he was making on the poet's art: his activity can indeed by summed up as well as summoned every time the "words" are tied together by one performative verb: "I tie." This word is, as it were, the flesh of all language, since it can then fill by one of its parts any sequence of consonants, and since it contains the seeds of artistic creation.

There remains one problem if we want to follow Dante's demonstration: how can he transform *avieo* into A E I O U? In his commentaries on the *Convivio, La Rotta Gonna,* André Pézard has been able to solve the mystery, and I shall henceforth follow his patient demonstration.[15] Pézard notes first of all that the trajectory coming from the A, going to the U, coming back to the I, going past it to reach E and fold back onto O figures a rough loop or noose:

Pézard tries several experiments with knots of various kinds, but none of them seems to follow a logical pattern to account for the order of the vowels. It is another passage from the *Convivio* that yields a first real clue: Dante compares the hierarchies of the souls in their ascending order, from animal to human and divine, to the nesting of geometrical figures, which become more and more complex every time an apex is added: "Therefore, just as when we take away the last side of a pentagon, what is left is a quadrangle, but no longer a pentagon; so when we remove the last faculty of the soul, that is reason, what is left is no longer a man, but only a thing with a sensitive soul."[16] Such a conceit exploiting the geometry of figures was common in scholastic thinking, and Joyce uses some of these *topoi* when he plays with "French triangles" (see p. 103). Stephen is driven by the same figures, which describe not only actual relationships but also rhetorical moves: "What the hell are you driving at? / I know. Shut up. Blast you. I have reasons. / *Amplius. Adhuc. Iterum. Postea*" (*U*, 9.846–48).

The context of *Convivio*, book 4, makes it plain that Dante has in mind the patterns of logic (and rhetoric) developed by the Schoolmen, who, as Stephen says, had been schoolboys first and had studied Aristotle, refining peripatetic syllogisms with new varieties of *Barbara, Celarent, Baroco*. In the basic logical square of most *Summulae logicae* of the time, the letters *A, E, I,* and *O*, stand for, respectively, universal affirmation, universal negation, particular affirmation, and particular negation. The interplay of the contraries (A and E, I and O) and of the contradictories (A and O, I and E) can define medieval logic as the art of reasoning in AEIO:

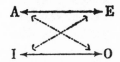

Such a logical square could not suffice when one wanted to go beyond the logic of statements toward a modal logic. The categories of modality (the possible, the contingent, the impossible, the necessary) implied in their deployment another apex in the figure: thus modalist logicians distinguished between A (positive mode, positive statement), E (positive mode, negative statement), I (negative mode, positive statement), and U (negative mode, negative statement), which still left room for O (negative particular statement, not to be confused with U, U stating, for instance, "It is not possible that *x* be not," that is, the reverse of O). When the five categories are gathered in a pattern, it is written as follows, in an order that explains Dante's knot with *avieo:*

This pattern underlies Buridan's list of seventy-two basic statements, which is constituted by a double star with five apexes, each angle standing as well for the V or *Verum,* and this in its turn gives a firm logical foundation to the older magical pattern called Solomon's pentangle, a graph elsewhere alluded to by Dante. Now when John Eglinton *roundly* accuses Stephen of exhibiting mere French *triangles,* he not only repeats Dante's gesture (*per modo volubile*) but also points toward *Finnegans Wake,* in which Joyce uses two triangles and two circles to describe Anna Livia's genitalia: ". . . you'd wheeze whyse Salmonson set his seel on a hexengown" (*FW,* 297.2–4). True, a leap has to be performed—a "salmon's leap," in *Finnegans Wake*—in order to jump from the principle of all veridiction to the ominous sexual seal of Solomon. This is nevertheless inevitable as soon as the tie of words binds the subject to his debt in language and generation: the pattern preconditions language in its capacity for telling the truth and for disclosing the secret of a sexual origin.

In what sense can authority and debt be said to to be linked, or tied together? Authority is not limited to a "power"—the power to be obeyed, for instance, which generally opposes reason and authority; it also signifies a "credit," the consideration or weight a theory carries, the credence held by a witness or a historian. Authority is founded at the intersection between the force of an enunciation and the credit given to it, which no doubt implies the same questions of belief Stephen was asking himself. Thus, a historian whose credit is sufficient becomes an "authority" in his field, and I can authorize myself with his name to give weight to a statement. This is precisely where Stephen stands: he is not so much looking for a "father" as for an "authority" that will enable him to authorize himself. He will speak on the authority of this symbolic name so as to speak in his name later. Such a gesture presupposes an enunciation, a statement and its modality. By naming thus, he will name himself and tie himself up, logically or dialectically, or even rhetorically, in a symbolic order. The authority of authors is underpinned by the logics of enunciative modalities.

Now a "symbolic father" seen from this perspective sums up two modal properties which, at first sight, appear irreducible, or difficult to reconcile. A father is, according to Stephen's sentence already quoted, "a necessary evil," but "paternity may be"—this time the statement is modalized—"a legal fiction." Just as Dante threads his loop between the heights of imperial authority and those of philosophical authority, Stephen takes on the entire art of the dialectician; neither a historian, one who utters the truth about real particulars, nor a philosopher, one who utters the truth about universals, Stephen asserts the necessity of the probable. He thereby covers himself with the authority of Aristotle, or eventually, and without ever naming him, of Freud, to confute the Platonism of his opponents:

> Here he ponders things that were not: what Caesar would have lived to do had he believed the soothsayer: what might have been: possibilities of the possible as possible: things not known: what name Achilles bore when he lived among women.
> Coffined thoughts around me, in mummycases, embalmed in spice of words. Thoth, god of libraries, a birdgod, moonycrowned. And I heard the voice of that Egyptian highpriest. *In painted chambers loaded with tilebooks.*
> They are still. Once quick in the brains of men. Still: but an itch of death is in them, to tell me in my ear a maudlin tale, urge me to wreak their will.
>
> (*U*, 9.347-58)

Stephen is not merely reducing Platonism to idle speculation; he attacks the structure of speculation as such and sees the dialectics of life and death inherent in writing in the paradox he formulates: writing is a "still life" but also a living death, which urges the reader to act. Stephen—always linked with Toth, as in the *Portrait*—does not enforce the metaphysical condemnation of writing (for which Thoth was rendered responsible in the Egyptian myths) we have now learned to associate with Platonism, nor does he adopt a radically optimistic position facing writing (he does not say, for instance, that writing keeps alive that which would otherwise perish, a discourse that is homologous with the first). He appears here as a "dialectician" in the Aristotelian sense; that is, as someone who reasons about the probable in a rigorous manner.[17] He is no "analytician," he does not meditate on eternal truths starting from assured premises: he is much too "haunted" for that, not only by his mother but also by the conjuration of literature which functions here exactly as the poison poured into the ear of the sleeping king in *Hamlet*, a murder that, for Stephen, is almost identical with its own disclosure by the murdered king to a still-innocent prince. "Wreaking their will," the texts initiate the series of performative gestures that all smack of a perverse confession with uncertain ends. Thus, they manage to write down in subjects what they hid and revealed at the same time: the cypher, the signature of the author, the name of the father, that ghost always lurking behind action: will, or Will's will, a William who makes the quick still and the still quick. "He points the deathbone and the quick are still. *Insomnia, somnia somniorum*" (*FW,* 193.29–30).

In the psychoanalytic configuration slowly unfolded by Stephen (and we never know whether he is describing his own family, Shakespeare's household, or a blend of these and Hamlet's situation), analytic judgments would be restricted to the mother's side, since certitude dominates, whereas the fathers all appear condemned to the realm of the probable: *pater semper incertus.* This would accord with what Freud has to say about the move from hieroglyphs, still pertaining to the triumph of material evidence in claims for affiliation, to the Semitic alphabet in *Moses and Monotheism; maternal* and *material* are quasi-synonyms that are displaced by the law of the Father and a transcendent principle that finds its sure guarantee in writing. But it may be possible that his move has replaced affiliation and the couple paternity/maternity by the principle of authority: one can no longer claim to be the real father, but can only claim authority for a child or book. Authority then conjoins two meanings generally felt to be antinomous: a maximum of uncertainty, of absence, a lack of "ground" (this would be confirmed by the literary portrayal of "authority" given by Thomas Mann in the *Magic Mountain* with the unpredictable but irresistible Peeperkorn) and a maximum of power, the judicial force of a pact binding the subject to a symbolic order. It is no accident, then, that the voice Stephen hears resounding through the library halls, the chambers stacked with manuscripts, tilebooks, and quartos, should come to him mediated through J. J. O'Molloy's recital of John F. Taylor's speech, and should be that of Moses.

This may be why Stephen feels the need to transform Shakespeare into a "Jew." If, on the one hand, he historicizes the playwright's stature, whose works are seen as responses to personal and especially familial dramas, he relies on the minutiae of historical chronicle to reach more sweeping statements concerning the divine nature of the artist. He thereby blends Sabellian modalist theology—for which Father, Son, and Spirit were but *modes* of a unique transcendent God—and Aquinian aesthetics, which are reread through Hegel: "He goes back, weary of the creation he has piled up to hide him from himself, an old dog licking an old sore. But, because loss is his gain, he passes on towards eternity in undiminished personality, untaught by the wisdom he has written or by the laws he has revealed. His beaver is up. He is a ghost, a shadow now, the wind by Elsinore's rocks or what you will, the sea's voice, a voice heard only in the heart of him who is the substance of his shadow, the son consubstantial with the father" (*U*, 9.474–81).

The "Pisgah sight" of Elsinore tells us that there still is something rotten in Dublin, an old strand by the sea on which straggling lost dogs dig for a phantom of divinity. By a properly dialectic inversion, the precise knowledge of Elizabethan mores and context is used to justify the metaphorical function of Shakespeare, slipping from Father to Son, from life to plays. For here the unnamed writer (Stephen refers to him only by the third person throughout his passage) can be identified with God only because he has relinquished all mastery and all knowledge of his texts—he is a ghost speaking to other ghosts.

How can a subject divided by his guilt and debt repossess this divinized projection of himself into two dialoguing ghosts? Simply because the skilled dialectician, aware of all the artful dodges evolved by the artist, soon learns how to use and to abuse double negations: neither son nor father, he is both at the same time; neither Plato nor Aristotle, he enacts the drama of his own death and dispossession, uniting Jesus with Socrates drinking hemlock. Perpetual oscillation between the divinized author and the divided subject. The artist as a "divineither." Should we replace the formula "Greekjew is Jewgreek" by "neither Greek nor Jew"?

Some elements of an answer lie scattered in the book and help us to understand how Aquinas (and Freud) concur to make Shakespeare a Jew of a particular type. The Telemachiad starts with the now classical opposition between Buck Mulligan, as the aesthete dreaming of Greek culture and of a spiritual renaissance for Ireland ("Ah, Dedalus, the Greeks. I must teach you. You must read them in the original" [*U*, 1.79–80]), and Stephen Dedalus, whose name has already translated a Greek myth into Latin) by playing the Jesuit, hostile to any manifestation of pagan *joie de vivre*, haunted by abstruse theological problems. And whereas Stephen shows a Shakespeare irretrievably divided against himself, therefore constituting a whirlpool of dialectic polarities ("darkening even his own understanding of himself. A like fate awaits him and the two rages commingle in a whirlpool" [*U*, 9.463–64]), a Matthew Arnold could pose Hebraism and Hellenism as a similar dialectical whirlpool, setting the boundaries and main concepts of our Western culture: "Hebraism and Hellenism—between these two points of influence moves our world. At one time it feels more powerfully the attraction of one, at another time of the other."[18] The intellectual history of the nineteenth century, from Hölderlin and Hegel to Newman, Arnold, and Pater, would indeed prove the generalization to be broad but true. This also applies to Bloom, who is less unambiguously a Jew than one might believe. For in the library episode, he is suspected of perversion, homosexuality, and voyeurism ("Did you see his eye? He looked upon you to lust after you," Buck tells Stephen [*U*, 9.1210]), whereas other insinuations—in Sirens, for instance—hint of incestuous tendencies. (As a matter of fact, the Homeric and Jewish exile of Bloom, symbolized by the absence of a full sexual relationship with Molly, has been complicated by Milly's puberty.) Like Shakespeare, Bloom is both a Jew and a Greek. Let us retrace the stages through which this theme passes.

In "Nestor," Mr. Deasy initiates the motif of the "epic of two races" by flaunting his naive anti-Semitism among garbled Irish history. By opposition, Stephen, who does "not know" what money is, is made painfully aware of his real debts, feeling closer to the Jewish moneychangers he had seen in Paris ("Their eyes knew the years of wandering and, patient, knew the dishonours of their flesh" [*U*, 2.372]) than to Irish patriots of any side. When he remembers Deasy's words in the next chapter, just as he appears anxious not to squander what he has been given ("By the way go easy with that money like a good young imbecile" [3.59]), he falls prey to an "incestuous" temptation and half-imagines, half-hears a conversation between his maternal uncle and him. Richie Goulding would be the first substitute father available after Stephen's decision to leave the Tower, but Goulding would represent the maternal regression Simon Dedalus brands with sarcasms suggesting incest (see p. 64).

In "Æolus," it is journalism which pertains to incest, according to Joyce's plan at least; it proceeds from a perverse crossing between literature and finance, and thus perverts language, since the enthymeme, or false syllogism, is its main trope. Now Stephen may appear as "enthymemic" too, and he does not refuse to play the go-between for Deasy's efforts in favor of Irish cattle. Dialectic is but a form of "enthymemics," as it were, but finds a way out of the impasse described in Stephen's parable, A Pisgah Sight of Palestine. As a literator, Stephen cannot avoid "incest," since he is caught up within the infinite regress of texts quoting texts. But the "Scylla and Charybdis" episode displaces the relative positions of incest and writing: incest is not just the crossing between money and text in an exhausted rhetorical culture; it inhabits the person of the universal creator and haunts the very mystery of paternity.

Stephen believes he quotes Aquinas when he states that, in contradiction to Freud's thesis, incest is not a fundamental issue structuring the development of the libido, but stems from hoarding, another economic image: it comes from "an avarice of the emotions" (*U*, 9.781). He thus answers Eglinton's challenge regarding Shakespeare: "Prove that he was a Jew" (9.763) by an enthymeme: All usurers are like Jews; Shakespeare was something of a usurer; therefore he was a Jew. But the gross fallacy of such a sleight-of-hand is balanced by a weightier argument, deriving from literature: Shakespeare could not have written so well about Shylock if he had not been a Jew himself. Stephen is ready to lay the blame on the "Christian laws" that bound the Jews' affections "with hoops of steel," but he agrees with Aquinas that "the love so given to one near in blood is covetously withheld from some stranger who, it may be, hungers for it" (9.781–83). Shakespeare, described as jealous and possessive, a capitalist and a usurer, becomes the Jew *par excellence* when he is shown to display the masochism of him who enjoys his own dispossession.

Just as the ghost of the author wishes to unite with his own transubstantial heir in *Hamlet,* in the general economy of Stephen's theologicophilolological mixture, the artist God, who has slightly bungled his creation, is just like Shakespeare, his own grandfather's father: "The playwright who wrote the folio of this world and wrote it badly (He gave us light first and the sun two days later), the lord of things as they are whom the most Roman of catholics call *dio boia,* hangman god, is doubtless all in all in all of us, ostler and butcher, and would be bawd and cuckold too but in the economy of heaven, foretold by Hamlet, there are no more marriages, glorified man, an androgynous angel, being a wife unto himself" (*U,* 9.1046–52).

Paradoxically, the universal necessity of a prohibition of incest proves and comforts the validity of such a no less universal drive towards self-generation and reproduction. Stephen remarks that in the records of perversions there may be testimonies of unnatural relationships between sons and mothers, fathers and daughters, and siblings in all possible combinations— as *Finnegans Wake* sets out to explore—but never between sons and fathers: they are united and separated by a similar "bodily shame," which consists of this same crossing of the mother's womb, a "doublecrossing" indeed, according to Dylan Thomas.[19] The only real "jewgreek" would then be the divine creator, incestuous and homosexual, who would found *a contrario* the absolute commandment forbidding the perversion he enacts. If paternity defines this vacuum, a vacuum that underpins the whole symbolic architecture of language and culture, one understands why Stephen refuses any approach of the father in terms of love: "Who is the father of any son that any son should love him or he any son?" (9.844-45). Paternity points to the void, the unconscience of origins, the unconscious hoarding of signs or letters, and yet it remains the model of any creative gesture. Should we smile to see the dignity and the otherness of our author soiled, degraded, polluted in this loop tied fast on itself, in a blasphemous incest, an incest that nevertheless obliges the divided subject to write the ultimately sacred book?

Perhaps Dante himself could now guide us through this unorthodox maze of authority? Let us follow him and start at the beginning, in the limbo in which, curiously, sits the human embodiment of philosophic authority for all poets, namely, Aristotle. His throne shines out in these dark places, and he also plays the part of a paterfamilias, which marks him off for the kind of symbolic paternity Stephen allegedly is in quest of, although in the third episode Stephen never refers to Aristotle directly, calling him only by that Dantean tag, "maestro di color che sanno." The authority proved by Dante's etymological deductions is never far from inverting historical sequence, since he is seen to have fathered the whole of philosophy, almost begetting his ancestors by some retrospective arrangement:

> vidi 'l maestro di color che sanno
> seder tra filosofica famiglia.
>   Tutti lo miran, tutti onor li fanno:
> quivi vid' io Socrate e Platone,
> ch 'nnanzi a li altri più presso li stanno.[20]

Because the Philosopher is not named, his anonymity enhances the universal reverence that surrounds him. Socrates and Plato, united as another mystical couple, initiate the following roll call of great thinkers, just before the perilous descent towards darkness.

At the other end of the periplus, Virgil having been relayed and replaced by Beatrice and the Virgin, Dante finally contemplates the mystic rose in the last Canto of *Paradiso*. Just as Stephen alludes to Aristotle by an oblique reference, he points to a similar paradox concerning Mary in a quotation lifted from the first line of *Paradiso*, 33:

> But here is the matter now. Or she knew him, that second I say, and was but creature of her creature, *vergine madre figlia di tuo figlio*, or she knew him not and then stands she in the one denial or ignorancy with Peter Piscator who lives in the house that Jack built and with Joseph the joiner patron of the happy demise of all unhappy marriages, *parce que M. Léo Taxil nous a dit que qui l'avait mise dans cette fichue position c'était le sacré pigeon, ventre de Dieu! Entweder* transsubstantiality *oder* consubstantiality but in no case subsubstantiality.
>
> (*U*, 14.301–8)

Stephen is not exactly attacking the Roman ruse, which consisted of replacing the mystery of the Trinity with the more homely and bathetic picture of a Virgin Mother closer to the heart of the populace. But in a way he has to cover the same ground as Dante, that is, to move up from a philosophical family sketched by the figures of Plato, Socrates, and Aristotle, toward a mystical family made up of the Father, the Son, and the Holy Spirit, with which the Virgin entertains certain affinities. The initial paradox of Immaculate Conception (referring to Mary's own birth, thus to saint Ann being a virgin when she conceived the Virgin) provides the theoretical locus for Stephen's own knot, binding him to generation and regeneration of the "word that shall not pass away" (14.293–94). Besides, Dante's last canto posits such a knot or tie, called *nodo* and not *legame* this time:

> Nel suo profondo vidi che s'interna,
> *legato* con amore in un volume,
> ciò che per l'universo si squaderna;
>   sustanze e accidenti e lor costume,
> quasi conflati insieme, per tal modo
> che ciò ch'i' dico è un semplice lume.

La forma universal di questo *nodo*
credo ch'i' vidi, perché più di largo,
dicendo questo, mi sento ch'i' *godo*.[21]

This passage describes the universal knot binding together what is necessary and what is accidental in one flame of love, a love which also "moves the stars." Dante obeys the same paradigm of authority he describes in the *Convivio,* since a proof of the validity of what is written or uttered lies in the performative action realized by the very telling or writing: the poet, unlike Stephen, believes his own theory, not merely because it is founded on sound authority but also because his enunciation of the vision brings such bliss, such "joyance" or joycity, to Dante—and to his reader, entranced by the same magnificent ascent towards light and beauty. The knot bridges the gap between the vision and the words making up the vision.

If Stephen still cannot believe his own words and cannot rely on a vision of love, it is because this theory would be undermined in its sophistry if the force of alterity and lack were brought to bear on it. When Stephen refuses the Marianist sop thrown to the crowds by Roman orthodoxy, it is primarily because he attempts to replace a descending dialectic, which presents Mary as the daughter of Christ, her son, with an ascending and patrilinear dialectic, which sees in the ghost of *Hamlet* his own father's father. Moreover, such a masculine tie is easier to loop back than a feminine one, since in order to become the daughter of her own son the Virgin requires the intermediary of a divine Father, whereas to become one's father's father, one needs a human mother, not a divine one, and if the artist has already been made divine by his works, the trick—the hattrick, Joyce would say—is soon done.[22] This is a trick not too different from that performed by Oedipus, who, after he has blinded himself to *see* and not to atone for his deed, disappears from his sacred grove at Colonnus.

A medieval song about the Virgin stated:

Virgin you are, and daughter and mother,
Virgin didst beget the fruit of life:
Daughter your son, mother your father.[23]

Stephen, who wanders around in brothels singing sacred psalms—as Joyce was wont to do, according to some eyewitnesses[24]—declares himself to be "the eternal son and ever virgin" (U, 14.343-44). Thus Stephen adds another paradox to the series I have traced, starting with the acknowledgment of a debt he does not intend to pay: his theory of paternity does not aim at transforming him into an artist, a father, and a master, but at underlining his unassailable virginity. Stephen's virginity cannot therefore be superimposed onto the purity that radiates from Dante's final vision. In his case, it remains suspended, an inviolable reserve preserved despite any possible cancellation. Dante's mystical rose supposes an order, a pattern integrating all its elements, blending trinity and unity. Conversely, in his dialectical games with gain and loss, reconciliation and sundering—and it is no coincidence that on the one occasion that Stephen repeats himself during his demonstration it is to stress the theme of sundering (see p. 9)—Stephen gropes for an insight into otherness, pure alterity, an Other that cannot be subsumed by the name of divine or humane love.

What are we to think of this young, arrogant prig who, although clearly aware of Bloom's race and origins, thanks him for his hospitality by singing an old ballad conveying a crude anti-Semitism? True, his main motive is to ward off any ritual soul-murder whereby he might have been tempted to offer himself up to the wanton satisfaction of a Jewish girl, played by Molly's Milly or Milly's Molly. He nevertheless seems to exchange places with Bloom and to leave the scene of "Ithaca" with the added weight of a double exile. Stephen takes charge of a wandering given up too soon by Bloom (if we must believe Tiresias, and Dante, depicting the sad fate befalling the undaunted adventurer that Odysseus still was after his return home).

Stephen's act cannot, however, be untied from the writing that inscribes it while tracing its signature in black and white. The fatigue and uncertainty of the orator at the conclusion of his Shakespearean purple patch enhance the dissociation of the voice from the name: "What's in a name? That is what we ask ourselves in childhood when we write the name that we are told is ours. . . . I am tired of my voice, the voice of Esau. My kingdom for a drink" (*U*, 9.927–81). Stephen rephrases the question asked by Telemachus in the *Odyssey*: who can know for sure whose son he is? But, as Eglinton notes, his Odysseus or Ulysses of a father is one who—thanks to Shakespeare, no doubt—has read Aristotle: "*Que voulez-vous?* Moore would say. He puts Bohemia on the seacoast and makes Ulysses quote Aristotle" (9.995–96). Stephen, a Bohemian "artist" born not far from the sea, begotten in a book called *Ulysses*, also quotes Aristotle in order to find his place in the middle of the tie that writes him down as a subject, a knot never tight enough, which can loosen his tongue and his hand. A pure utterance, left to itself, would be meaningless, but the first condition for the tie of the I between A, E, and O, U is the tracing of a few letters, even if they are imaginary, in space. In that sense, the name-of-the Father exists only when it insists as written by a subject, underwritten by an author warranted, empowered, authorized to his own division.

Moreover, why should Stephen, who is the first-born of his family, see himself as Esau, ready to bargain his theories for a glass of beer? Like Shakespeare, he secretly desires his dispossession, a disinheritance in favor of more cunning rivals, in order to enact an exile ensured against all calls back home: assuming the disguise of the black sheep or of the scapegoat, he keeps company with Christ, Parnell, Socrates, and all betrayed great men, who all testify to the cruel fate awaiting the author. But at the same time, Stephen is a Jacob whose ruse has been so successful that he has even managed to disguise his own voice, which points toward a still-future writing in which he cannot yet find his bearings. Stephen, a horn-mad Esau ceaselessly willing that the Jacob hidden in him shall overthrow him, sign in his place, by proxy as to speak, reaches self-generation through an intense dialectical passion—in the sense in which one speaks of the Passion of Christ—of his subjectivity. He sets in motion the whole pathos of Hegel's "unhappy consciousness" or a conscience torn apart by perversion and desire in the hope of being carried away toward a radical otherness.

Such would be the lesson taught by the "Ithaca" episode, the most masterful (or is it authoritative?) of all the chapters, and apparently Joyce's favorite passage in the book. The scientific catechism of questions and answers dissects, reduces, multiplies, disseminates, grinds, and mixes characters and motivations, objects and substances, memories and plans until they become "heavenly bodies." The calculations performed by a kind of delirious demiurge ("Reduce Bloom by cross multiplication of reverses of fortune . . . and by elimination of all positive values to a negligible negative irrational unreal quantity" [*U*, 17.1933–35]) all tend toward the infinitization of textual atoms drifting from the rest of the book into the widening whirlpools. Infinity is a weapon used by Joyce against the reassuring promises of synthesis or atonement which are endlessly deferred, set adrift in the spatial transmigration affecting everything. This time, the idle speculations on "possibilities of the possible as possible" (*U*, 9.349–50) disclose a new principle of serialization. This is also why the ultimate weapon wielded by Bloom against Boylan and the suitors is not a bow and arrows but his differential positioning in an ever-widening sequence of hypotheses. When Bloom enters Molly's bed and lies beside her warm body, we are not told that he smiles, only that he might have smiled at the thought of another male form in his place before him:

If he had smiled why would he have smiled?
    To reflect that each one who enters imagines himself to be the first to enter whereas he is always the last term of a preceding series even if the first term of a succeeding one, each imagining himself to be first, last, only and alone whereas he is neither first nor last nor only nor alone in a series originating in and repeated to infinity.

(*U*, 17.2126–31)

Bloom's and Stephen's sundering proceeded in itself from a principle of verticality: their first glance when leaving the house is for "the heaventree of stars hung with humid nightblue fruit" (17.1039), then for Molly's lamp on the first floor. The difference of level is here again swept away in the serial inventory that imitates Dante insofar as it, too, encompasses the stars and what, behind them, may move them; but a lever is thus found to disarticulate the still-centered Aristotelian cosmos in which the knot is also a rose; and the decentered cosmos of *Ulysses* just needs the tranquil self-rotation of Molly's terrestrial singsong, which alone can "countersign" it for eternity.

The cyclical infinity inherent in this type of serialization cannot be ascribed to Hegelianism any longer; it must be referred back to Vico. Heidegger has shown that the concept of experience evolved by Hegel means that the parousia of the absolute has always already happened. In a way, Hegel, who does not believe in any radical beginning and who presents science or philosophy as a "circle or circles," is, strictly speaking, the only thinker who may be said to have summed up the entire history of philosophy, since he has tried to retrace all its thinking experience in his dialectical language. "The one Western thinker who has enacted a thinking experience of thought is Hegel," Heidegger writes in a text that points out similarities between Hegel and Aristotle.[25] Now, Joyce, although he had been introduced to Hegel's aesthetics, as already stated, never seems to have considered Hegel's role as fundamental in philosophy, since he reserves such eminence for Aristotle. In 1917, as he was in the midst of the redaction of *Ulysses*, he was able to tell Georges Borach: "For two hundred years we have not had any great thinker. This is a bold remark, since it includes Kant. All the great thinkers of this century and of the last from Kant to Benedetto Croce have only been trifling. The greatest thinker of all times is according to me Aristotle. He has defined everything in a wonderfully clear and simple way. Later whole volumes have been written to reach the same conclusions."[26] Here at least we find someone who has been utterly convinced by Dante's authoritative statement!

Croce's name may, however, help us understand why Hegel is not mentioned in such a context. Croce is commonly held to be a "Hegelian'" philosopher, and it is true that his most theoretical works are in one way or another discussions with Hegel. For Joyce, no doubt, Croce is alluded to not only as a philosopher of history but as someone who attempted an original and synthetic theory of aesthetics. It is probably through Croce that Joyce was able to perceive the importance of Vico; Croce's book

The Philosophy of Giambattista Vico, was published in 1911, and fully documents the background of his famous chapter on Vico in his earlier (and very influential) *Aesthetics*, which Joyce had read.[27] In the former book, Croce parallels Vico with Hegel and generally makes use of Hegelian terminology in order to bring to light the consistency of Vico's thought. For instance, he notes the quasi-overlap between Vico's conception of "Divine Providence" and Hegel's "cunning of Reason." In his book on Hegel, Croce states that "Vico was the precursor of Hegel,"[28] and it seems that for him the obscurities of Vico (which "consist in the obscurity of his ideas") could be dispelled by Hegel.[28] On the other hand, Croce mounts a violent and thorough criticism of Hegel in the field of art; for him, Hegel is the typical case of a philosopher who is incapable of understanding art without reducing it to philosophy. The very title of his book, *What Is Living and What Is Dead of the Philosophy of Hegel,* shows that Croce wishes to weed out the Hegelian system, and the first lack in Hegel is his philosophy of language. For Hegel, according to Vico, art is a mere "philosophical error, or an illustory philosophy,"[29] and in that respect Hegel is not too far from Aristotle (or, for that matter, in a context which implies Joyce more intimately, from Aquinas read by Bosanquet):

> For this reason, it is not altogether wrongly that the system of Hegel (whose twin principles of the concrete concept and the dialectic, are of frankly aesthetic inspiration) has appeared to be a cold intellectualism irreconcilable to the artistic consciousness. . . .
>
> The characteristic of the Aristotelian logic is its syllogistic, or Verbalism, the confusion into which it falls between logical thought and speech, and its claim to establish logical forms, while limiting itself to verbal forms. Hegel did not and could not criticize this error, because he was without the instrument of criticism, which can be furnished only by a valid philosophy of language.[30]

Thus Hegel is seen as a mortician, an embalmer; for him the only good artist is a dead artist, for art in itself is already dead. The death of art is required for philosophic *Aufhebung,* or sublation, *and* sublimation. "The Aesthetic of Hegel is thus a funeral oration: he passes in review the successive forms of art, shows the progressive steps of internal consumption and lays the whole in its grave, leaving Philosophy to write its epitaph."[31] In opposition to this movement stands Vico, the "inventor" of the science of aesthetic. For Vico, artistic creators are likened to God the Creator in that they produce Fables that are imaginative universals, hence philosophic universals. Language and poetry are identified, and his Philosophy of the Spirit becomes a philosophy of the aesthetic spirit.

Joyce agreed that Vico provided a valid philosophy of language, even if he was at times mistaken in his etymologies and historical surveys: it is a philosophy of language one can *use* for the pleasure it offers, without having to believe all of its theses. Thus, for Joyce it is the language of *Finnegans Wake* which takes Vico as model, with its stress on playful circularity and the constant interaction of life and death and regeneration, not only because Vico brings the dynamics of language lacking in Aquinas and Hegel but, more specifically, because Vico's philosophy carries out the aesthetic Hegel ought to have written.

Finnegans Wake signals the abandon of Joyce's aesthetic discourse as such; there cannot be any hope of holding a discourse describing the function of the artist or of the creator: the versions and perversions are so numerous, parodies of all kinds abound, all the critical approaches are alluded to without ever allowing one to stand out. And naturally, it would be extremely dangerous to think that Shem the Penman stands as a spokesman for Joyce's aesthetic beliefs. Any theoretical aloofness meets its own dissolution in the tide of puns. In this sense, Vico enables Joyce to go beyond the gap between an aesthetic theory and the fiction which stages it. What remained as the naive exposition of a system in *Stephen Hero* was already taking a more subtle, more cunning shape in the rhetorical maneuvers of the *Portrait*. *Ulysses* opens out by a disjuncture between the two meanings of aesthetic: sensory perception and discourse about the beautiful. They have to be tied together through the attempt to reconcile the subject and his symbolic determinations, according to what I have sketched for Stephen Dedalus. In

Finnegans Wake, Vico's historical philosophy allows Joyce to dispense with (not to overcome; his move is much more economical) the speculative system altogether and to advance toward the dialogism of interpretations. To shift from Hegel to Vico therefore means to abandon reflexive circularity, to do away with the incestuous and perverse tricks of the God as artist, who begets himself in his closed system, in order to found another circularity, hermeneutical in essence. The main character becomes the reading or speaking subject, no longer a mirror or an echo of the writing subject but his accomplice, his complementary and contradictory accessory.

Now Vico merely succeeds in overstepping the speculative apparatus at large, understood as the circle of consciousness that always finds again the tracks of absolute knowledge no matter where it goes, because his postulate of a cyclical history presupposes a philosophy of authority. Vico constantly opposes philosophy, dealing with the necessary truths of nature and contemplating universal reason and philology, dealing with the creations of the human mind and observing the grounds for an awareness of certainty. In a movement toward a more rigorous scientificity, philology borrows its methods from philosophy before swallowing it. The seventh paragraph of Vico's *New Science* should be quoted:

> Moreover, it may here be pointed out that in the present work, with a new critical art that has hitherto been lacking, entering on the research of the truth concerning the authors of these same nations . . . philosophy undertakes to examine philology (that is the doctrine of all the institutions that depend on human choice; for example, all histories of the languages, customs and deeds of people in war and peace), of which, because of the deplorable obscurity of causes and almost infinite variety of effects, philosophy has had almost a horror of treating; and reduces it to the form of a science by discovering in it the design of an ideal eternal history traversed in time by the histories of all nations; so that, on account of this second principal aspect, our Science may be considered a philosophy of authority.[32]

Vico starts from an almost theological axiom: only God can possess the full science or understanding of things because he is their Author. The one necessary condition to the knowledge of a thing is to make it; hence Vico's recurrent formula: *verum ipsum factum*. This appears as an explicit refutation of Cartesianism; there can be no direct insight into an *ego cogito* that would not have made itself prior to examination. On the other hand, it frees the subject for an indefinite examination of all that men have made, all that is encompassed by their "choice" and free will, which, as the passage shows, includes history and civilizations. For Vico, when someone has done something, he can then become the authoritative narrator of his own deeds. The principle has momentous consequences, for it enables him to move from a theology of the author of the universe toward the authority of historical witnesses. Indeed, authority almost entails a duty to tell, an obligation to narrate. Another passage develops this view:

> Our science therefore comes to describe at the same time an ideal eternal history traversed in time by the history of every nation in its rise, development, maturity, decline and fall. Indeed, we make bold to affirm that he who meditates this Science narrates to himself this ideal eternal history so far as he himself makes it himself by that proof "it had, has, and will have to be." For the first indubitable principle posited above is that this world of nations has certainly been made by men, and its guise must therefore be found within the modifications of our own human mind. And history cannot be more certain than when he who creates things also narrates them. Now, as geometry, when it constructs the world of quantity out of its elements, or contemplates that world, is creating it for itself, just so does our Science, but with a reality greater by just so much as the institutions having to do with human affairs are more real than points, lines, surfaces, and figures are. And this very fact is an argument, O reader, that those proofs are of a kind divine and should give thee a divine pleasure, since in God knowledge and creation are one and the same thing.[33]

The philosopher transformed into a philologist, equipped with a sound theory of language, now engaged into the hermeneutics of human reality, can become the Creator of the History he narrates. The "divine pleasure" is not set aside for the end of history, as in Hegel's apocalyptic progression toward absolute knowledge; it is available to any reader, who must only superimpose his interpretative action onto the creative gesture in order to become God himself. Thus, even the punning approximations and inaccuracies, the gratuitous or blundering similarities between different periods or names can find an authority and dignity which are to be measured by the pleasure taken in the writing or the reading.

The "ideal reader" of *Finnegans Wake*, with his ideal insomnia or "wake," participates in this divine enjoyment, recreating language and history. In the logic of recourses, of *corsi* and *ricorsi storici*, of universal and ideal history, Vico replaces Hegel, a Hegel who still loses himself in speculation, drunk with the wine of absolute knowledge, while his sons Shem, Ham, and Japhet dance in a frenzied round to follow in the traces of bewildering, entertwined circular patterns outside the patriarch's tent. Hence this passage, which parodies Hegel through the drunken speech of one of the four Irish Masters, those annalists of the early days, or one of the four evangelists: "gynecollege histories (Lucas calling, hold the line!) . . . for teaching the Fatima Woman history of Fatimiliafamilias, repeating herself, on which purposeth of the spirit of nature as difinely developed in time by psadatepholomy, the past and present (Johnny MacDougall speaking, give me trunks, miss!) and present and absent and past and present and perfect *arma virumque romano*" (*FW*, 389.10–19).

Virgil remains a disoriented guide for a senile Dante, who gropes his way out of history, a history that woman has hysterized into feminine Fatima; and the development of the spirit through nature and time is summed up by the curious term of "psadatepholomy." one can hear "pseudo-telephony" in it, and we are reminded that all this seems to be uttered in a telephone call to the deity to "hold the line," a phony telephony, so to speak, between "Edenville" and the "omphalos."[34] The communication really conveys a "tip": "P.S. a date? follow me!" The *post scriptum* of history attract attention, and there is the promise of a meeting which at the same time is a date, renewing with eschatological promise in the guise of Christ telling Peter, "Follow me." All this is deployed on the background of classical history, with Ptolemaeus Soter, who is already linked with television in another context (*FW*, 254.22–23), and to whom an incestuous sister who is no other than Cleopatra suggests that it is time he should leave her the throne. The hysteria of history, according to Luke, or to John (or T. S. Eliot), can never free itself from an incestuous family circle.

But insofar as these stories are polyphonically multiplied by new possible layers of meaning, without ever fixing themselves on such and such a particular incest or perversion, there is an excess of meaning in the text by comparison with what its author may have intended, and this excess is in turn exceeded by what readers can write into it. The insertion of a serialist infinity within the intertwining narrations needs Vico's rhythmical beat to explode the totality of the text. From time to time, Joyce felt obliged to explain that he did not "believe" the theories of Vico, that they had only been "imposed" on him through "the circumstances" of his life, magically repeating Stephen's denegation. Beyond the ambiguities of such a reference to a biography exploited and quarried for many false leads, Joyce shows that the constitutive division of the author's enunciation does not prevent the reader's divinization.

Now *Finnegans Wake* is a unique book in that anyone who wishes to penetrate it must, by a long and almost tedious process of reciprocal interpenetration or biological anastomosis, arrive at the point when a reader's authority is established. The reader has to authorize himself to the status of reader; not merely because the text requires culture and also an effort that some may deem disproportionate, in excess of any possible fun derived from the puns, but also because this provides an experience of reading which then radically alters any subsequent reading. Once I have become, thanks to *Finnegans Wake*, the author of my reading, I can keep an awareness of this recurring dissolution in the text, which, far from comforting my own illusory mastery over texts and meanings, underlines the fact that I am porous, open to alterity, read and written in advance by other texts. Stephen Dedalus gains a sense of authorship only when he refuses all the shelters and ruses of a cunning feminine reason, fleeing from Molly's deep night, into which Bloom is smothered at the end of "Ithaca." Stephen is sent like a wandering missile on an unforeseen orbit, and nothing announces that he is going to sit down at some makeshift table and immediately start writing the book one is still holding. Perhaps he is authorized only to keep silent, for he may well be the first reader of *Finnegans Wake*.

Stephen is a virgin and will remain a virgin; he is not wanting in experience, but he has nothing more to prove by a more radical gesture than this minimal refusal of compromise. For the parousia of the absolute has already taken place in its circle of circles. Stephen's "No" as voiced in the "Nothung" of "Circe" recalls Siegfried to hint also that the new freedom opens onto a new knot: "knot-hung!" The unhappy conscience will have to learn how to survive in the scission which patterns desire, a desire that murmurs into his ear the guilty tales of an innocence never completely lost. The play of such innocence devoted to the production of texts is another metaphor for reading, a serial and ludic reading, a reading haunted by the ghosts of two rival bogeymen, those of Shakespeare the Jew and Hegel the Greek. But who is the son of a Hegel who wrote the durn thing anyhow?

CONCLUSION

I have started this book with a remark which some will take as a provocation, others as a triviality: that Joyce forces criticism to acknowledge its theological nature. After all the readings that have been deployed, it now may appear that this "theology," if it is granted as such, is a perverted theology and, besides, that in this perversion lies the main chances of a possible "modernity" of literature. For Bloom and Stephen are not "the Jew" and "the Greek" linked in a sort of parodic or dialectical couple; they are the "perverted Jew" and the "perverted Greek." Bloom is defined as a "perverted jew" by Martin Cunningham (*U*, 12.1635); Stephen, whose "jesuit strain" has been "injected the wrong way" (1.209) is supposed to adhere to a "perverted transcendental-ism" (14.1223). Bloom is described as "perversely idealistic" as a consequence of a self-abuse (*U*, 15.1781) in "Circe," while Stephen hesitates, a would-be "lover of an ideal or a perversion" (9.1022). How can this insistence on the theme of perversity lead to a concept of modernity?

Perversion is founded on a structure of thought which is over-hauled despite a lack of belief in its efficacy; the efficacy of language will be left to divided speaking and writing subjects. Perversion is Joyce's way of avoiding the aporias of "high modernism," of bypassing Pound's or Eliot's fundamentally reactionary beliefs in primitive myths and ritual. Just as Pound, Yeats, and Eliot wished to salvage "original" values and see the present and the past in one sweeping mythological Vision, Joyce defends a "modernity" with roots in past times. But these two concepts of "modernity" – or, for that matter, of "modernism" – do not overlap.

No one is quite sure whether it helps much to pigeonhole Joyce as a "modernist." True, he has been claimed as such by his friends. But it seems more relevant to go back to the notion Joyce himself had developed about "modernity," a notion which, for instance, clashes with Eliot's. Whereas Eliot tends to push "modernism" towards a renewed Maurassian "Classicism," Joyce, in his conversations with Arthur Power, repeatedly and forcibly attacks Romanticism *and* Classicism in the name of a more rigorous notion of modernity:

> But as our education was based on the classical, most of us have a fixed idea of what literature should be, and not only literature but also of what life should be. And so we moderns are accused of distortion; but our literature is no more distorted than classical literature is. All art in a sense is distorted in that it must exaggerate certain aspects to obtain its effect and in time people will accept this so-called modern distortion, and regard it as the truth.
>
> (*CP,* 74)

One may not grant immediately that this "distortion" corresponds to what I called "perversion." Yet, I wish to show that this is precisely the criterion by which Joyce distinguishes himself from all his fellow modernists and situates his writing precisely at the hinge between art and life, masculinity and femininity, subjectivity and objectivity. When Joyce says "we moderns," this is not meant as an allusion to the "movements" of the Zurich Dadaists, the London Vorticists, or the Paris Surrealists, but is a reference to a general context encompassing Proust, Gide, and Picasso, for instance. He indeed sees himself as the contemporary of *The Waste Land* (*CP,* 100–101) and of *A la recherche du temps perdu,* with greater emphasis on the second "masterpiece" of modernism, although it suffers from "overelaboration" in Joyce's view. Joyce defends Proust's "innovations" as not being experimental: "It was not experimentation . . . , his innovations were necessary to express modern life as he saw it. As life changes, the style to express it must change also" (*CP,* 79). However banal these statements may sound, Joyce's strict adherence to the myth of a direct encounter with "Life" is combined with a deep skepticism concerning the truth value of "facts" that are organized in systems of belief thanks to the agency of ideologies.[1]

What I would like to argue is that Joyce's sense of being "a modern" is inseparable from a crisis in faith, a crisis that took the very name "modernism" and developed a debate within the Catholic and Protestant churches at the end of the nineteenth century. The debate over "modernism" pretended to reconcile religious orthodoxy with the new dogmas of science, such as Darwinian evolutionism.[2] It was this subversive tendency that brought about a return to Thomism as the major philosophy in Catholic schools and universities. Joyce, in that sense, can be called the heir of modernism—a modernism that was almost over as he started his career—and Aquinas the first real "postmodern" philosopher. It is in this wider perspective that Joyce's statements on the equivalence of "modern times" and the Middle Ages can take all their significance. His own version of Viconian cyclicity is that Europe will sooner or later return to medievalism: "The old classical Europe which we knew in our youth is fast disappearing; the cycle has returned upon its tracks, and with it will come a new consciousness which will create values returning to the mediaeval" (*CP,* 92). Joyce felt keenly that his books would have been more appreciated in the fourteenth or fifteenth century and that Dublin was a privileged place because it still was a medieval city. This view leads to very perceptive political intuitions:

Ulysses also is mediaeval but in a more realistic way, and so you will find that the whole trend of modern thought is going in that direction, for as it is I can see there is going to be another age of the extremes, of ideologies, of persecutions, of excesses which will be political perhaps instead of religious, though the religious may reappear as the political, and in this new atmosphere you will find the old way of writing and thinking disappear, is fast disappearing in fact, and *Ulysses* is one of the books which has hastened that change.
(*CP,* 93)

Medievalism for Joyce is emblematized by the pubs around Christ Church he used to frequent as a young man, where he "was always reminded of those mediaeval taverns in which the sacred and the obscene jostle shoulders" (*CP,* 92), a parodic combination he ascribes to the fact the Irish have never been subjected to the Lex Romana as the other European nations have. His writing is thus closer to the spirit of Rabelais or Cervantes than to anything that has derived from the "modern" mind of the Renaissance. What is of paramount importance is that Joyce never parades a faith or a neo-Catholic belief; if he reinscribes "evil" in his writings, it can only be in the perverse and historical mode which is his, without "believing in it." As *Finnegans Wake* puts it, in a strange French parenthesis that serves as a gloss on prayers, Pater Nosters, and Hail Marys: "as the b——r had his b——y nightprayers said, three patrecknocksters and a couplet of hellmuirries (*tout est sacré pour un sacreur, femme à barbe ou homme-nourrice*)" (*FW,* 81.27–29). All is sacred/accursed for whom curses, be it a bearded woman or a male nurse! The strange bisexual "buggers" who let out these "bloody" prayers are the ideal butts of Dublin gossip, and yet they manage to carry out the book's main ambiguities and tensions. The "*Nom de nombres!*" (*FW,* 285.3) of these curses (*nom de nom* being a still current French swear word based on God's name) spells out the impish parodies of the Cartesian consciousness as *ego cogito:* "cog it out, here goes a sum. So read we in must book. It tells. He prophets most who bilks the best" (*FW,* 304.31–305.2). Coleridge had written, "He prayeth best, who lovest best," in his

"Rime of the Ancient Mariner," but here prayer has turned into a perverted prophecy based on the building of capitalism being identical to universal *Bildung* on the one hand, and on the practice of swindling, forging, cheating, and disappointing on the other hand. Joyce's book is indeed a fake prophecy in which it is impossible to "believe" but which should nevertheless pave the way to a new and "modern" consciousness. Love remains that "mystery" Stephen cannot hear, although the ghost of his mother has already answered his prayer by quoting to him his own words (or Yeats's, rather):

THE MOTHER
... You sang that song to me. *Love's bitter mystery.*

STEPHEN
(*eagerly*) Tell me the word, mother, if you know now.

(*U*, 15.4188–92)

This is typical of Joyce's perverse strategies: one cannot hear what is already written, one cannot see what is merely spoken. The "tell me all" of the washerwoman gossiping about the archetypal family of the *Wake* must indeed stay a frustrated demand, endlessly disappointed, for there can be no "bridge" between the two talkers, to take up Stephen's joke about the "pier" as a "disappointed bridge" (*U*, 2.39).

In *S/Z*, Roland Barthes attacks the idleness forced upon us by a classical writing that has programmed everything and leaves the reader passive. If we are careful not to fall prey to a simplified version of the so-called transparency of "classical" texts (which Barthes's reading itself undermines when pointing out the complexity of codes at work in "Sarrazine"), and if one stays wary of historical oversimplifications, the "modernity" of Joyce's writings may appear, in a way, a typical modernist gesture giving back meaning to archaic forms.[3] Thus, like the medieval texts that lacked correct punctuation, needed to be read alongside numerous glosses and in often contradictory versions, *Finnegans Wake* proposes an evolutionary book that has to be reshaped by every reader who will learn to master its idiolect, to inhabit its pages, to live with or within its universe. The same could be said of *A la recherche du temps perdu*. The writing of the "Moderns" in that sense tends to make the reader not just a consumer but a producer of a text considered as "writerly" or "writable" and not merely "readerly" or "readable," to take up Barthes's terms.[4] *Finnegans Wake* would not only be the "writerly" text *par excellence* but would reflect on this process, which is made an element in the textual problematics caught up between performativity and reflexivity: "His producers are they not his consumers? Your exagmination round his factification for incamination of a warping process" (*FW,* 497.1–3). The very form of the rhetorical question—which also alludes to the collection of essays on *Work in Progress* Joyce had himself planned (no author has been more concerned than Joyce as to what critics would say about his work; consequently, he projected another collection of four long essays on *Finnegans Wake* which all the Joyceans dream of writing)—shows that Joyce privileges neither producer nor consumer in a process that warps words, falsifies their meanings, and distorts contexts and structures.

The text hesitates between the "unreadable-writable" which any reader has to discover at the cost of excessive investment and "ideal insomnia" (*FW,* 120.14) and the "risible-readable"—the laughter that takes us unawares when we suddenly come across an unsuspected pun, or finally see a different meaning in a phrase read over a hundred times. As Freud has shown, the more one looks for the meaning of a joke, the less one laughs, for laughter comes from an economy, which it is impossible to calculate when dealing with *Finnegans Wake*. Its paradoxical and eccentric echonomy entails a constant mobilization and a cumulative discharge of sporadic laughter which is liberated in fits and is triggered off by sense discovered in apparent nonsense. Although the process takes some time (but not in the sense of a reader's competence, since any "first reader" can trust his or her beginner's luck), no place has been consecrated by wit and prepared in advance for the readers, the author having relinquished his prerogatives to them. Thus the entire "risicide" (*FW,* 161.17) textual strategy constituting a "risible universe" (419.3) should ideally tend towards an unstable mixture of laughter and despair such as Joyce is rumored to have experienced at the end of his life.[5]

That notion that "writerly" should be rewritten as "risibly" or "wrisible" corresponds to the peculiar type of perverse laughter Stephen Dedalus seems eager to produce, as for instance when he recites to his class his celebrated "riddle" about a "fox burying his grandmother under a hollybush" and stands up, giving a "shout of nervous laughter to which their cries echoed dismay" (*U*, 2.116–17). When we read *Finnegans Wake*, we may as often feel dismay as experience this "nervous laughter," since we are bowling along "bumpily, experiencing a jolting series of prearranged disappointments" (*FW*, 107.33). The carefully contrived slips of the pen move along bumpily, joltingly, in a prearranged structure which lets accidents occur of themselves for a reader who makes sense of them.

Finnegans Wake thus completes the work accomplished by *Ulysses* as it "hastens" all the more the changes it tried to bring about. Unlike *Ulysses*, which still relied partly on a realistic mode of presentation, in its first half at least, the last book puts an end to the dichotomy between reader and author by abolishing the opposition between text and commentary, novel and criticism. Criticism is digested ("carefully digesting the very wholesome criticism" [*FW*, 163.36]), absorbed, consummated, and consumed in a perpetual self-commentary that says more about itself in advance and by prolepsis than one can say about it. Criticism is exhausted in a perverse play with true or false references which finally dissolve it. And the text lets us know that if we want to enjoy it, we shall have to be "uncritical" enough, but if we wish to understand it, we shall have to turn into critics, a disjunction Freud recognized as crucial when talking about jokes:

> Nor have we any need to enter further into the question of how pleasure could arise from the alternation between "thinking it senseless" and "recognizing it as sensible." The psychogenesis of jokes taught us that the pleasure in a joke is derived from play with words or from the liberation of nonsense, and that the meaning of the joke is merely intended to protect that pleasure from being done away with by criticism.[6]

Nevertheless, criticism remains "ineluctable," for it can be called "wholesome" and even nourish the reading—and the writing. If criticism manages to account for the reading-writing process, totalizing the fragments and fragmenting the wholes, it engages in a systematic dismemberment that creates its own memory while opening up to the alterity of authority.

NOTES

Preface

1. "La Missa Parodia de *Finnegans Wake,*" *Poétique,* no. 17 (1974): 75–95. This article, among other things, attempted to formalize David Hayman's operative categories used to describe Joyce's compositional processes in his Introduction to *A First-Draft Version of Finnegans Wake* (Austin: University of Texas Press, 1963).

2. In my forthcoming *Joyce upon the Void: The Genesis of Doubt* (London: Macmillan, 1991).

3. "Silence in Dubliners" was published in *James Joyce: New Perspectives,* ed. Colin MacCabe (Bloomington: Indiana University Press, 1982), 45–72, and "A Portrait of the Artist as a Bogeyman" in *Oxford Literary Review* 7, nos. 1– (1985): 62–90 (also published in *James Joyce: The Augmented Ninth,* ed. Bernard Benstock [Syracuse: Syracuse University Press, 1988], 103–34. Some parts of the central chapters of *Joyce: Portrait de l'auteur en autre lecteur* had already been published in English as "A Clown's Inquest into Paternity—Fathers, Dead or Alive in *Ulysses* and *Finnegans Wake,*" in *The Fictional Father,* ed. Robert Con Davis (Amherst: University of Massachusetts Press, 1981), 73–114.

4. See Jacques Derrida, *Ulysse Gramophone* (Paris: Galilée, 1987), 73–78, translated by Tina Kendall and Shari Benstock as "Ulysses Gramophone: Hear Say yes in Joyce," in Benstock, *Joyce: The Augmented Ninth*, 27–75.

5. James Joyce, *A Portrait of the Artist as a Young Man: Text, Criticism, and Notes*, ed. Chester G. Anderson, Viking Critical Library (New York: Viking, 1977), 181.

Introduction

1. Jacques Derrida, "Two Words for Joyce," in *Post-Structuralist Joyce*, ed. Derek Attridge and Daniel Ferrer (Cambridge: Cambridge University Press, 1984), 147.

2. Roland Barthes, "The Death of the Author," trans. Stephen Heath in *Image-Music-Text* (New York: Hill and Wang, 1977), 142–48. Also more recently translated by Richard Howard in *The Rustle of Language* (Berkeley and Los Angeles: University of California Press, 1989), 49–55. See also Michel Foucault, "What Is an Author?" trans. Josué V. Harari in *The Foucault Reader* (New York: Pantheon: 1984). Both Foucault and Barthes tend to replace the author with the reader. Their combined theses form the theoretical basis on which Vicki Mahaffey has built her excellent reading of "authority" in Joyce's works, in *Reauthorizing Joyce* (Cambridge: Cambridge University Press, 1988).

3. Peggy Kamuf, *Signature Piece: On the Institution of Authority* (Ithaca: Cornell University Press, 1988), 5–12.

4. Gustave Flaubert, *The Selected Letters,* ed. and trans. Francis Steegmuller (New York: Vintage Books, 1957), 194. See also Richard K. Cross, *Flaubert and Joyce: The Rite of Fiction* (Princeton: Princeton University Press, 1971), esp. "Invisible Novelists," 177–92.

5. Flaubert, *Selected Letters*, 126.

6. I have attempted to work with this concept and to link it to Joyce's theory of female "indifference" in "Bruno no, Bruno si: Note on a Contradiction in Joyce," *James Joyce Quarterly* 27, no. 1 (1989): 31–39. This will be developed in *Joyce upon the Void: The Genesis of Doubt* (forthcoming).

7. For an excellent reading of the epiphanies as opening up onto the Lacanian concept of the Real, see Catherine Millot, "On Epiphanies," in Benstock, *James Joyce: The Augmented Ninth*, 207–9, and "Epiphanies," in *Joyce avec Lacan*, ed. Jacques Aubert (Paris: Navarin, 1987), 87–95.

8. Flaubert, *Selected Letters*, 163. Flaubert's technique of empathic

projection, which enhances distance while abolishing it, is very close to Joyce's methods, especially in his preparation for the "Nausicaa" episode of *Ulysses,* as for instance when Flaubert writes, "For two days now I have been trying to live the dreams of young girls" (ibid., 128).

9. Ibid., 153.

10. Jacques Derrida, *Edmund Husserl's Origin of Geometry: An Introduction,* trans. J. P. Leavy (Stony Brooks: Nicolas Hays, 1978), 71.

11. See Manfred Pütz's seminal essay "The Identity of the Reader in *Finnegans Wake*," *James Joyce Quarterly* 11, no. 4 (1974): 287–393.

12. See T. S. Eliot's tantalizing note to *The Waste Land* in which he states, "What Tiresias *sees*, in fact, is the substance of the poem" (*Collected Poems, 1909–1962* [London: Faber, 1963], 82). This suggests that the reader should become blind, like Tiresias, in order to read all the meaning.

13. Derrida, "Two Words for Joyce," 149.

14. Ibid.

15. Derrida, "Ulysses Gramophone," in *James Joyce: The Augmented Ninth,* 73. Derrida has referred in some detail to Bloom's idea of recording people's voices so as to listen to them after their deaths: "Besides how could you remember everybody? Eyes, walk, voice. Well, the voice, yes: gramophone. Have a gramophone in every grave or keep it in the house. After dinner on a Sunday. Put on old greatgrandfather. Kraahraark! Hellohellohello amawfullyglad kraark awfullygladaseeagain hellohello amawf krpthsth" (*U,* 6.962–65). The Joycean spirit of parody then prompts Derrida to dedicate his reading of this quote to the real Stephen Joyce, who was in the room ("Ulysses Gramophone," p. 73, n. 9). One should not forget, however, that the other medium envisaged by Joyce is photography (another type of *graphein*), which should help to recall someone's eyes. The articulation between eyes and voice will be developed in Chapter 2, and the ghostlier presence of Othello lurking behind the recorded "hello," in Chapter 3.

16. Louis Gillet, *Stèle pour James Joyce* (Marseilles: Sagittaire, 1941), 101.

17. See my "Joyce the Parisian," in *The Cambridge Companion to James Joyce,* ed. Derek Attridge (Cambridge: Cambridge University Press,1990), 93–100.

18. Notebook VI.B.14.9, *The James Joyce Archive,* ed. Michael Groden, 63 vols. (New York: Garland, 1978-), vol. 32. I refer to the 63 volumes of the *James Joyce Archive* by the volume numbers provided by the *James Joyce Quarterly*

19. Jacques Derrida, *L'Ecriture et la Différence* (Paris: Seuil, 1967),

228. Also in English as *Writing and Difference*, trans. Alan Bass (Chicago: University of Chicago Press, 1978).

20. G. W. F. Hegel, "Die Welt des sich entfremdeten Geistes," in *Phänomenologie des Geistes* (Frankfurt: Ullstein, 1970), 294.

21. The relevance of Hugo von Hofmannsthal's famous "Lord Chandos's Letter" to Joyce has been pointed out by Hermann Broch in his essay on Hofmannsthal (written between 1947 and 1950), in which he stresses the convergence between the two writers to the point of surmising that Joyce had had a "Chandos experience" himself. See Hermann Broch, *Schriften zur Literatur, I: Kritik*, ed. Paul Michael Lützeler (Frankfurt: Suhrkamp, 1975), 311–12.

22. Edgar Allan Poe, *Great Short Works* (New York: Harper and Row, 1970), 472. All my references are to this edition.

My reading of this tale was already forming the end of the original introduction to *Portrait de l'auteur en autre lecteur*, 19–21, but it has since then benefited from Stanley Cavell's illuminating comments in a recent paper, "Being Odd, Getting Even" (1986), first published in *Reconstructing Individualism*, ed. Thomas C. Heller et al. (Stanford: Stanford University Press, 1986), and now taken up in *In Quest of the Ordinary: Lines of Skepticism and Romantism* (Chicago: University of Chicago Press, 1988). I quote from this later collection of essays.

Although I do not follow Cavell in all his analyses, I feel strongly the affinity between his problematics of skepticism versus transcendentalism and the position of Joyce. I have also, in a very different key, used another story by Poe, "The Murders in the Rue Morgue," in order to show that the progressive, "genetic" aspect of Joyce's last work could be understood as the outcome of a "double murder" which triggered his orangoutang-like performance, playing murderously with all sorts of languages. See my "Pour une cryptogénétique de l'idiolecte joycien," in *Genèse de Babel: Joyce et la Création* (Paris: Editions du CNRS, 1985), 49–91, and in *Joyce upon the Void*.

23. Cavell, "Being Odd, Getting Even," 123.

24. The now classic Lacanian approach to perversion is to be found in the collection of essays by P. Aulagnier-Spairani, J. Clavreul, F. Perrier, G. Rosolato, and J.-P. Valabrega, *Le Désir et la perversion* (Paris: Seuil, 1967). Since this impressive synthesis, one French analyst and theoretician in particular, Denis Vasse, has kept elaborating this notion (in terms not that far from Cavell's concept of "acknowledgment" and "avoidance"). See, for instance, *Un parmi d'autres* (Paris: Seuil, 1978), and *Le Poids du réel, la souffrance* (Paris: Seuil, 1983).

1. Maurice Blanchot, *L'Ecriture du désastre* (Paris: Gallimard, 1980), 187. Also available in English as *The Writing of the Disaster,* trans. Ann Smock (Lincoln: University of Nebraska Press, 1986).

2. Hermann Broch, "James Joyce und die Gegenwart," in *Schriften zur Literatur, I: Kritik,* 63–94. See also my article "Joyce and Broch; or, Who Was the Crocodile?" *Comparative Literature Studies,* 19, no. 2 (1982): 121–33, in which I attempt to describe the theoretical framework in which Broch's reading of *Finnegans Wake* can be understood.

3. *Pound/Joyce: The Letters of Ezra Pound to James Joyce with Pound's essays on Joyce,* ed. Forrest Read (London: Faber, 1968), 27–28.

4. Stephen's "silence" is thereafter marked by the shift to the mode of the diary instead of direct speech or dialogues.

5. John Henry Newman, *Critical Essays,* 1:128, quoted by Günter Biemer in *Newman on Tradition,* trans. K. Smith (London: Burns and Oates, 1967), 90.

6. *James Joyce's Scribbledehobble: The Ur-Workbook for "Finnegans Wake,"* ed. Thomas E. Connolly (Evanston: Northwestern University Press,1961), 25.

7. See R. I. Moore's fascinating paper "Heresy as Disease," in *The Concept of Heresy in the Middle Ages (11th–13th Century)* (The Hague: Leuven University Press, 1976), 1–11. This conception of heresy as a contagious disease seems to be shared by Mr. Tate, the English master in *A Portrait,* when he states his diagnosis of Stephen's paper with the words: "This fellow has heresy in his essay" (*P,* 81). Heresy is never far from dogma, in the same way as "canker" and "cancer" contribute an ironic epitaph to Wolsey's grave in Leicester Abbey (*P,* 10). See also Annie Tardits's more recent synthesis of the problematics of heresy from a Lacanian point of view, in "L'appensée, le renard et l'hérésie," in *Joyce avec Lacan,* ed. Jacques Aubert (Paris: Navarin, 1987), 107–58.

8. By "Other" I refer to the Lacanian concept of *L'Autre* which has been translated as "the Big Other" or the "capitalized Other." I prefer to leave the term its fluidity, crucial to Lacan's strategies. Nevertheless, it remains very important to distinguish between the "other" of the imaginary realm and the "Other" that defines the unconscious as made up of language and determined by the Law and the Name of the Father. What remains untranslatable is the systematic echo introduced by Lacan between *l'objet petit a* and the *petit autre* of imaginary identifications.

9. For a more detailed consideration of the relation between neuro-

sis and perversion in Joyce, see Colin MacCabe, *James Joyce and the Revolution of the Word* (London: Macmillan, 1979), 32–8, 104–29.

10. Gustave Flaubert, *Trois contes,* in *Oeuvres complètes* (Paris: Seuil, 1964), 169.

11. Ibid., p. 175.

12. Ibid., p. 176.

13. Joyce alludes to Leo Taxil's spoof on the New Testament, *La Vie de Jésus* (Paris, 1884), in which Mary confronts an angry Joseph, who refuses to believe in immaculate conception. She answers that it is the "pigeon" who has made her pregnant. See "It Loses Something in Translation: Italian and French Profanity in Joyce's *Ulysses*," by Marisa Gatti-Taylor, in *Joyce, Modernity and Its Mediation,* ed. Christine van Boheemen (Amsterdam: Rodolpi, 1989), 141–49.

14. See Matthew Hodgart, *James Joyce: A Student's Guide* (London: Routledge and Kegan Paul, 1978), 45–46, and John Garvin, *James Joyce's Disunited Kingdom* (London: Macmillan, 1976), 37–45.

15. Blanchot, *L'Ecriture du Désastre,* 51.

Chapter Two Thy Name is Joy

1. See Michael Groden, *"Ulyssess" in Progress* (Princeton: Princeton University Press, 1977).

2. James Joyce, *Collected Poems* (New York: Compass, 1957), 63.

3. This photograph, made in 1938, was part of a color series Gisèle Freund devoted to Joyce.

4. Clive Hart quotes Frank Budgen's conversation in *Structure and Motif in Finnegans Wake* (London: Faber, 1962), 163.

5. Louis Gillet, *Stèle pour James Joyce* (Marseille: Sagittaire, 1941), 141.

6. *Selected Letters,* 361. In this same letter, Joyce writes in a self-abasement typical of "mourning and melancholy": "I was very fond of him always, being a sinner myself, and even liked his faults" (361). I shall take this up in Chapter 7, "Language of Earse."

7. Jacques Lacan, "Le Sinthome," *Séminaire* of January 13, 1976, published in *Ornicar,* no. 7 (1976): 15.

8. I try to develop this in an analysis of Joycean "bisexuality" in *"Finnegans Wake:* Labi sexualité–états d'un vestiaire," in *Cahier de L'Herne James Joyce,* ed. Jacques Aubert and Fritz Senn (Paris: L'Herne, 1985), 453–82.

9. I translate from Jacques Lacan's "Foreword to Robert Georgin, *Lacan* (Lausanne: Cistre-L'Age d'Homme, 1977), 15–16.

Chapter Three *The Figures of Incestitude*

1. See Jane Ford, "Why Is Milly in Mullingar?" *James Joyce Quarterly* 14, n. 4 (1977): 436–49.

2. Don Gifford and Robert J. Seidman quote this song in *Notes for Joyce: An Annotation of James Joyce's "Ulysses"* (New York: Dutton, 1974), 248.

3. See Richard Ellmann, *Ulysses on the Liffey* (London: Faber, 1972), n.p., for the Italian scheme Joyce sent to Linati. "Notte Alta" refers to "Ulisse (Bloom)" and "Alba (dawn)" to "Telemaco (Stephen)."

4. Jacques Lacan, *Ecrits: A Selection,* trans. Alan Sheridan (London: Tavistock, 1977), 20–25, 66–68, 81–87.

5. *Letters,* 2:107–8. This letter is dated September 19, 1905, and is thus later than the fragment referred to on p. 63. According to this letter, all "mystical" resemblance vanishes without the mediation of a name. It is as if Joyce had to be made aware of the fictive nature of paternity before choosing a name for his son. And in Lucia's case, the situation is quite different, this stage of doubt having been overcome.

5. Lacan, *Ecrits,* 149.

Chapter Four *Circe's Stagecraft*

1. The concept of "textual unconscious" was first used in a psycho-analytic and genetic perspective by Jean Bellemin-Noel in *Vers l'Inconscient du texte* (Paris: Presses Universitaires de France, 1979). See especially pp. 191–202.

2. See Joyce's Trieste notebook in *The Workshop of Dedalus,* ed. Robert Scholes and Richard M. Kain (Evanston: Northwestern University Press, 1965), 97.

3. I have developed Joyce's plays on Jousse and Vico in "Joyce: Les Lèvres circoncises," in *Leçons d'écriture: Ce que disent les manuscrits,* ed. A. Grésillon and M. Werner (Paris: Minard, 1985), 107–28.

4. Lacan, *Ecrits,* 273–74.

5. Gustave Flaubert, *La Tentation de Saint Antoine,* ed. E. Maynial (Paris: Garnier, 1954), 2. Flaubert does not use italics, but different fonts, with a bigger type for the characters' speeches.

6. See *Joyce's "Ulysses" Notesheets in the British Museum,* ed. Phillip F. Herring (Charlottesville: University Press of Virginia, 1972), 286.

7. See the Linati scheme in Ellmann, *Ulysses on the Liffey,* n.p. Ellmann translates this as "vision animated to bursting point."

8. This aspect of "Circe" has been explored in detail by Hugh Kenner,

Ulysses (London: Unwin Critical Library, 1980), 118–27, and by C. H. Peake, *James Joyce, the Citizen and the Artist* (London: Edward Arnold, 1977), 263–76.

9. See Richard Ellmann's footnote to *Letters,* 3:104.

10. Hans Walter Gabler comments on Joyce's practice of quoting the preceding chapters in this way: "Yet the implications of the rewriting of *Ulysses* in 'Circe' are surely that the preceding narrative of Bloomsday is made to function as if it constituted not a fiction, but itself an order of empiric reality." Gabler, "Joyce's Text in Progress," in *The Cambridge Companion to James Joyce,* 232.

11. Joyce, "The Holy Office," in *The Critical Writings of James Joyce,* ed. Ellsworth Mason and Richard Ellmann (New York: Viking, 1959), 149, 152.

12. James Joyce, Notes to *Exiles* (Frogmore, St. Albans: Granada Publishing, 1979), 147.

13. *Ridda,* or "reel," is described as the antidote to Circe's charms in the Linati scheme.

Chapter Five Spinning Molly's Yarn

1. Maurice Blanchot, *L'Entretien infini* (Paris: Gallimard, 1969), 35–45.

2. Maurice Blanchot, *Le Livre à venir* (Paris: Gallimard, 1959), 16–17. Blanchot comments on Kafka's idea that "the Sirens have a more terrible weapon than their song: it is their silence." See Franz Kafka, "Das Schweigen der Sirenen," in *Hochzeitsvorbereitungen auf dem Lande,* ed. Max Brod (Frankfurt: Fischer, 1980), 58–59.

3. See Paul Faure, *Ulysse le crétois* (Paris: Fayard, 1980), 24 et seq.

4. See Colin MacCabe, *James Joyce and the Revolution of the Word,* 80–90.

5. Ezra Pound, "Canto I," *The Cantos* (London: Faber, 1978), 7.

6. See James Van Dyck Card, *An Anatomy of "Penelope"* (London: Associated University Presses, 1984), 38–55.

7. See my *"Finnegans Wake:* Labi Sexualité," in Aubert and Senn, *Cahier de L'Herne James Joyce,* 453–82.

8. Stanislaus Joyce, *My Brother's Keeper,* ed. Richard Ellmann (New York: Viking, 1958), 69; italics mine.

9. Sigmund Freud, *Jokes and Their Relation to the Unconscious* (1905), trans. James Strachey (London: Routledge and Kegan Paul, 1966), 37.

10. Carl G. Jung, *Die Bedeutung des Vaters für das Schicksal des Einzelnen* (Leipzig and Vienna: F. Deuticke, 1909), 30.

11. "You who bow down at altar / Remember me and pity Him /

Who took my flesh and bone for armour / And doublecrossed my mother's womb." Dylan Thomas, "Before I Knocked," in *Collected Poems* (New York: New Directions, 1957), 9.

Chapter Six Idiolects, Idiolex

1. Umberto Eco, *La Structure absente*, trans. Esposito-Torrigliani (Paris: Mercure de France, 1972), 129–30.

2. Norman Page, *Speech in the Novel* (London: Longman, 1973), "Speech and Character: Idiolect," 90–112.

3. Stuart Gilbert, *James Joyce's "Ulysses"* (Harmondsworth: Penguin, 1963), 173.

4. See Danis Rose's edition of *The Index Manuscript: Finnegans Wake Holograph Workbook VI B 46* (Colchester: Wakesnewslitter Press, 1978), 96.

5. P. W. Joyce, *English as We Speak It in Ireland* (Dublin: Longmans and Gill, 1910).

6. James Joyce, "Ireland, Island of Saints and Sages" (1907), in *Critical Writings*, 156.

7. Ibid., 173.

8. See also Dominic Manganiello, *Joyce's Politics* (London: Routledge, and Kegan Paul, 1980).

9. In *Dante sous la pluie de feu* (Paris: Vrin, 1950), André Pézard demonstrates that if Brunetto Latini (Brunet) is found in the fifteenth circle of Hell among the sodomites, even though he was Dante's teacher in rhetorics, it is only because Dante reproaches him for having abandoned his native language and having written his *Livre du trésor* in French. Stephen quotes Brunetto in an Italian translation of this same work (*U*, 9.374–75), which is a neat way of correcting Dante's curious condemnation.

10. Quoted by Richard Ellman, *James Joyce* (London and New York: Oxford University Press, 1959), 1:410.

11. Added to *Our Exagmination Round His Factification for Incamination of Work in Progress* (London: Faber, 1972), 193–94.

12. *Letters*, 1:273–74. For other specific glosses by Joyce, see *Letters* 1:247–48, and *Selected Letters*, 329–32.

13. *Critical Writings*, 258–68.

14. See Roland McHugh, *The Sigla of "Finnegans Wake"* (London: Arnold, 1976).

15. See P. W. Joyce, *A Short History of Ireland from the Earliest Times to 1608* (London: Longmans, Green, 1893), chap. 7, "The Laws of

Compensation and Distress" (pp. 47–55), and chap. 8, "Grades and Groups of Society" (pp. 55–60).

Chapter Seven The Language of Earse

1. See Ellmann, *James Joyce*, 1:411, for a clear summary.

2. Ibid.

3. See Petr Skrabanek's list of Slavonic words, "Slavansky Slavar," *A Wake Newslitter* 9, no. 4 (1972): 51–68.

4. According to Richard Ellman, "Joyce's Library in 1920," in *The Consciousness of Joyce* (London: Faber, 1977), 131.

5. See Brendan O Hehir, *A Gaelic Lexicon for "Finnegans Wake" and A Glossary for Joyce's Other Works* (Berkeley and Los Angeles: University of California Press, 1967), 182.

6. See John T. Noonan, Jr., *Contraception: A History of Its Treatment by the Catholic Theologians and Canonists* (Cambridge: Harvard University Press, 1966), 91.

7. See Margot Norris, *The Decentered Universe of "Finnegans Wake"* (Baltimore: Johns Hopkins University Press, 1976), 104 and passim.

8. Joyce plays on the famous misspelling of the word *hesitancy* as "hesitency" by Pigott, one of Parnell's accusers. See James S. Atherton, *The Books at the Wake* (London: Faber, 1959), 102 et seq.

9. "It is also the defence and indictment of the book itself." *Letters*, 1:406.

10. These terms are borrowed from Otto Rank, though with different emphasis. See Jean Kimball, "James Joyce and Otto Rank: The Incest Motif in *Ulysses*," *James Joyce Quarterly* 13, no. 3 (1976): 366–79.

11. Jacques Mercanton, *Les Heures de James Joyce* (Lausanne: L'Age d'Homme, 1967), 36.

12. Stanislaus Joyce, *My Brother's Keeper*, 224.

13. Atherton, *The Books at the Wake*, 31.

14. Ibid., 179–80.

15. Freud's source is Ernst Sellin, *Moses und seine Bedeutung für die isrealitisch-jüdische Religionsgeschichte* (Leipzig-Erlangen: Werner School, 1922), 16 and passim. Freud's main arguments in his own *Moses and Monotheism: Three Essays* (London: Hogarth, 1966; vol. 23 of the *Standard Edition* of Freud's works), 7–137, are based on Sellin's theses.

16. Freud, *Moses and Monotheism* 43n.

17. Ellmann, *James Joyce*, 1:737

18. Ibid., 180. John Joyce agreed reluctantly, and once only. See also an interesting account of Joyce's patrilinear mythology in Colbert

Kearney's paper "The Joycead," in *Coping with Joyce: Essays from the Copenhagen Symposium,* ed. Morris Beja and Shari Benstock (Columbus: Ohio State University Press, 1989), 55-72.

19. Ellmann, *James Joyce,* 1:755.

Chapter Eight A Portrait of the Author as a Bogeyman

1. See note 2 to the Introduction.

2. Barthe, "The Death of the Author," in *Image-Music-Text,* 148.

3. "Writing is that neutral, composite, oblique space where our subject slips away, the negative where all identity is lost, starting with the very identity of the body writing." Ibid., 142.

4. According to Roland Barthes, totality is both frightening and ludicrous: a monster, in fact. See his "Le Monstre de la totalité" in *Roland Barthes par Roland Barthes* (Paris: Seuil, 1975), 182.

5. See Jacques Aubert, *Introduction à l'esthétique de James Joyce* (Paris: Didier, 1973).

6. Jacques Derrida, "Violence and Metaphysics," in *Writing and Difference,* trans. Alan Bass (Chicago: University of Chicago Press, 1978), 227-28

7. Emmanuel Levinas, *Totalité et infini,* 2nd ed. (The Hague: M. Nijhoof, 1965), xv.

8. This comes from the Gorman-Gilbert schema; see Ellmann, *Ulysses on the Liffey,* n.p.

9. For this point, see the excellent analysis by Richard Ellmann in *The Consciousness of Joyce* (London: Faber, 1977), 45-72.

10. According to Gifford and Seidman's *Notes for Joyce,* p. 204, the main allusion is to *The Egoist*—a hint that may well be intended if one keeps in mind the main play on self and others.

11. For a general survey—which, incidentally, does not mention this striking echo between "Scylla and Charybdis" and the *Convivio*—see Mary T. Reynolds, *Joyce and Dante* (Princeton: Princeton University Press, 1981).

12. Dante, *Convivio,* trans. William W. Jackson (Oxford: Clarendon Press, 1909), 209. Both Dante and Joyce are attentive to the *poetic* value of their theory of vowels. The vowels tie up, as it were, the authority of the poet above all, *poet* being understood in its etymological sense of "maker" with words. Joyce, it is well known, had been inspired by Rimbaud's sonnet on vowels, although it inverts the order of the last two vowels and begins with "A Noir, E blanc, I rouge, U vert, O bleu: voyelles . . ." In fact, the inception of the "A.E.I.O.U." theme is to be

found in Joyce's marginal vocalizations in the early episodes of *Ulysses*. These appear in the margins of the first draft of "Proteus," when Stephen is trying to imitate the "silent roar" of the planets: "His lips lipped and mouthed fleshless lips of air: mouth to her moomb. Oomb, allwombing tomb. His mouth moulded issuing breath, unspeeched: ooeeehah: roar of cataractic planets, globed, blazing, roaring way-awayawayawayawayaway" (*U*,3.401–4). Above a series of crossed-out attempts at onomatopeic plays on "moombh" is a very clear (uncrossed) line with "a. e. i. o. u." Joyce has then probably decided to preserve this and to use it in the next episode devoted to Stephen, "Scylla and Charybdis." See the *James Joyce Archive* 12, Buffalo V.A.3–15.

13. Dante, *Convivio,* 209–10. I refer in brackets to the Italian text of the *Convivio,* from *Opere de Dante Alighieri,* ed. F. Chiapelli (Milan: Mursia, 1965), 234

14. Ibid.

15. André Pézard, *La Rotta Gonna: Gloses et corrections aux textes mineurs de Dante* (Paris: Sansoni et Didier, 1967), 1:237–60.

16. Dante, *Convivio,* 217.

17. According to Aristotle's *Poetics,* poetry is a more "philosophic" genre than history or chronicles because the object of poetry is general, not particular, just as it is probable and not necessary, inevitable, or in-eluctable (*Poetics* 9.51a36 et seq.).

18. Matthew Arnold, *Culture and Anarchy,* ed. J. Dover Wilson (Cambridge: University Press, 1971), 130. The phrase is also used as an epigraph by Derrida in his article on Levinas, "Violence and Metaphys-ics," in *Writing and Difference,* 79. See also David J. DeLaura, *Hebrew and Hellene in Victorian England: Newman, Arnold, and Pater* (Austin: University of Texas Press, 1969).

19. See note 11 to Chapter 5, above.

20. Dante, *Inferno* 4.131–35. Laurence Binyon renders those lines thus:

I saw the Master of those who know: he sate
Amid the sons Philosophy to him bore.
All do him honour, all eyes on him wait.
Here I beheld Plato and Socrates
Who of all are nearest to his high estate.

Dante, *The Selected Works,* ed. Paolo Milano (London: Chatto and Win-dus, 1972), 24.

21. Dante, *Paradiso* 33.85–93; italics mine. In Binyon's version:

I beheld leaves within the unfathomed blaze
   Into one volume bound of love, the same
   That the universe holds scattered through its maze.
Substance and accidents, and their modes, became
   As if together fused, all in such a wise
   That what I speak is one simple flame.
Verily I think I saw with mine eyes
   The form that knits the whole world, since I taste,
   In telling of it, more abounding bliss.

22. See pp. 92–93, above.

23. Quoted by André Pézard in a footnote to his translation of Dante's *Paradiso*, in Dante, *Oeuvres Complètes*, trans. A. Pézard (Paris: Gallimard, Pléiade, 1965), 1663.

24. Hence Gogarty's limerick about Joyce: "There was a young fellow called Joyce / Who possesseth a sweet tenor voice / He goes to the kips / With a psalm on his hips / And biddeth the harlots rejoice." Quoted by Ulick O'Connor, *The Times I've Seen: Oliver St John Gogarty* (New York: Ivan Oblensky, 1963), 55.

25. Martin Heidegger, *Holzwege* (Frankfurt: Klostermann, 1980), 319. See also ibid., 111–204.

26. I translate from the German text of the complete conversations noted by George Borach when he was Joyce's friend in Zurich, as reproduced in *Die Toten: Ein James Joyce Lesebuch* (Zurich: Diogenes, 1979), 234.

27. Benedetto Croce, *The Philosophy of Giambattista Vico* (Bari: Laterza, 1911), trans. R. G. Collingwood (London: Latimer, 1913); and Benedetto Croce, *Aesthetic*, trans. Douglas Ainslie (1909; reprinted New York: Noonday Press, 1969), 220–34.

28. Benedetto Croce, *What Is Living and What Is Dead in the Philosophy of Hegel* (Bari, 1906), trans. Douglas Ainslie (London: Macmillan, 1915), 72; Croce, *The Philosophy of Giambattista Vico*, 38.

29. Croce, *What Is Living and What Is Dead in the Philosophy of Hegel*, 129.

30. Ibid., 131–32.

31. Croce, *Aesthetic*, 303.

32. *The New Science of Giambattista Vico*, revised translation of the 3rd edition (1744) by Thomas Goddard Bergin and Max Harold Fisch (Ithaca: Cornell University Press, 1968), sec. 7, p. 6. (I do not reproduce the comments or interpolations added by the translators between brackets.)

33. Ibid., sec. 349, pp. 104–5.

34. "Put me on to Edenville. Aleph, alpha: nought, nought, one" (*U*, 3.39–40). See also Derrida's comments on Joycean "telephones" in *Ulysse Gramophone*, 79–88.

Conclusion

1. I develop the connection between Joyce and skepticism in my forthcoming *Joyce upon the Void: The Genesis of Doubt.*

2. See, for instance, *Au coeur de la crise moderniste: Le Dossier inédit d'une controverse,* letters and texts by M. Blondel, H. Brémond, F. von Hügel, A. Loisy, F. Mourret, and J. Wehrlé; ed. R. Marlé (Paris: Aubier-Montaigne, 1960).

3. See Lorraine Weir's perceptive summary of the issue of modernity in her excellent *Writing Joyce: A Semiotics of the Joyce System* (Bloomington: Indiana University Press, 1989), 8–10.

4. Roland Barthes, *S/Z*, trans. R. Miller (London: Cape, 1975), 4–5.

5. Brenda Maddox, in her recent book on Nora (*Nora: A Biography of Nora Joyce* [London: Hamish Hamilton, 1988]), while trying to make a feminist case for Nora in a very biased way, has also stressed this duality and has emphasized the fact that the constant idiosyncratic laughter which seized Joyce when he was writing his *Work in Progress* seemed to disturb Nora. Nora told Mrs. Giedion-Welcker that she could not sleep at night: "I go to bed and then that man sits in the next room and continues laughing about his own writing. And then I knock at the door, and I say, "Now, Jim, stop writing or stop laughing" (*Nora*, 426).

6. Sigmund Freud, *Jokes and Their Relation to the Unconscious*, 131.

Designed by Chris Hotvedt
Composed by A. W. Bennett, Inc.
in Garamond Antiqua text and display
Printed on 50-lb., Glatfelter, B-16
and bound in Holliston's Roxite A
by Thomson-Shore, Inc.